PUERTO RICO'S CONSTITUTIONAL PARADOX

This book explains how the People of Puerto Rico managed to adopt a constitution whose content and process were both original and colonialist, participatory and undemocratic, as well as progressive and anticlimactic.

It looks in detail at the rich contradictions of the Puerto Rican constitutional experience, focusing on the history and content of the 1952 Constitution. This constitution is the only constitutional document written by the Puerto Rican People themselves after more than 500 years of Spanish and US colonialism.

By exploring Puerto Rico's unique history and constitutional experience the book shines a spotlight on key emerging themes of comparative constitutional studies in this area: state constitutionalism, the persistence of colonial relationships in the Caribbean, and the continued development of constitutionalism in Latin America.

The book delves deep into the particular experience of Puerto Rican constitutionalism which combines elements of colonialism, democratic tensions, and progressive policies. It explains how these features converge in a constitutional project that has endured for 70 years and continues its contradictory development. It considers issues such as the island's colonial history, including its conflicting relationship with democratic values and the constant presence of social movements and their struggles.

It also explores the content of the 1952 Constitution, focusing on its progressive substantive policy, particularly its rights provisions, its amendment procedures, and the governmental structure it set up.

Volume 2 in the Constitutionalism in Latin America and the Caribbean series

Constitutionalism in Latin America and the Caribbean

Series editors:

Richard Albert
Carlos Bernal
Catarina Santos Botelho

The Constitutionalism in Latin America and the Caribbean series publishes outstanding scholarship on the law and politics of the many varieties of constitutionalism in Latin America and the Caribbean. From single-jurisdiction and cross-national studies to inquiries into the relationship between constitutional and international law in multilevel legal orders in the region, the series welcomes submissions that identify, contextualise, illuminate, and theorise the origins, challenges, foundations, and future of constitutional law and politics in these understudied – but fascinating and important – parts of the world. Scholarship published in this series covers the range of methodologies in law and politics, including but not limited to comparative, doctrinal, empirical, historical, and theoretical perspectives. The series editors invite preliminary inquiries as well as full proposals for monographs and edited volumes in what aims to be the leading forum for the publication of exceptional public law scholarship on Latin America and the Caribbean.

Recent titles in this series:

Constitutional Erosion in Brazil: Progresses and Failures of a Constitutional Project
by Emilio Peduso Neder Meyer

Puerto Rico's Constitutional Paradox: Colonial Subordination, Democratic Tension and Promise of Progressive Transformation
by Jorge M Farinacci-Fernós

Puerto Rico's Constitutional Paradox

Colonial Subordination, Democratic Tension and Promise of Progressive Transformation

Jorge M Farinacci-Fernós

·HART·

OXFORD · LONDON · NEW YORK · NEW DELHI · SYDNEY

HART PUBLISHING

Bloomsbury Publishing Plc

Kemp House, Chawley Park, Cumnor Hill, Oxford, OX2 9PH, UK

1385 Broadway, New York, NY 10018, USA

29 Earlsfort Terrace, Dublin 2, Ireland

First published in Great Britain 2023

A catalogue record for this book is available from the British Library.

A catalogue record for this book is available from the Library of Congress.

Library of Congress Control Number: 2022947593

ISBN: HB: 978-1-50995-346-2
ePDF: 978-1-50995-348-6
ePub: 978-1-50995-347-9

Typeset by Compuscript Ltd, Shannon

Acknowledgements

TO MY PARENTS. Both were incredibly gifted jurists, generous, loving, and, above all, tireless *luchadores*. They constantly reminded me that the Puerto Rican story is a combination of many factors, experiences, and contradictions. Hopefully, its future is one free of colonialism and exploitation.

I would like to thank professors Joel Colón-Ríos and Carlos Ramos González for their incredibly valuable feedback and comments. I would also like to thank my research assistant, Génesis Rivera Carrasquillo, for all her help.

Contents

Table of Cases

Puerto Rico

United States

1

Concepts and Structure

I. OVERVIEW

SINCE THE ARRIVAL of the Spanish in the late fifteenth century, Puerto Ricans have written and adopted only a single constitution for themselves,[1] and this was done as late as 1952.[2] That constitution is still in effect today, with negligible modifications, including a recent unilateral and extratextual alteration made by the US Congress in a stunning display of colonial power that has not been seen since the adoption of the constitution seven decades ago.

Because of the ongoing colonial relationship between Puerto Rico and the US, as well as its own democratic shortcomings, the authority, legitimacy, and integrity of the 1952 Constitution are perpetually in doubt. Some, like Joel Colón-Ríos and Martin Hevia, question whether Puerto Rico's 1952 Constitution can even be called a constitution in the normative sense of the word, since it cannot be considered as 'an actual supreme law'.[3] Of course, the same can be said of other sub-national constitutions like those of Illinois or Ohio, but the argument is particularly valid in a colonial context like Puerto Rico. At the same time, the adoption process and, especially, the substantive content of the Constitution still command important – though qualified – popular support,[4] which may account for its relative longevity.

This interesting combination reflects the contradictory nature of the Puerto Rican constitutional project and experience, as well as its history and society overall. In Puerto Rico, colonialism co-exists with a proto-democratic

[1] The concept of Puerto Rico or Puerto Ricans, as currently known, can be traced to the middle of the nineteenth century. Until 1952, 'constitutional' norms were entirely imposed from the outside, first by Spain, and later on, by the US.

[2] Even the task of identifying and naming the document adopted in 1952 is a controversial endeavour. Depending on one's particular view of Puerto Rican history and its future, it can be identified as the 'Constitution of Puerto Rico', the 'Constitution of the Commonwealth of Puerto Rico' (*Estado Libre Asociado de Puerto Rico*) and several other variants. For purposes of simplification, and in a possibly vain attempt to remain 'neutral', this book will mostly use the term '1952 Constitution'.

[3] J Colón-Ríos and M Hevia, 'The Legal Status of Puerto Rico and the Institutional Requirements of Republicanism' (2011) 17 *Texas Hispanic Journal of Law and Policy* 1, 2.

[4] For the purposes of this book, *substantive content* refers to the rights and policy provisions of the constitution, while *structural content* refers to those parts of the constitution that deal with the State, its branches of government, and the overall political system.

political system, as well as intense social conflicts and transformative aspirations. The 1952 Constitution reflects these characteristics, while it also attempts to address them.

In general terms, it can be stated that the 1952 document actually produced three different constitutional phenomena: (1) a *colonial* constitution; (2) a democratically deficient or *(un)democratic* constitution; and (3) a *transformative*, *progressive*, and *social* constitution. Until now, most of the available scholarship has heavily focused on the first of these, sometimes mentions the second, and almost always ignores the third. This book attempts to bring together all three elements in a single narrative, in order to have a complete picture of the Puerto Rican constitutional project as it stands today. This includes recognising the importance of the social and substantive aspects of the 1952 Constitution, while also addressing the colonial and democratic components.

This trichotomy also impacts how the 1952 constitutional project is currently seen by Puerto Rican society and it permeates the actual content of the Constitution itself, including its substance, structure, and amendment mechanisms, as well as its ongoing development and enforcement. It has also had a direct impact on the nature of Puerto Rican society and its conflicted relationship with the US.

The 1952 Constitution's creation process was also characterised by intense contradictions. On the one hand, it employed important democratic and participatory devices that allowed the Constitutional Convention that drafted it to reflect many – though not all – of the deeply held policy views of the social majority. On the other hand, its deliberations were inherently subject to the watchful eye of the US Congress, not to mention that the resulting political structure adopted by the Convention fell somewhat short of its own democratic credentials.

It should also be added that the process of creation took place in an atmosphere of significant political repression against the island's militant pro-independence movement, which boycotted the constitutional creation process, thus weakening its claim to legitimacy. Since then, the independence movement has had a conflicted relationship with the 1952 Constitution. The Constitution's eventual underenforcement by Puerto Rican courts adds to the constitutional project's internal and external contradictions, as well as the difficulty of charting its future course.

In that sense, the contradictory nature of the Puerto Rican constitutional project exists on several levels. How can a colonial constitution represent or generate an authentic exercise of self-determination? How can a democratic creation process that incorporated important sectors of society produce an undemocratic governmental structure that mostly relegates popular participation to a passive, even secondary, role? How can a progressive constitution that aims for social transformation survive the watchful eye of a reactionary, Cold War-era, federal Congress?

These types of contradictions, both internal and external, require a comprehensive conceptual approach that facilitates a complete analysis of the Puerto Rican constitutional experience. In particular, an analysis of Puerto Rican constitutionalism necessitates intersecting two sets of relevant elements. The first set consists of *constitutional components*. These refer to the stages and features that make up the Puerto Rican constitutional project and experience as a whole. In particular, I refer to: (1) pre-adoption history; (2) the creation process; (3) structure and amendment mechanisms; (4) substantive content; (5) post-ratification events; and (6) current developments.

The second set consists of *conceptual factors*. Specifically, these are: (1) colonialism; (2) democratic elements; and (3) progressive and social content. Each one of these conceptual factors is present in all of the constitutional components. As such, it would be beneficial to analyse each factor separately and discuss how they impact each component individually.

The structure of this book will reflect this approach. Specifically, each chapter will address a particular constitutional component individually through the prism of each one of the previously identified conceptual factors. The result is an enriched understanding of the dynamic, paradoxical, and contradictory nature of the ongoing and *sui generis* Puerto Rican constitutional project. It may also shed light on where the island's constitutional project and society are heading or, at least, its possible horizons.

II. CONSTITUTIONAL COMPONENTS

A. General Pre-adoption History

Constitutions do not materialise from the aether.[5] While they can signal the start of a new historical phase in the life of a particular community, they can also be the culmination of one – or even several – complex historical processes. This is particularly significant when it comes to societies that have not enjoyed a robust constitutional history, experience, or culture. In Puerto Rico's case, this void is due to a centuries-old denial of both sovereignty and real self-determination, one of the results of a seemingly permanent colonialism under different imperial powers.

In other words, while pre-adoption history is usually essential in order to obtain an understanding of a particular society's current constitutional project, it becomes absolutely critical in relation to a community that, in more than 500 years, has only experienced a single constitutional process that, in addition,

[5] H Lerner, *Making Constitutions in Deeply Divided Societies* (Cambridge University Press, 2011) 26 ('Constitutions are rarely, if ever, written on a clean slate').

was characterised by strong contradictions and limitations. As we will see throughout this book, even the concept and existence of 'Puerto Rican constitutionalism' is permanently and inherently contested and problematic.

As discussed in greater detail in the paragraphs below, colonialism is not just a political problem that relates to a denial of self-government and sovereignty to a particular political community. It is also a cultural and economic phenomenon that can produce and exacerbate social ills, including dysfunctional economic structures, as well as crises of collective identity and ideas of self-worth. It also generates internal contradictions in the society on which it has an impact. Even in its most 'benign' form, colonialism produces negative consequences. Puerto Rico is no exception.

This explains, for example, how the colonial economic crises of the early twentieth century created the conditions for a strong and militant labour movement that managed to directly influence the content of the 1952 Constitution, thus accounting for part of its social and progressive characteristics. Simultaneously, this same colonial structure has prevented Puerto Ricans from actually overcoming the social ills that the Constitution was meant to address. In fact, that colonial system has, arguably, contributed to the continued existence of a dysfunctional society and economy.

This example merely reaffirms the importance of pre-adoption history, particularly social history, in any thorough analysis of Puerto Rico's current constitutional project. In Puerto Rico's case, even though the current constitution was adopted relatively recently, the relevant pre-adoption period stretches for more than four centuries.

Although the modern concept of 'Puerto Rico', or, more accurately, 'Puerto Ricans', is a mid-nineteenth century phenomenon, it would be a mistake to start our historical analysis there. A complete study of the historical processes that culminated with the adoption of the 1952 Constitution must start considerably earlier. Puerto Rico's constitutional project has been a long historical journey, and it remains unfinished.

Unlike the other constitutional components, pre-adoption history allows us to leave the dry arena of law and politics, and access other important social, economic, cultural factors, inter alia, that allow us to paint a more complete picture of Puerto Rico's ongoing, incomplete, and contradictory constitutional project. As we will see, the contradictory nature of this project is not inherent or natural: it is historically conditioned and rooted, thus requiring a holistic historical analysis.

In that sense, Puerto Rico has two forms of pre-adoption history: (1) the general and overarching historical events and experiences that help us to understand the society that existed in 1952 and also explain what transpired during the constitutional drafting process; and (2) the more immediate antecedent events and circumstances that generated the relevant social, material, and ideological forces that would lead the constitutional project, including the formulation of a coherent social majority with its goals and preferences.

The recognition that pre-adoption history plays a critical role in any analysis of an individual society's constitutional project allows us to appreciate the historical significance, limitations, and possibilities of that society's specific constitutional creation process. This is no different for Puerto Rico. In these circumstances, one begins to see that the outcome of a particular process of this nature is not a random occurrence that is the result of the execution of someone's individual will; it is, instead, a historically conditioned social and collective process that constitutes the culmination of a concrete historical experience.

B. Creation Process

How a constitution is drafted and adopted is almost as important as – and in some cases even more important than – the actual content of its text. It is here that legitimacy and authority are first obtained. As Elkins et al explain, '[p]ublic involvement in constitution making is increasingly considered to be essential for the legitimacy and effectiveness of the process'.[6] It will also be vital for the legitimacy of the resulting text and of the constitutional project in general.

In that sense, the creation process determines whether the constitution really is the work of 'We the People' or whether it is merely a technical legal event of secondary relevance, which runs the risk of failing to take root in a particular society, thus dooming it in the long run. In many cases, this distinction will determine whether a particular constitution will be short-lived or whether it will manage to endure through several generations.

The constitutional creation process can be divided into two phases: (1) the immediate antecedent events that directly led to the drafting process; and (2) the drafting process itself, followed by adoption and ratification.

The first period is mostly *informal* in nature, except for the legal and political acts that actually and officially authorised or initiated the constituent process. This antecedent stage includes the social and public discussions, debates, and deliberations regarding the nature and expected content of the constitutional text and structure. In other words, it is during this phase that the different social, political, and civic forces interact in the public sphere to shape the direction and orientation of the drafting process that will follow. This includes the public comments, expressions, and proposals that are made as part of the selection process for delegates to the constitutional convention. It is here that social majorities are finally articulated, and policy consensus are created and strengthened.[7]

[6] Z Elkins et al, 'The Citizen as Founder: Public Participation in Constitutional Approval' (2008) 81 *Temple Law Review* 361.

[7] See Z Elkins et al, *The Endurance of National Constitutions* (Cambridge University Press, 2009) 86; Y Ghai and G Galli, *Constitution Building Process and Democratization* (Institute for Democracy and Electoral Assistance, 2006) 9.

But this first stage of the creation process also includes the structural and legal basis that paves the way for the actual drafting enterprise. This stage determines, for example, whether the drafting process will constitute a truly sovereign exercise of the constituent power or whether, on the other hand, it is merely a more limited exercise of constituted power that traces back to a preexistent and authoritative source of sovereignty. In the case of Puerto Rico, obviously the colonial nature of its relationship with the US is key.[8]

The second stage of the creation process deals with the actual drafting and consideration of the constitutional text. Again, this has formal and informal articulations. The former refers to the official proceedings and workings of the deliberative body itself. This includes the deliberations of its committees or commissions, the actual drafting of the text, the discussion of amendments, and debates on the floor of the convention. In modern times, these formal components of adoption history are documented in official, public, and mostly reliably accurate records.

But very few modern constitutional creation processes are limited only to legal and formal proceedings within an elected deliberative body formally tasked with writing the constitutional text. There are also informal social processes that occur simultaneously, which can exert considerable influence on the drafting process. This includes social mobilisations and public debates that do not stop when the election of delegates is over and the drafting body begins its deliberations. While these public discussions mould pre-election consensus concerning important policy issues and questions, they also help push particular positions while the delegates are debating and deliberating on specific provisions and amendments. Constitution-making is not a static phenomenon.

These public debates are also vital for securing compromises and for making sure that important matters are not unjustifiably left on the cutting-room floor. In addition, they are crucial in maintaining enough popular support for the constitutional project, which is essential for obtaining public ratification after the drafting process is over. Finally, they constitute self-aware attempts by the drafters to influence future judicial interpretations and enforcement by filling the authoritative legislative record with remarks, clarifications, and explications. It is a fluid and multi-layered process that looks simultaneously to the past, present, and future.

The creation process also encompasses different modes of public participation and contributions, whether direct or indirect, that make their way into the constitutional text or, at the very least, the legislative record. These mechanisms of public participation and contribution constitute an organic link that connects

[8] This also has an impact on the level of constituent authority that the framing body has and, thus, the level of constituent power it can exercise. See RS Kay, 'Constituent Authority' (2011) 59 *American Journal of Comparative Law* 715.

the different informal social deliberations with the formal drafting process itself. They also enhance the democratic credentials of that process.

In some circumstances, international or supernational events and actors will also be relevant to the creation process. This is particularly true when it comes to subnational or colonial political units that must comply with the legal and political requirements of a separate or superior sovereign. The actual role of these outside forces merits analysis, not only in terms of their direct impact on specific articulations of the text or structure of the constitution but also with regard to their overarching influence and control in a particular historical context.

Popular ratification is a key element of the creation process. It confirms that the text to be adopted can really be said to reflect and represent 'We the People'. One the one hand, ratification is never a foregone conclusion. If the drafting body has insufficiently engaged with the public, there is a risk that an unsurmountable gap will separate the framers and their text from the People and their views. If this happens, the text can actually be rejected in a referendum, thus stopping the constituent process in its tracks.

Conversely, if the drafting process incorporated mechanisms for popular participation and discussion, then ratification can even become inevitable. This includes looking into how the framers present their product to the public for their consideration. This will aid in the ratification and can also shed light on the meaning of the constitutional text itself. In any event, an analysis of the ratification process is an unavoidable endeavour.

The same thing can be said about immediate post-ratification events. Some of the most critical formative moments for a new constitution are its first steps after being born. It is here that the formal constitution begins its transition into the real one, and where the final battles are fought in terms of what the constitution means and, more importantly, what it will actually do.

C. Governmental Structure and Amendment Mechanisms

While written constitutions around the world vary in terms of their substantive content and policy provisions (or whether to have them at all),[9] all of them, at least, address and establish the structures of government for their respective political communities. In the classical sense, a constitution *constitutes* the instruments of political government.[10] In modern times, these instruments tend to be of a democratic nature.

In other words, a fundamental component of any analysis of a constitutional system is the political structure it establishes. This implies several conceptual layers of analysis. First is to assess whether the political or

[9] See JM Farinacci-Fernós, 'Post-Liberal Constitutionalism' (2018) 54 *Tulsa Law Review* 1.
[10] Modern substantive constitutions also *constitute* society itself, *including* the political structure of government. ibid.

governmental system established by the constitution is democratic in nature or not, or at least proto-democratic.[11] While we will address *democracy* as a distinct conceptual factor a little later on in this chapter, here it is sufficient to state that a democratic or proto-democratic structure incorporates, at the very least, ideas such as the consent of the governed, political accountability, popular consultation or participation, as well as free and frequent selection of governmental leadership.

Second, what is the type and level of distribution of political and governmental power? Are there separate branches? What are their functions and how do they interact? How are the different offices and leadership positions specifically selected? In democratic systems, this includes an analysis of constitutional-level electoral rules, procedures, and structures.

Third, how is power to be exercised by different political actors and institutions? This includes an analysis of failsafe mechanisms and other constitutional limitations and safeguards with regard to the exercise – in this case – of public power. Some constitutions also address the use of private power, particularly in societies that have experienced instances of excessive or abusive exercises of private, mostly economic, power, whether from corporations, monopolies, landowners or financial institutions, inter alia.

Finally, an analysis of a particular constitutional system requires an assessment of the existing mechanisms for constitutional change – mostly, but not exclusively, the formal ones adopted in the text itself. This includes interpretive commands for courts or other bodies charged with constitutional enforcement, as well as specific amendment mechanisms that cover possible procedural and substantive requirements or limitations, and potential overhaul or even replacement.[12]

Almost by definition, constitutionally prescribed amendment procedures are, at least initially, an instance of constituted power.[13] Whether these processes can, eventually, develop a life of their own and *become* a separate and distinct instance of constituent power is a separate issue regarding constituent authority that necessarily transcends the formal processes established by the constitution in the first place. This applies both to discrete amendment mechanisms and broader revision, overhaul, or even replacement procedures.

But the constituent power-constituted power dichotomy, and its relation to constituent authority, is insufficient when it comes to a thorough analysis of a constitution's formal modification mechanisms and procedures. Even when dealing with an instance of constituted power, there are important differences,

[11] For our purposes here, non-democratic governmental structures include non-symbolic monarchies, theocracies, military governments, and other similar designs. Official one-party systems are more complex but should not automatically be described as inherently non-democratic.

[12] See JM Farinacci-Fernós, 'The Constitution is Dead, Long Live the Constitution! The Creation, Endurance and Modification of Modern Revolutionary Constitutions' (2020) 25 *Barry Law Review* 35.

[13] O Doyle, 'The Boundaries of Constituent Authority' (2019) 20 *German Law Journal* 161, 163.

designs, and approaches that merit individualised study and evaluation. This makes up an essential part of any thorough analysis of a particular country's constitutional project.

D. Substantive Content

As discussed above, not all constitutions incorporate substantive policy provisions. Some, like the Australian Constitution, simply limit themselves to establishing the structures of government, leaving everything else – particularly policy matters – to the ordinary, normally democratic, political process through the structures and mechanisms created, precisely, by the constitutional text.[14]

But the Australian model, as the closest thing to a pure example of this phenomenon, is extremely unusual and rarely reproduced. Most classic or framework constitutions incorporate some sort of policy content, though they do it almost exclusively though individual rights provisions, which are sometimes limited. In turn, these rights tend to be mostly of a civil and political nature and simply facilitate the proper operation of the governmental structure established in the main parts of the framework constitution, without directly addressing substantive issues.

Modern constitutionalism has, for the most part, chosen a different path: in addition to the establishment of a governmental structure and the adoption of basic political rights related to its adequate function, these constitutions also incorporate a considerable number of substantive policy provisions. These provisions address a whole set of social, economic, cultural, and environmental issues that were previously left, almost exclusively, to the ordinary political and legislative processes. This shift represents an expansion of the constituent power and the very notion of direct self-government and popular sovereignty.

Constitutions are no longer just governmental charters that, in addition, guarantee basic (mostly individual) political rights. The normative power and historical experience of constitutional entrenchment has led many political communities to transform their constitutions into substantive designs for their respective societies that also act as a democratic safeguard against possible future malfunctions of the ordinary political process. In particular, they allow social majorities to entrench their deeply held views on important policy matters, regardless of the opinions of future legislators who may not share those majoritarian preferences. Constitutions are no longer just charters about government: they are assertive blueprints for society and its future.

[14] See J Goldsworthy, 'Australia: Devotion to Legalism' in J Goldsworthy (ed), *Interpreting Constitutions: A Comparative Study* (Oxford University Press, 2007) 109. While the Australian constitutional text does refer to religious liberty and the right to vote, these do not alter the general characterisation of the document as a whole.

As a result, modern constitutions are full of substantive policy content. Issues such as economic activity, labour relations and conditions, wealth distribution, social organisation, environmental protections, among others, have now become constitutional subjects. In that sense, a distinct inquiry into the particular substantive content of modern constitutions is warranted, separate from an analysis of its framework provisions that deal with the structures of government and formal mechanisms for constitutional alteration.

Substantive policy mostly comes in two possible textual vehicles. First, it may be set out as judicially enforceable rights provisions. These include socioeconomic and cultural rights, which can come in both negative and positive, as well as vertical and horizontal, forms.[15] Whether it is access to water or overtime pay provisions, these rights can have a direct impact on the development of society and the quality of life of its inhabitants.

Second, these substantive policy provisions can take the form of general constitutional commands that transcend the individual rights paradigm. These provisions can simply establish or require systems, programs, entities, institutions, and structures that have direct policy implications. For example, they can, inter alia, require state ownership over particular economic sectors, establish a public education or healthcare system, or address issues of land ownership.

E. Post-ratification Events

If pre-ratification history is crucial to understanding how a particular constitution came into being, post-ratification events allow us to see the actual impact of a constitution on the society it governs. In other words, both the experiences and practices of a particular society under a new constitutional regime facilitate obtaining a full grasp of the entirety of that society's real experience regarding its constitutional project.

In that sense, post-ratification events can reveal several important elements. For example, how have the relevant institutional actors interacted with the constitution, including their views regarding its content and their understanding as to its proper role in society. While not necessarily dispositive regarding the formal content of the constitution – since institutional actors can misinterpret or underenforce specific constitutional provisions, or even the text in general – it can be extremely important to determine what the practice of the constitution has been. In the end, a constitution is both what it *should* be and what it actually *has* been.

[15] For a more in-depth analysis of the interaction between the negative-positive, horizontal-vertical, political-socioeconomic aspects of modern constitutional rights, see JM Farinacci-Fernós, 'Looking beyond the Negative-Positive Rights Distinction: Analyzing Constitutional Rights According to their Nature, Effect and Reach' (2018) 41 *Hastings International and Comparative Law Review* 31.

Institutional actors include courts, political forces, governmental entities, civil society, and other elements of the community. Studying their role is particularly important when dealing with a community's first autochthonous constitutional experience, as in the case of Puerto Rico. The lack of historical antecedents and experiences means that the practical gloss developed by these institutional actors is all the more important, in the absence of a larger constitutional culture to serve as a concrete background with regard to the role and meaning of the constitution.

Judicial decisions are a crucial part of the post-ratification period. This includes issues such as interpretive methodology, dominant legal philosophies, and even the development of a constitutional ideology and identity, as well as the public's response to these decisions. They can also help to identify any possible gap between the *promise* of the constitution and the *reality* of its enforcement and implementation. In turn, this gap can either weaken the constitution – by eroding the confidence of the public as to its content and the historical project underlying it – or strengthen it, by generating a popular movement that demands its adequate enforcement.

Another relevant post-ratification event is how the constitution has impacted on the general culture of a particular community, and whether it has been able to garner sufficient ongoing support from the public to command their fidelity and protection. In other words, whether – and to what extent – the constitution has taken root in society, and indeed which version of the constitution is in effect. This creates a double feedback loop: the constitution moulds society, and social events have an impact on the development of the constitution.

In colonial societies, post-ratification events also include the dynamics of the relationship between the imperial power and the colonial possession. Almost by definition, these post-adoption dynamics have constitutional implications for the imperial power as well, which also merit analysis as part of the constitutional experience of the colonial possession.

The adoption of a constitution by a colonial entity can have an impact on the metropolitan power in different ways. For example, it can require an adjustment in its domestic law regarding its territories. Also, it can influence the political persuasions of both its public and leadership, which can lead to a constant reassessment of the relationship itself.

F. Recent Constitutional Developments

Constitutions exist in the real world – here and now. Every society's constitutional experiment is, by definition, an ongoing, fluid, and historically contingent endeavour. This requires the conceptual separation of general post-ratification events – which start immediately after adoption of the constitutional text – and the most recent constitutional occurrences of the present.

This is particularly important in societies that are in a constant process of self-definition and self-determination, including post-revolutionary or post-conflict societies and internally polarised ones, as well as those that are subject to substantial external pressures such as colonialism. In these scenarios, the constitutional structure is more likely to be in constant flux and subject to potentially substantial transformations.

Also, by focusing on recent constitutional developments, we are able to capture a society's constitutional experience at a very particular historical juncture that allows for a more complete assessment of the entire constitutional experiment as a whole. In that sense, by focusing on the most recent constitutional developments, events, and occurrences, one is able to fully appreciate the complexities, contradictions, and potential of a particular constitutional project.

III. CONCEPTUAL FACTORS

In order to fully understand Puerto Rico's 'three constitutions', we must first clarify what we mean by colonialism, democratic elements, and potentially transformative progressive or social content. These will be the central concepts through which we will individually analyse all of the components of Puerto Rico's complex and contradictory constitutional project.

A. Colonialism

This is not a book *on* colonialism, but it does require a specific and practical discussion *about* colonialism, particularly, in the context of Puerto Rico's constitutional history and its current predicament. Our approach to the concept of colonialism, then, is select and very particular; specifically, in terms of explaining Puerto Rico's conflicted relationship with the US and with its own colonial past under Spanish rule.

Since the arrival of the first Spanish explorers at the end of the fifteenth century, Puerto Rico has never been able to enjoy truly full sovereignty. Colonialism, in one form or another, has been a constant historical reality. It is virtually impossible to understand Puerto Rican history in general, and its constitutional experience in particular, without direct and consistent references to colonialism. Colonialism is the original sin of Puerto Rican constitutionalism.

What do we mean by *colonialism*? Has it meant the same for 500 years or has it evolved both as a historical and context-specific, practical phenomenon? Does it vary depending on the region of the world in which it is being implemented? There are no universal answers to the basic questions regarding the meaning of colonialism.

For example, Mitchell Purdy adopts a definition of colonialism that sees it as the 'policy or practice of acquiring full or partial political control over another country, occupying it with settlers, and exploiting it economically'.[16] In the Puerto Rican experience, while Spanish colonisation was accompanied by substantial immigration from the metropolis into the island, colonialism under the US flag has been somewhat different. While there has been a recent wave of mostly wealthy Americans moving to Puerto Rico to benefit from its generous tax incentives, most of the Puerto Rican territory has not experimented significant settler colonialism.[17] This may be changing as we speak.

Colonialism is not a static or settled concept; it has evolved historically. In that sense, Puerto Rico has lived through different forms and stages of colonialism. In its general, short form, colonialism can be defined as the political and economic subordination of one political unit by another – normally a more powerful one – and mostly for the benefit of the metropolitan power. This type of relationship will often exhibit different negative characteristics, such as, inter alia, undemocratic or authoritarian governance practices, cultural assimilation, displacement or even oppression, economic exploitation, physical occupation, political repression, and control through – mostly imposed – legal mechanisms and structures. It also includes the ability of the metropolitan power to directly intervene in the affairs of the colonial possession, such as the application to the latter of the former's legislative enactments.

Colonialism can also have an impact on the mindset of the colonised, to the point that the latter actually accept or tolerate their condition. This adds to the complexities of the colonial condition, where it becomes very difficult to separate self-determination from the effects of a cycle of dependency. In that sense, colonialism can actually reinforce itself, allowing for an argument that, because the colonised acquiesce to their condition, it is legitimate to continue the relationship.

As a result, with regard to the particular case of Puerto Rico, the concept of 'colonialism' can even be ideologically contestable and problematic. This is part of the war of words that characterises the Puerto Rican debate regarding its political situation and future. Is Puerto Rico a nation, country or subnational unit, or all, or none, of the above? Should we mainly focus on the nomenclature and concepts created by US domestic law – such as 'territory', 'secession', 'separation' or 'statehood' – or should we instead turn to terms found in international law, such as 'colony', 'annexation', 'self-determination' or 'occupation'?

[16] M Purdy, 'An Alternative Road: How the West can Draw from China's Belt and Road Initiative to Improve the Efficiency of Western Foreign Aid to Africa' (2022) 30 *Michigan State International Law Review* 125, 144, quoting from the *Oxford English Dictionary*.

[17] See TG Reed, 'Fair Use as Cultural Appropriation' (2021) 109 *California Law Review* 1373, n 54, defining settler colonialism as 'a historically created system of power that aims to expropriate Indigenous territories and eliminate modes of production in order to replace Indigenous peoples with settlers', quoting DI Saranillio, 'Settler Colonialism' in SN Teves et al (eds), Native Studies Keywords (University of Arizona Press, 2015) 284.

Even the choice of words to be used supposes an ideological commitment to a particular version of Puerto Rico's history. Did the US 'invade' Puerto Rico in 1898 or should we only state that they merely 'arrived' or 'disembarked'? Are the US armed forces an occupying force or are they our fellow citizen-soldiers who happen to be based on the island? Is it independence or separatism?

This war over words has been a constant in Puerto Rican political discourse. This includes attempts to define colonialism *from the specific Puerto Rican experience and perspective*. For example, Pedro Malavet uses the term *colony* in reference to 'a polity with a definable territory that lacks legal and political sovereignty because that authority is exercised by a people other than the inhabitants of the colony'.[18] Specifically, Malavet believes that 'Puerto Rico, with a definable territory as well as an identifiable culture that is different from that dominating in the colonial power (the United States), is a "cultural nation" that lacks sovereignty; it is therefore an "American colony"'.[19] Others see Puerto Rico more as a post-colonial entity that has yet to achieve full sovereignty.[20]

Malavet's approach to the colonialism question seems founded on his view that:

> [t]he fundamental basis of imperialism is generally the racial supremacy of one group over all others. In the United States, imperialism extends to the internal and external conquests of those racially classified as nonwhite by those racially classified as white.[21]

The economic and class issues appear to be somewhat secondary in this approach.[22] In other words, Malavet seems to characterise the national question in Puerto Rico from a mostly racial perspective, all the while recognising that 'Latino' is a multi-racial concept that, *in the US*, has been socially constructed in racial and ethnic terms.[23] According to him, this has resulted in an 'othering' of Puerto Ricans, regardless of skin colour.[24]

Of course, imperialism and colonialism are not just systems of national oppression based on racial or ethnic considerations; they are also systems of economic exploitation. According to Achiume and Carbado, 'imperialism is

[18] PA Malavet, *America's Colony: The Political and Cultural Conflict Between the United States and Puerto Rico* (New York University Press, 2007) 4.

[19] ibid.

[20] See J Blocher and M Gulati, 'Puerto Rico and the Right of Accession' (2018) 43 *Yale Journal of International Law* 229, 253 ('it is a former colony'; 'transitioned from a colonial status to self-governance status').

[21] Malavet (n 18) 3. He explicitly adopts a 'LatCrit' approach to the Puerto Rican colonial question.

[22] See ibid 10. While the author does state that 'most Puerto Ricans on the island are members of an economic underclass,' he pays very little attention to the Puerto Rican upper classes.

[23] ibid 23.

[24] ibid 7.

defined to emphasize capitalist expansion and economic exploitation, and colonialism is defined to emphasize territorial conquest and acquisition'.[25] In Puerto Rico, both phenomena are present, particularly the former. This economic exploitation, carried out by private forces under the protection of the metropolitan government, creates social responses, including labour militancy. This merely reinforces the idea that a study of Puerto Rican colonialism cannot limit itself to formal legal or political considerations. It must also consider its economic and social aspects, particularly when dealing with the colony of a capitalist superpower that has evident imperialistic characteristics.

This book also takes a side regarding the issue of colonialism in Puerto Rico.[26] While US domestic law identifies Puerto Rico as a self-governing (sort of) 'territory' of the US, it is difficult to deny the colonial nature of that relationship. To deny Puerto Rico's colonial condition would add insult to injury.[27] In the end, regardless of the word chosen to describe the situation, the complete subordination of Puerto Rico's political and economic system to that of the US is hardly a debatable or controversial view, and it is an integral part of any complete and honest assessment of the Puerto Rican constitutional project.

B. Democratic Tension

It would seem almost oxymoronic to propose the possibility of a democratic version of colonialism. Almost by definition, colonialism is the denial of collective self-determination and full democratic self-government. But history is full of contradictions; it is part of the dialectic energy that drives human civilisation. As a result, even though they both inhabit a similar conceptual space, democracy requires a separate analysis from colonialism. Democratic spaces can exist within a colonial situation.

The idea or concept of *democracy* is probably one of the most contested in modern human political debate. As with colonialism, this book does not propose to unpick that Gordian knot or to dive into the inner workings of this philosophical discussion. Since this book's main analytical focus is on the Puerto Rican constitutional experience, the definition of democracy we adopt needs to be relevant and specific to that inquiry.

With that context in mind, 'democracy' refers to the existence of a system of government where power is exercised with some basic measure of consent,

[25] ET Achiume and DW Carbado, 'Critical Race Theory Meets Third World Approaches to International Law', (2021) 67 *UCLA Law Review* 1462, 1470; *cf* JT Gathii, 'Imperialism, Colonialism, and Ingternational Law' (2007) 54 *Buffalo Law Journal* 1013, 1019–20.

[26] Even not taking a side is taking a side.

[27] However, this book does not adopt the classic nationalist narrative regarding the Puerto Rican colonial situation, which tends to develop a moral dichotomy along national lines. In my estimation, it is imperative to also consider the internal class contradictions in Puerto Rican society, including powerful economic interests that are aligned with the US, as well as the social and economic component of Puerto Rico's colonial relationship with the US.

accountability, and popular participation with regard to decision-making and the selection of governmental actors. Since '[d]emocracy is in the details',[28] a very useful approach would be to think of democracy as a fluid continuum instead of a fixed set of precise requirements. On the other side of this scale are different versions of authoritarianism and tyranny.

I strongly resist the idea that liberal democracy lies at the furthermost point on the 'democratic' side of the continuum. That political system has no inherent claim to optimal democratic status.[29] Precisely because of this, most political systems – including liberal democracies – have internal democratic tensions or deficits. In fact, some non-liberal or post-liberal systems can actually have a *better* claim to optimal democratic status.

These contradictions, which produce democratic tensions or deficits, can have multiple forms and articulations. For example, representative democracies can fail to adequately reflect the policy preferences of the social majority. This can be the result of gerrymandering, economic disparities that affect access to legislators, and coopting by corporate interests. It should also be noted that undemocratic structures can actually produce democratic outcomes.

These paradoxes require more careful analysis and characterisation. Instead of lumping them up together in an attempt to assess some sort of 'democratic' bottom-line or net result, we should embrace these contradictions as constitutive of a particular society's political structure and culture and see them as they are. In other words, contradictions and tensions are not always things to be solved, but to be understood and accounted for.

For the purposes of this book, then, we will assess the democratic characteristics and credentials of all the different constitutional components we identified in the previous part. It is precisely from this individualised analysis of the democratic content of these components that we can attest to the substantial democratic tensions that underscore the current Puerto Rican constitutional project.[30]

C. Transformative Progressive and Social Content

As noted above, modern constitutions are full of substantive content, ranging from economic policy provisions to a constantly expanding list of individual

[28] L Henkin, 'A New Birth of Constitutionalism: Genetic Influence and Genetic Defects' in M Rosenfeld (ed), *Constitutionalism, Identity, Difference and Legitimacy* (Duke University Press, 1994) 52.

[29] See Farinacci-Fernós (n 9). Precisely because of this, most democratic systems – including liberal democracies – have internal tensions, contradictions, and faults. Non-liberal and post-liberal democratic systems have, at least, an equal claim to the 'democratic' label. As such, each system must be analysed on its own terms, resisting the temptation to put a thumb on the scale just because one is confronted with a liberal democratic system.

[30] In many instances, the net result may be characterised as proto-democratic, partially democratic, or democratically flawed.

and collective rights.[31] Although it is not inherently so, most of that content has – from a historically descriptive perspective – leaned ideologically to the Left.[32] As we will see in this book, Puerto Rico's constitutional text is a prime example of this phenomenon. Its content can be described as explicitly progressive with a definite social, working-class fingerprint. Though it cannot be described as revolutionary, it nonetheless has considerable transformative potential.

What do we mean by *progressive* or *social*? These concepts have ideological, historical, and even material connotations that require further explanation and analysis. While not synonymous, they are ideologically and historically linked.

When a constitution addresses substantive policy issues, as opposed to purely procedural or structural matters that can be dealt with through narrower grounds such as coordination-based approaches, it is inevitably forced to make a value judgement with regard to those issues, even the more controversial ones. In other words, it has to take sides. Neutrality scarcely works when adopting substantive policy provisions.

For example, if the constitutional text deals with matters regarding labour rights, it has to either harm or benefit the working class, at least for the most part. The same can be said about issues regarding property, wealth distribution, social services, economic activity, the death penalty, and so on. Any constitutional provision that deals with these issues requires, necessarily, a taking of sides, even if only incidentally. Is private property sacred or is its protection conditioned by its social function? Will the economic system incorporate equality-generating mechanisms, or will it be *laissez-faire*? Will there be a public healthcare or education system, or will they be left entirely or principally to the private sector? Will the death penalty be abolished, allowed, or even required? These are not pure dichotomies; there is plenty of room within the spectrum. But it is almost impossible to arrive at a truly neutral point. In some instances, being 'neutral' is also taking sides.

The fact that many modern constitutions address these sorts of policy issues makes them substantive in nature. But that mere fact does not tell us *which* positions have been taken as to the specific policy matters. This requires an additional step: making an actual value judgement with regard to those positions. This allows us to know if we are dealing with a primarily conservative or progressive constitution. The fact that it is substantive simply tells us – at least as a preliminary matter – that it probably cannot be considered truly 'neutral'.

[31] See Farinacci-Fernós (n 9).

[32] JM Farinacci-Fernós, 'Originalism in Puerto Rico: Original Explication and its Relation with Clear Text, Broad Purpose and Progressive Policy' (2016) 85 *Revista Jurídica Universidad de Puerto Rico* 203.

When, for example, a constitution positions itself on the side of social justice, an equitable distribution of wealth and power, or the defence of the interests of working-class people, then it can be described as a *progressive* constitution. This is not just a general description of the constitution as a whole. It can also mean that the constitution specifically possesses progressive *content*, which can be extracted from its individual provisions and its combined effects. The result is a potentially transformative constitution. As noted above, this has ideological, historical, and material implications.

With regard to ideology, we must remember that modern constitution-making is not merely a legal endeavour; it is also a political phenomenon. Furthermore, it can even be described as the highest mode of political expression, which makes the process socially and historically transcendental. As a result, intense ideological struggles are fought and many of the results are entrenched as constitutional provisions.

This ideological component is closely related to historical considerations and factors that can also veer in a progressive direction. Precisely because constitution-making can be regarded as the highest form of political activity, it can become ground zero for the effective mobilisation of numerically superior, but historically power-deprived, social forces and groups. As such, many of their grievances, interests, goals, and projects tend to be, as a historical matter, on the side of distribution, communitarianism, and social justice.

In the end, constitutions are about power. And not just political power, but economic and material power as well. As such, a progressive constitution can have a direct impact on the distribution of wealth, goods, and other material things of value, such as property, income, and access to or control of physical spaces and governmental resources. In other words, constitutions can also have a role to play in class struggle and economic disputes. A substantive constitution that takes a progressive bent will most likely affect, even if only indirectly, the actual distribution of power in a particular society.

Progressive constitutionalism, precisely because it intends to substantially transform society, requires that multiple institutional actors engage in affirmative action to actually make it happen. Progressive text will not be enough; it also requires entities, such as courts, to commit to its implementation. This is a potentially weak spot for progressive constitutionalism: it is vulnerable to institutional sabotage or underenforcement, thus frustrating its transformative goals.

IV. INTEGRATED ANALYTICAL STRUCTURE

Chapter 2 of this book discusses the Puerto Rican historical experience prior to the process that culminated in the adoption of the current Constitution in 1952. This includes an analysis on how the colonial relationship between Puerto Rico and the US has been a constant feature of all aspects of daily life on the island, whether political, social, economic, or cultural. This is but the starting point of how colonialism, democratic tensions, and transformative social aspirations have had multiple points of interaction with Puerto Rico's history in general and the 1952 Constitution in particular.

More importantly, we will see that it was during these preceding historical stages that the contradictory nature of the current Puerto Rican constitutional project first emerged and materialised. While little remains of the formal legal structures and content adopted during Spanish colonisation and domination, the cultural and social experiences related to colonialism, democratic deficits, and social aspirations remained and, to some extent, guided Puerto Rico's interactions with the new imperial power during the twentieth century.

Chapter 3 deals with the 1952 constitutional creation process, again through the lens of colonialism, democratic tension, and progressive policy. Here, the contradictory nature of the Puerto Rican constitutional project will be most evident: the creation of the Constitution of Puerto Rico was a highly democratic and participatory event but, simultaneously, that same process was directly subject to the limitations of colonialism which, by definition, is a most undemocratic system. More importantly, we will note that the resulting structure in relation to the organisation of the Puerto Rican government can also be characterised as democratically deficient. In other words, a highly democratic process generated a democratically deficient political structure. This democratic process was also characterised by authoritarian tendencies, particularly with regard to the pro-independence movement.

But the 1952 creation process also channelled, and sometimes even generated, important social and political forces that helped mould the actual content of the Constitution itself. This situation accounts, for example, for much of the progressive and socially oriented content of many of the 1952 Constitution's substantive provisions, particularly in the Bill of Rights. This influence was both informal and formal, and included the submission of proposals and petitions by members of the public, as well as diverse social, labour, civic, and community groups.

Chapter 4 addresses the actual content of the 1952 Constitution, focusing first on the governmental structure and formal amendment mechanisms. It is here that many of the colonial and undemocratic features of the Puerto Rican Constitution will become most evident. Both because of congressional command and colonial assimilation, the Puerto Rican governmental structure closely mirrors both the federal and state systems in the US. Ironically, many autochthonous innovations with regard to the political, electoral, and governmental systems actually diminished the democratic credentials of the Constitution. This includes, for example, a considerably consolidated executive, a distrust of an active citizenry that self-governs through direct participation, an electoral system that disincentivises multi-party contests, and a seemingly unbounded trust in the virtues of representative, indirect democracy.

The chapter analyses the Puerto Rican version of the separation of powers, the functions, and interactions of the three established branches, the electoral system, and the particulars of the operation of the government and the exercise of public power, including its structural safeguards and limits.

Furthermore, Chapter 4 addresses the procedural and substantive components of the 1952 Constitution's formal mechanisms for amendment, revision, overhaul, and possible replacement. As we will see, Puerto Rico's colonial relationship with the US further complicates this issue, because these procedural and substantive components have two different sources: (1) the text and structure of the 1952 Constitution itself; and (2) the relevant federal legislative enactments.

Chapter 5 continues the discussion on the content of the 1952 Constitution, turning its attention to issues of actual substantive policy. In the Puerto Rican experience, the main source of substantive policy are rights provisions mostly found in Article II of the Constitution (Bill of Rights), although there are other relevant parts as well.

In addition to incorporating, and substantially expanding both in terms of number and reach, the basic catalogue of civil and political rights – including guarantees related to criminal prosecutions and procedures – the 1952 Constitution also adopted several rights provisions that deal with matters such as education, labour conditions and relations, the treatment of minors, environmental protections, the rehabilitations of felons, and other human rights. It also addresses more general issues such as limitations on corporate power – particularly with regard to land ownership – and wealth distribution.

Chapter 6 focuses on the experiences of the Puerto Rican constitutional project after ratification of the Constitution in 1952 and how they have impacted on the operation of the Constitution itself. Puerto Rican constitutionalism did not stop in 1952. On the contrary, considering that the 1952 text is the only constitution that Puerto Rico has ever written for itself – notwithstanding the inherent limits of a colonial constitution as an adequate expression of self-government and popular sovereignty – the experiences in Puerto Rico after 1952 are crucial to understanding the reality of its ongoing constitutional project.

This includes how the Supreme Court of Puerto Rico, as the main constitutional institution charged with its ultimate interpretation and enforcement, has handled that task. In particular, it analyses the methodological approaches carried out by the Court, how it has dealt with the differences between the Puerto Rican text and its federal counterpart in the context of the island's colonial condition, and the general role of the 1952 Constitution in the everyday life of Puerto Ricans. It also studies many of the Court's failings, including problems of underenforcement, assimilation, and reproduction of the Constitution's most undemocratic features.

Chapter 6 also examines the interaction between the constitutional project and the colonialism debate – both in Puerto Rico and in the US – as well as the history of self-government and nation building under the 1952 regime. This includes the relevant historical events that have contributed to Puerto Rico's constitutional life. Finally, it studies the 1952 Constitution's role in shaping everyday life on the island.

Chapter 7 discusses more recent and current developments regarding the Puerto Rican constitutional project and experience. In particular, it focuses on key events that are very closely related to the main conceptual factors identified in this introductory chapter and their corresponding paradoxical nature.

With regard to colonialism, it discusses recent US Supreme Court decisions that have cemented the territorial nature of Puerto Rico's relationship with the US. At the same time, movements to overcome the current colonial situation are still developing and, for the first time in decades, Puerto Rico's territorial status has become more visible in the US political debate.

In terms of democratic tensions, Chapter 7 also analyses the momentous events of the so-called 'Summer of 19' that saw a clash of popular democratic aspirations with undemocratic constitutional arrangements. These events culminated in the first-ever resignation of an elected Governor because of popular mobilisations and pressure.

The chapter also discusses the substantial paradigm shift that has occurred in Puerto Rico's electoral politics, which has seen a considerable and consistent weakening of the historical two-party system into a plausible, but still tentative, multi-party environment. The combined effect of these events has, for the first time since the adoption of the 1952 Constitution, generated serious cross-party discussions regarding the possibility of amending or even revising the current electoral and governmental structure established in that document.

Finally, with regard to progressive or social content, Chapter 7 addresses the role of the 1952 Constitution in the socioeconomic crisis that has engulfed Puerto Rico during recent years. In particular, it deals with the use of the police powers to address the COVID-19 pandemic and the political consequences generated by the contradictions between the Constitution's social character and the severe austerity measures enacted by the Fiscal Control Board established in the federal PROMESA statute[33] approved by the US Congress in 2016.

In this regard, it seems that the 1952 Constitution's colonial nature has, at least partially, neutralised its social character. At the same time, it is interesting to note that the Bill of Rights still commands popular support, which at least hints that the substantive part of the 1952 Constitution's historical project still stands, though weakened. This constitutes a historical crossroads for Puerto Rico in terms of determining whether the Bill of Rights will founder along with the Commonwealth status, or whether it will survive in the Puerto Rican People's attempt to rebuild their society away from inequality and social injustice.

Chapter 7 also shares some final thoughts that propose a general assessment of the Puerto Rican constitutional project and possible alternatives towards the future. The story of Puerto Rican constitutionalism is still being fought, and recent events add to the mix of contradictions that permeate it. Where we go from here is still up to us, sort of.

[33] Puerto Rico Oversight, Management, and Economic Stability Act (PROMESA), Public Law No 114-187 (2016).

2

Puerto Rico before 1952

I. A HISTORY OF SUBORDINATION AND AUTHORITARIAN ANTECEDENTS: SPANISH COLONIALISM AND EARLY US DOMINATION

WHAT IS CURRENTLY known as 'Puerto Rico' grew mostly, though not exclusively, from the descendants of pre-Colombian indigenous communities, Spanish incomers, and African slaves. Other immigrant populations have also informed this constantly evolving manifestation of nationhood, from Corsican coffee farmers during the end of the nineteenth century to Dominican labourers in the latter stages of the twentieth century. There are many other demographic and cultural contributions. The concept of 'Puerto Ricans' must also take into consideration the experiences of people who left the island, mostly to the continental US, to seek out better living opportunities and conditions. These communities and their experiences, centred in places like New York City, Chicago, Hartford, and, more recently, Orlando, among others, also form part of the larger Puerto Rican story.

For more than 500 years, only two imperial powers have exercised sovereignty over the island: Spain and the US. No independent Puerto Rico has truly existed in modern times. It should be no surprise, then, to learn that a society that has been subject to colonialism for over five centuries has also had a weak relationship with democratic institutions and practices. Puerto Rico is no exception. The island's history on this matter has been a mixed bag, combining democratic instincts and aspirations with undemocratic institutions, experiences, and cultures of governance.

Of this period, the first four centuries were dominated by the Spanish Empire. This presence was characterised by the absence of a truly autochthonous legal system, the inconsistent application of colonial law that partially mirrored the Castilian system, and a ruthless colonial administration. Constitutionalism was unknown to Puerto Ricans during Spanish rule, except for rare and limited moments during reform processes that took place in peninsular Spain and had partial ripple effects on the island. These reforms tended to be mild and short-lived.

Authoritarianism was characteristic of the Spanish colonial presence in Puerto Rico, as it was elsewhere in the Americas. The colonial project that mostly eradicated the local indigenous population – and entirely destroyed their social, economic, and political system – was more concerned with economic exploitation, military fortification, and political control than in developing a just, or even functional, society.

During the early stages of Spanish colonialism, Castilian law was extended to the island. Since the Spaniards had no previous experience with overseas Empire of such magnitude as the Americas, their first instinct was to apply their legal system to it. Of course, it should be noted that the Castilian-led, Spanish legal system was still underdeveloped after centuries of Moorish occupation and the slow-moving *Reconquista* that eventually re-established Hispanic hegemony over the Iberian Peninsula.

But the extension of Castilian law to the Americas proved to be short-lived. The geographical, social, and demographical characteristics of the new continent required a different approach. The result was Indies law, which was Castilian in nature but unique in its actual content, structure, and operation. This started a centuries-old process of legal separation between peninsular and colonial law. This distancing led to the mostly ad hoc rule of colonial institutions and actors, particularly the royal governors. The legal system that eventually emerged was, as could be expected, substantially authoritarian and colonialist.

When the gold supply in Puerto Rico was exhausted, Spain's attention with regard to the island's role in its Empire shifted to trade and military considerations. This further entrenched the authoritarian and undemocratic nature of the Spanish colonial presence.

In terms of trade, the mercantilist system was particularly inefficient in Puerto Rico, which led to the creation of an informal economy outside the capital, San Juan, particularly in the western town of San Germán.[1] There, a contraband-centred economy blossomed, one that was far more efficient than the official trade system based in San Juan. Because of the economic benefits generated by the contraband model, the Spanish authorities in San Juan mostly tolerated it, at least for a while.

But as San Germán's economy flourished, particularly in contrast with its counterpart in San Juan, the town's inhabitants attempted to establish more proto-democratic control over their own affairs. Until then, all colonial institutions were decidedly undemocratic. The sole, partial, exception were the townships or *cabildos*. In these townships, a basic proto-democratic culture emerged, but was quickly snubbed out by the Spanish authorities operating from San Juan.

During the nineteenth century, the Puerto Rican legal system was primarily centred around executive decrees adopted by royal governors, who were mostly military men. These decrees, also known as *bandos*, mostly focused on controlling social activity and maintaining the political order. As such, they were substantially authoritarian, conservative, and repressive. For example,

[1] For many years following the arrival of the Spanish, Puerto Rico only had two official townships: San Juan and San Germán. It currently has 78.

they outlawed meeting at night and blasphemies. They also implemented forced labour regimes that generated considerable social resistance.

These experiences highlight Puerto Rico's limited, and somewhat dysfunctional and strained, historical relationship with democracy. The Spanish combination of authoritarianism and colonialism constituted a permanent obstacle to any sort of true democratic development. Such was the general state of affairs until the start of the nineteenth century, when revolutionary events in Europe and the Americas changed the political and legal landscape.

The revolts in the 13 British colonies and in Haiti, coupled with the revolution in France, created a crisis within the Spanish Empire, already severely weakened by a long process of economic, military, and geopolitical setbacks. The final straw was the Napoleonic invasion of the Iberian Peninsula. This combination of revolutionary ideas with metropolitan impotence and crisis, as well as the accumulated experience of colonial authoritarianism and mismanagement, led to the explosion of a massive independence movement in the Americas.

By the end of the first quarter of the nineteenth century, Spain was left only with its Caribbean possessions. After the Dominican Republic successfully gained its independence, only Cuba and Puerto Rico remained. The combination of the emergence of a reformist movement in Spain and the need to hold on to its remaining colonial possessions led many in the Spanish leadership to consider changing their attitudes regarding Puerto Rico.

Reforms such as the *Real Cédula de Gracia* (1815) and the inclusion of Puerto Rican delegates during the Cadiz Cortes (1810–12) signalled a modest attempt to reform the nature of Spanish colonialism in the Americas. But these reforms were mostly short-lived, as Spain consistently returned to its more authoritarian and undemocratic tendencies, both in the Peninsula proper and, more intensely, in Cuba and Puerto Rico, as well as in its other remaining territories in the Pacific.

As noted above, the modern concept of 'Puerto Rico' emerged during Spanish rule, particularly during the latter half of the nineteenth century, as with most instances of the phenomenon of nationhood across the globe. The development of a distinct Puerto Rican nationality, coupled with the authoritarian nature of Spanish colonial rule, sparked a movement that sought separation from Spain, whether through outright independence or the struggle to achieve considerable autonomy.

This movement culminated in an unsuccessful uprising in 1868 known as the *Grito de Lares*. This revolt combined challenges to Spain's colonial rule with proto-democratic grievances and aspirations. One of the ideological leaders of the uprising, the famed abolitionist Ramón Emeterio Betances, issued his *Diez Mandamientos de los Hombres Libres*, which laid out the main political and programmatic tenets of the insurrection. Among these were the abolition of slavery, the recognition of important political rights and individual liberties such as freedom of speech, press, and association. It also included demands regarding self-rule and political representation.

The call for the abolition of slavery warrants further discussion, as it is related to the emergence in Puerto Rico of demands for social reform, mostly centred around exploitative economic and political systems. It represents the culmination of a longer process of resistance to other forms of exploitation and subordination.

Since the early days of Spanish colonialism, the dominant economic system in Puerto Rico had been built around the exploitation and subordination of non-European peoples. It first centred on the indigenous *taíno* population, and then on African slaves.

It should be noted that the Spanish colonial project had substantial religious characteristics. One of the justifications for the subordination of entire indigenous populations was that their souls were at risk, since they had not yet received the 'good news' of Jesus Christ. After receiving papal blessing, the Spaniards adopted a legal system that characterised indigenous peoples as incapable minors who needed to be tutored by individual Spaniards. Though still considered human beings with souls and 'free will', the Spanish system of *repartimiento* and *encomienda* constituted practical slavery and brutal exploitation. After failed attempts, mostly by religious figures, to regulate the treatment of the *taínos* and improve their living conditions, their population was virtually wiped out, which is when Spain turned to the importation of African slaves.

The institution of slavery in Puerto Rico had its own unique, and contradictory, characteristics. Like the *taínos*, slaves were considered persons, not things. Yet, they were capable of being individually owned by their masters. Slavery in Puerto Rico coexisted with wage labour and different forms of servitude. This signalled the slow and painful transition from feudalism to capitalism.

The contradictory nature of the institution of slavery in Puerto Rico can be appreciated from the fact that, while slaves were considered to be persons that could be owned, they also had a legal status that afforded them certain rights. Among these were the right to marry, an education, to purchase or receive their freedom, and to enjoy religious holidays. On the one hand, this meant that slavery in Puerto Rico was not as brutal as, say, in the southern US. On the other hand, it meant that this detestable institution managed to endure under the guise that it was relatively 'benign'.

The revolt in the town of Lares in 1868 was part of this difficult transition. This explains why many of the claims made during the insurrection relate to economic grievances and calls for the abolition of slavery. When one adds the fact that Spanish rule, after the reformists' attempts faded away, was particularly repressive – which accounts for the inclusion of liberal and political demands during the 1868 process – one can appreciate the state of affairs in Puerto Rico at that time: the clash between an authoritarian, colonial, and exploitative social, economic, and political system on the one hand, and proto-democratic, pro-independence, and reformist movement that was taking shape in the island, on the other.

After the 1868 rebellion was crushed, Spain responded with greater repression and harsher control measures. Still, a new nationality had been born which questioned its allegiance to peninsular Spain and would become the nucleus of a Puerto Rican national resistance sentiment that survives to this day. It also represented the existence of an important spark of rebellion among Puerto Ricans.

By the end of the century, Spain had allowed the formation of local political parties, as long as they did not openly contest Spanish rule. This marked a very feeble attempt to develop a plural political system, which was far from being democratic. But it at least permitted the development of a more open political culture that could usher in future reform.

By 1897, Spain was desperately holding on to its two last American territories: Cuba and Puerto Rico. Aware that its grip on Cuba was slipping away, the Spanish government offered Puerto Rico an Autonomy Charter (*Carta Autonómica*) that, for the first time in centuries, allowed the Puerto Rican People to achieve a significant – albeit still incomplete – level of self-government and a limited taste of democratic practice, at least as compared to the previous historical practice under Spain. This was meant to encourage Puerto Ricans to maintain their links with Spain and not go down Cuba's revolutionary path of separation. Through the Autonomy Charter, Puerto Ricans elected their first island-wide government, which signalled the potential start of a new era of self-rule, democratic development, and liberal reforms.

But these steps proved, once again, to be short-lived. Just a few months later, on 25 July 1898, the US invaded Puerto Rico as part of the Spanish-American War. Resistance was minimal, evidencing the exhaustion of the Spanish colonial model. On 10 December 1898, the US and Spain signed the Treaty of Paris, which officially ended the war.

Through the Treaty of Paris, Spain formally transferred sovereignty over Puerto Rico to the US.[2] As a result, from 1898 to 1900, Puerto Rico was subject to direct US rule through a military government. The autonomous government that had been set up through the Charter managed to co-exist briefly with the military rulers but was eventually abolished. The disbanding of the autonomous institutions did not generate any real popular opposition or pushback. Unfortunately, the autonomous government had not been able to create sufficient social support or institutional roots to withstand the transcendental paradigm shift that followed the war.

Whether Spain had the legal right to transfer of sovereignty over Puerto Rico to the US through the Treaty of Paris has been long disputed. The main

[2] Puerto Rico's relationship with the US preceded the formal handover made in 1898. During the latter part of the nineteenth century, the US was one of Puerto Rico's main commercial partners. This reflected the increased presence, influence, and importance of the US in the Western Hemisphere. It also meant that the US had important economic interests in the island. This situation, in turn, meant Puerto Rico gradually moved into its orbit and, eventually, geopolitical designs and objectives.

argument is that Spain had already relinquished sovereignty over Puerto Rico through the 1897 Autonomy Charter. In that sense, it could not transfer what it no longer possessed. Puerto Rico had become, at least, a semi-sovereign and self-governing political entity that was no longer wholly beholden to the Spanish crown. Any change of sovereignty would thus require Puerto Rican consent, ideally without the presence of an occupying military force.

As such, the argument goes, the US presence in Puerto Rico began illegally, since neither the Puerto Rican People nor its autonomous government gave their consent to such presence. The natural consequence of this argument is that the 25 July disembarkation was actually an invasion of autonomous Puerto Rico and not just of Spain itself or one of its colonial possessions. And since Puerto Rico was not a party to the Treaty of Paris, it never formally consented to the presence of the US on the island. This means that the US was occupying Puerto Rico in an unlawful manner.

While the validity of this argument is beyond the scope of this book, it serves as an example of how the colonial character of Puerto Rico's relationship with the US, and the political, social, and legal disputes that it has created, has been a constant feature of Puerto Rican constitutional development since the very beginning of the US presence on the island. Colonialism has been a constant, and unwelcome, travelling partner of constitutionalism in Puerto Rico. More to the point, constitutionalism in Puerto Rico was born and has grown under the shadow of colonialism.

Local reaction to the US occupation was mixed, and a generalised 'wait-and-see' policy gained traction. On the one hand, there was the view that here comes a friendly, fellow American republic that will help Puerto Rico get rid of its harsh European colonial master. Whether it would end with Puerto Rico becoming an independent republic or an equal part of the American federation, the idea of liberal reform of the current system was widely welcomed and even expected. On the other hand, the rise of US imperialism had been evident, given its territorial ambitions in the Pacific and the Americas. Some sectors feared that Puerto Rico had just replaced one colonial master with another, and that colonial subordination would continue, albeit under a different flag and language.

The struggle against colonialism would continue nearly uninterruptedly, although now within a new paradigm. New contradictions also arose at this time. Many of those who advocated independence from Spain now championed annexation with the US. Others who fervently opposed separation from Spain now advocated a self-governing Puerto Rico. An important, though probably not majoritarian, portion of the population that favoured independence from Spain maintained that view with regard to the US.[3]

[3] For a different perspective, see PA Malavet, *America's Colony: The Political and Cultural Conflict Between the United States and Puerto Rico* (New York University Press, 2007) 50, where he seems to argue that there was more consistency with regard to the different groups' positions as to Puerto Rico's relationship with both Spain and the US.

From 1898 to 1900, Puerto Rico was subject to US military occupation and direct colonial rule. Ironically, this anti-democratic reality was accompanied by important substantive reforms, such as the legalisation of divorce and labour unions. In that sense, substantive progress came hand in hand with authoritarian colonialism. Democracy and self-rule would develop slowly on the island, under the watchful eye of the US government.

The first two years of US domination after the war were utterly undemocratic and authoritarian. This period was marked by direct colonial rule through military institutions, hardly the stuff of democratic governance. Generals and admirals ruled by decree over the conquered land without a hint of consent of the governed. It seemed less like liberation and more like occupation and colonisation.

Ironically, as we saw, some of these undemocratic measures were actually progressive in nature. For example, one of the very first military decrees legalised labour unions and divorce, which had been banned under Spanish rule. Another example was the military government's decree that gave debtors a year to address their outstanding debts.[4] This was in line with the US commanding general's 'manifesto emphasizing the invader's benevolent intentions towards the country's inhabitants. The ambiguous terminology of the proclamation could satisfy a broad range of Creole expectations, but it did not explicitly commit itself to recognizing the political sovereignty of Puerto Ricans'.[5]

This has been sort of a constant of US colonialism in Puerto Rico: undemocratic mechanisms that periodically generate progressive results. More recently, after the Puerto Rico Supreme Court, in a 5–4 decision,[6] turned down the request by one member of a same sex couple to adopt the daughter of the other, the US Supreme Court recognised the constitutional right of same sex couples to marry.[7] In other words, while a Puerto Rican institution (whose members are appointed and confirmed by elected local officials) denied a progressive proposal, an American institution (the selection of whose members Puerto Ricans have no direct or indirect participation in) granted important substantive rights to a historically marginalised sector of the population. Such is the stuff of colonialism.

Colonialism did not impact exclusively on the political scene. It also had long-lasting legal, economic, and cultural effects. US capital and economic interests have always been dominant in the island since the 1898 invasion – even before – and Puerto Rico's legal system continues to be subordinate and constantly influenced by US law. In other words, the Puerto Rico-US relationship

[4] F Picó, *History of Puerto Rico: A Panorama of Its People* (Markus Wiener, 2014) 239.
[5] ibid 235–36.
[6] *Ex parte AAR* 187 DPR 835 (2013).
[7] *Obergefell v Hodges* 576 US 644 (2015). Shortly after this decision was issued by the US Supreme Court, the Puerto Rican Supreme Court recognised that it applied to Puerto Rico as well: *Charbonier Laureano v Gobernador* 193 DPR 516 (2015).

has been characterised by an imperialist and overt version of colonialism. This includes intermittent periods of political repression and attempts at cultural assimilation, including designs to replace Spanish as the native language.

The goal of the American government's project in Puerto Rico – if one can speak in such singular terms – is contested. Some suggest that '[a]fter the Spanish-American War, the US' imperial aspirations led it to attempt to "Americanise" the Puerto Ricans by imposing on the island a narrow vision of "American" culture, principally through legal and educational programs'.[8] To be sure, such endeavoors were made. For example, the University of Puerto Rico, for decades the crown jewel of Puerto Rico's public repertoire, was originally founded as a pedagogical school meant to produce teachers who would help assimilate the local population. Eventually, the UPR transformed itself into an engine of cultural resistance and social transformation.

Yet, it could also be argued that the early US occupation of Puerto Rico was partially reluctant to assimilate the local population, out of fear that it could lead to an undesired annexation of Puerto Rico as a federated state. In other words, that the US colonial project was one of domination more than assimilation or incorporation. The absence of any significant population movement from the mainland to the island may be indicative of this.

Another example of this phenomenon dates back to the 1940s, when the US-appointed colonial government attempted to make English the only language allowed in public schools. Aside from its asinine characteristic in practical terms – almost all public-school teachers knew very little English – it was also a political blunder. This naked, and unnecessary, attempt to destroy and supplant Puerto Rico's Hispanic culture sparked nationalist sentiment, which eventually halted the assimilation attempt.

Yet, it should be noted that Puerto Ricans did not necessarily miss their old European master. However, the Puerto Rican nationality that had been born in the nineteenth century was Spanish-speaking, among other cultural characteristics that were inherited from Spain. The resistance to the blatantly colonial and imperialist attempt to replace Puerto Rico's native tongue with the language of the new imperial power reflected the endurance of this nationality that, while politically subordinate to American control, held the line when it came to basic cultural identity and self-worth.

American capital also displaced, quite ruthlessly, local economic interests. US companies, particularly in the sugar industry, quickly became dominant. This generated a constant problem of capital flight, lack of reinvestment, and the pauperisation of large sectors of the Puerto Rican working class which, in turn, also produced important labour militancy. As is discussed in greater detail in Chapter 3, this mix of national identity and class tension was clearly present

[8] Malavet (n 3) 3. This view is consistent with a nationalist narrative of the US's design over Puerto Rico. This narrative mostly structures its analysis on national, cultural, and racial considerations.

during the 1952 constitutional process, which would account for much of its progressive substantive content.

The total domination of the Puerto Rican economy by US capital has entrenched the colonial relationship, by making Puerto Rico wholly dependent on American markets, products, and corporations, not to mention the dependency by a substantial sector of its population on federal social assistance programs. As a result, the Puerto Rican economy has never been allowed to develop fully as an autochthonous phenomenon, thus generating a vicious cycle of dependency and subordination, as well as resistance.

II. PUERTO RICO'S TERRITORIAL STATUS PRIOR TO 1952

Article IV, Section 3 of the US Constitution deals with Congress's powers over the territories 'and other Property belonging to the United States'.[9] The main characteristic of these territories is that they are subject to the plenary powers of Congress. This means that, unlike when it acts as the legislature of the US federation – and thus subject to the limitations of Article I – in the context of Article IV, Congress acts here as the territorial legislature. As such, Congress can exercise general police powers and decide on how such a territory is to be governed, regardless of the views of the people living in that territory. When it comes to the territories, all Article I bets are off. The same thing can be said for democratic considerations.

The American imperialist experiment that began at the close of the nineteenth century tested the structural limits of the US Constitution. Until that period, the US was made up of individual sovereign States and territories. As for the territories, historically these were sufficiently populated and politically organised entities that, after a transition period, became full members of the US federation.[10] In other words, the territorial condition was not designed to be indefinite or permanent. Congress's plenary powers were meant to be exercised until the sufficiently populated territory became fully organised politically and able to govern itself. Afterwards, the territory would be admitted as a State.

But the acquisition of populated lands outside the continental US, mostly inhabited by non-Anglos, generated resistance within certain sectors the US as to the possibility of admitting some or all of these communities as States. This resistance produced the infamous *Insular Cases*,[11] which have cast a longstanding shadow over Puerto Rico for more than a century.

[9] The mere fact that territories and properties are lumped together in the same provision is telling.

[10] R Serrano Geyls, 'The Territorial Status of Puerto Rico and its Effects on the Political Future of the Island' (2005) 39 *Revista Jurídica Universidad Interamericana de Puerto Rico* 13.

[11] See, eg, *Downs v Bidwell* 182 US 244 (1901). See also, E Rivera-Ramos, *The Legal Construction of Identity: The Judicial and Social Legacy of American Colonialism in Puerto Rico* (American Psychological Association, 2001).

In 1900, Congress approved the Foraker Act, which established Puerto Rico's first civilian government under US domination. For legal purposes, this Act created what is now known as the 'Government of Puerto Rico', which is why it is considered an organic statute. As a result, the previous legal order that existed under Spain and the Autonomy Charter were completely wiped away.

One interesting, but limited, possible exception is the Supreme Court of Puerto Rico. While the Foraker Act officially established a new judicial body, it was a sort of continuation of the old *Audiencia*, which was the colonial tribunal under Spanish rule. This was the result of a decision made in that respect by the military government between 1898 and 1900. The re-named *Audiencia* was allowed to operate, subject to two conditions: (1) the judges had to pledge loyalty to the US; and (2) they could only adjudicate private law claims. Therefore, for all intents and purposes, the Foraker Act constituted a clean break from Spanish colonial institutions, including the Judicial Branch.

The democratic nature of the civilian government established by the 1900 Foraker Act was marginal at best. Both the Governor and the Supreme Court were entirely appointed by the President of the US and confirmed by the federal Senate, regardless of the will of the Puerto Rican People. As to the Legislative Branch, only the lower house was selected by popular election.[12] Meanwhile, the upper house, called the Executive Council, was wholly appointed by the President and confirmed by the Senate, and was composed of six Americans and five native Puerto Ricans.

In other words, from 1900 until 1917, the only partially democratic institution on the island was the lower house of the Legislature. Moreover, the powers of this chamber were considerably limited, particularly when it attempted to confront the aggregated force of the unelected bodies. There were significant clashes in which the lower house attempted to reign in the rest. For example, it deliberately withheld its approval of the island's budget, in a failed attempt to gain democratic concessions in return. It should be noted that the 1952 Constitution includes a provision that states that, if the Legislature cannot agree on a particular budget, the previous year's budget would be reauthorised. This was the direct result of the House of Delegates' unsuccessful democratic rebellion at the start of the century.

As if this wasn't enough, the Foraker Act did not include a Bill of Rights. Combined with the fact that most federal constitutional rights were not applicable to Puerto Rico,[13] this intentional omission meant that, for almost 20 years, Puerto Ricans were deprived of almost all constitutional rights, whether federal or local. On the one hand, this did not present a radical departure from previous

[12] It should be noted that universal suffrage was finally adopted in Puerto Rico in 1935. Before that date, many groups were denied the right to vote, including women, the illiterate, and the propertyless.

[13] This was one of the direct holdings of the *Insular Cases*.

practice – after all, Spain had also failed to extend any form of constitutionalism to the island. On the other hand, it helped fuel resentment among the population regarding the colonial condition and the failure of the American republic to live up to its professed ideals of democratic reform.

As noted above, the new statute included an appointed Governor and Supreme Court. Both were to be nominated by the President of the US, with the advice and consent of the federal Senate. All other judges would be appointed by the Governor, subject to confirmation by the insular Executive Council. This made the heads of two of the branches of government directly selected by and accountable to the President of the US. In that sense, the colonial nature of the Foraker Act was plain and obvious. Not only did Congress get to decide how the island would be governed, but it also chose a structure that denied Puerto Ricans the opportunity to fully govern themselves.

As for the Legislative Branch, only one chamber – the House of Delegates – was to be elected by the Puerto Rican People and the other, the Executive Council, was to be appointed by the President of the US, subject to senatorial confirmation. The Executive Council would serve both as the upper chamber of the Legislature and the Governor's Cabinet. This structural creativity was evidence of Congress's leeway under the Territorial Clause.

An interesting detail about the Executive Council deserves further elaboration. According to the Foraker Act, the Council would be made up of 11 members, all of them appointed by the President and subject to at-will removal. Of those 11 seats, the Act required that 'at least five ... shall be inhabitants of Porto Rico'.[14] The remaining six members could be non-residents.

While the President could decide to appoint more than five native Puerto Ricans, the congressional design and actual presidential practice was that the remaining six members of the Council would be non-Puerto Ricans. This structure has two important consequences. First, it seems to presume that there will be a natural voting divide between Puerto Ricans and non-Puerto Ricans. And second, that if that divide were to materialise, the non-Puerto Rican block should be assured a one-seat majority. It appears that Puerto Ricans could not be trusted to have control over such an important government institution. Colonialism does not trust the colonised.

The Foraker Act did not change Puerto Rico's status as a US Territory under Article IV of the Constitution. On the contrary, the Act was adopted, precisely, under Congress' powers under the Territorial Clause. Under the Foraker Act, only one half of one of the three branches of government was to be selected by the Puerto Rican People. The remaining structures of government were to be directly filled by the US President. The Foraker Act represented a period of direct

[14] Foraker Act, Public Law No 56-191, § 18 (1900). Notice the reference to 'Porto Rico', as a sort of Americanised version of the correct spelling 'Puerto Rico'.

US colonialism, with the singular difference that, unlike the 1898–1900 period, it was civilian in nature.

It should be noted that the new US domination over the island was not accompanied by a mass population influx coming from the US. While the new rulers would be non-Puerto Ricans, the vast majority of the island's population would be made up of native Puerto Ricans and immigrants from neighbouring Caribbean countries. In that sense, US colonialism has mostly been political and economic, instead of demographic. Again, it is an imperialist version of colonialism that was typical of the period. Among other things, it was meant to prevent any move to incorporate the island as a federated state.

The Foraker Act did not extend US citizenship to Puerto Ricans. Nor did it contain a Bill of Rights that protected citizens against the actions of the local government created by the Act. This raised the question as to whether *federal* constitutional rights applied to the island.

As a result, shortly after the adoption of the Foraker Act, cases worked their way up to the US Supreme Court questioning Puerto Rico's precise legal situation and whether the US Constitution was fully applicable to the island. One of the key questions raised was whether Puerto Rico was on its way to becoming a state of the Union, as had been the historical practice until then with regard to populated and politically organised territories? The answer was not wholly clear. For example, the Foraker Act was actually titled 'An Act *temporarily* to provide revenues and a civil government for Porto Rico, and for other purposes' (emphasis added).

The same US Supreme Court that announced the separate but equal doctrine in *Plessy v Ferguson* decided the question in the *Insular Cases*. Specifically, it adopted a proposal first made in the *Harvard Law Review* to split the Territorial Clause atom.[15] This meant distinguishing between *two* types of territories for purposes of Article IV of the federal Constitution and, most importantly, the issue of the application of federal constitutional rights to the territories and their road towards statehood.

First, there were the *incorporated* territories. This first articulation mirrored historical practice and referred to territories that had started the process of becoming a US state. Because of their incorporated status, these territories were subject to the full protections of the federal Constitution. The incorporated territory status was meant to be temporary and transitional, as the precursor to full-fledged statehood. This was the historic definition of the territorial status, particularly those that had achieved sufficient population numbers and an acceptable level of internal political organisation.[16]

[15] See SE Baldwin, 'The Constitutional Questions Incident to the Acquisition and Government by the United States of Island Territory' (1899) 12 *Harvard Law Review* 393.

[16] See Serrano Geyls (n 10).

Second, there were the *unincorporated* territories. In these instances, the march toward statehood had not begun nor was there any guarantee that it would ever begin in the first place. As such, they could remain territories of the US, subject to Congress' plenary powers, on a permanent and indefinite basis. Because of their unincorporated status, these territories were not subject to the full protections of the federal Constitution. This new classification was meant to allow the US to acquire new territorial possessions and permanently govern its inhabitants, without any commitment to statehood or even democratic self-rule. It is the imperialist version of the Territorial Clause.

In order to distinguish between these two types of territories, the Supreme Court designed a test that enumerated several factors. Chief among them was whether Congress had granted US citizenship to the inhabitants of the territory. Since the 1900 Foraker Act had not done so with the regard to the residents of the island, the Supreme Court held that Puerto Rico was actually an *unincorporated* territory of the US, and thus, (1) subject to the plenary powers of Congress, (2) only *fundamental* constitutional rights would apply,[17] and (3) Puerto Rico could remain in that status indefinitely. According to the Court, Puerto Rico belonged to, but was not a part of, the US. This was colonialism at its finest and its lowest.

Full of explicitly racist language, the *Insular Cases* are, incredibly and shamefully, still good law in the US to this day.[18] Colonialism has thus become, and continues to be, an accepted feature of the US constitutional structure.[19] Puerto Rico is one of its current and long-lasting victims.

The Foraker Act lasted until 1917. This meant that the first 20 years of US presence in Puerto Rico were not accompanied by any real development in constitutional law, much less a culture or practice of constitutionalism. The organic act that created the local Puerto Rican government was devoid of a Bill of Rights, and the federal Bill of Rights did not automatically extend to the island. Only fundamental rights were applicable. And since this was before the US Supreme Court adopted its modern incorporation doctrine, very few rights were available to Puerto Ricans living on the island. For the first 20 years under US rule, constitutionalism was still an unknown concept for the Puerto Rican People.

In 1917, Congress replaced the Foraker Act with another organic statute known as the Jones Act. Also approved under the authority of the Territorial Clause of Article IV, the Jones Act made three substantial changes to the previous legal regime. First, it allowed Puerto Ricans to elect the entire Legislative

[17] For a critical view of this statement, see CD Ponsa-Kraus, 'The "Insular Cases" Run Amok: Against Constitutional Exceptionalism in the Territories' (2022) *Yale Law Journal* 2449, 2468. The author stresses that this conclusion is based on a misreading of the *Insular Cases* where the US Supreme Court emphasised that fundamental rights would apply to these territories, but did not necessarily mean that only fundamental rights would apply.

[18] For example, the *Insular Cases* were instrumental in the US Supreme Court's ruling in *Boumediene v Bush* 553 US 723 (2008).

[19] Ponsa-Kraus (n 17) 2488.

Branch, now made up of a Senate and a House of Representatives. This meant that at least one of the three branches of government would be wholly democratic in nature and directly accountable to the electorate. Second, the Jones Act, unlike its predecessor, included a Bill of Rights. Since the organic act serves as the foundation for the government of Puerto Rico, its Bill of Rights served as the equivalent of a constitutional charter of basic rights. And finally, it extended US citizenship to all Puerto Ricans living on the island. To a certain point, it seemed like a wholesale departure from the legal regime set up by the Foraker Act.

Not long after the adoption of the Jones Act, cases were presented in the federal Judiciary questioning whether Puerto Rico had stopped being an unincorporated territory of the US and had been fully incorporated, as per the doctrine announced in the *Insular Cases*. This would mean that: (1) the US Constitution would apply full force to the island; and (2) Puerto Rico had started its process of admission as a state of the federation. Since the *Insular Cases* had identified the conferral of citizenship as the key factor that distinguished between unincorporated and incorporated territories, many felt that Puerto Rico had changed categories.

But in *Balzac v Porto Rico*,[20] the US Supreme Court concluded that Puerto Rico was still an *unincorporated* territory of the US. According to the Court, the conferral of citizenship was merely a 'clue' as to whether incorporation had, in fact, taken place. This factor was not considered to be determinative. On the contrary, the Court now held that in order for a territory to be characterised as incorporated, an express statement from Congress that incorporation had occurred and that the process of admission into the Union as a State had begun was required. Since neither the Jones Act nor any other Act of Congress included such an express statement, the Court ruled that Puerto Rico had not been incorporated. The Court emphasised that the granting of citizenship was related to the inhabitants of Puerto Rico, not the status of the territory itself.

Undoubtedly, the unincorporated/incorporated territory dichotomy was a judicial *fiat* in an attempt to keep Puerto Rico within US control but outside the full protections of the Constitution or the prospect of statehood. That a substantially populated and sufficiently politically organised territory of the US could be permanently treated as such was new in the US constitutional experience. Meanwhile, the goalposts kept being moved, to impede Puerto Rico's admission into the American federation. This further strengthened anti-colonial sentiment on the island and the view that the US considered Puerto Rico as its property and Puerto Ricans as inferior.

An important clarification is warranted here. The naked colonialism of the unincorporated territory category, while motivated by hostility to the people who inhabited the island, had, and still has, mostly legal effects on the *territory*

[20] *Balzac v Porto Rico* 258 US 298 (1922). Notice, again, the use of the Americanised and incorrect identifier 'Porto Rico'.

itself and not formally on its people. In other words, from a purely constitutional law perspective, what establishes the legal content of citizenship is not *who* has it, but *where* they are. For example, if a Puerto Rican moves to the continental US, he or she can exercise his or her citizenship fully. They can vote in federal elections and receive economic benefits in equal conditions. They are also subject to federal income tax. On the flip side, if a Californian relocates to Puerto Rico, they would not be able to vote in federal elections and their benefits are subject to differential treatment, according to Congress' judgment, subject to the highly deferential rational basis review.[21]

As a result, legally, it is not Puerto Ricans who are treated differently, but any person who happens to reside in Puerto Rico. Of course, this does not hide the fact that, as a practical matter, Puerto Rico is mostly inhabited by Puerto Ricans. As such, the colonial nature of the *Insular Cases* still impacts how Puerto Ricans live and how Puerto Rican constitutionalism has developed. Recent decisions by the US Supreme Court have not changed this reality.[22]

While the *Insular Cases* and their progeny mostly focused on the differences between the two type of territories, there is still the question of what they have in common as territories. The quick answer lies in the contrast with federated states: neither type of territory has voting representation in the US Congress, nor do they have participation in the Electoral College or the Article V amendment mechanisms.

Professor Ponsa-Kraus suggests that the key may rest with the concept of annexation, which, according to her, occurs even in the context of unincorporated territories.[23] In other words, that Puerto Rico, like the other acquisitions that followed the Spanish-American War, has 'been annexed but not incorporated'.[24] Unfortunately, Ponsa-Kraus does not elaborate on the implications of this statement. In particular, what are the effects of Puerto Rico's annexation absent incorporation? It seems that the reference to annexation is meant to reiterate that Puerto Rico is somehow within the US, thus turning the Puerto Rican question mostly into a matter of domestic US constitutional law, as opposed to international law. In other words, that Puerto Rico is not separate from the US.

This brings us to two important international law considerations: (1) the right to self-determination; and (2) the illegality of colonialism. Unlike individual

[21] See *Califano v Torres* 435 US 1 (1978); *Harris v Rosario* 446 US 651 (1980).

[22] See Ch 7.

[23] In order to avoid terminological confusion, it should be noted that, as used here, annexation is separate from admission as a state of the Union (statehood). This is evidence of the conceptual differences between domestic US legal parlance and international law. For example, in international law, *statehood* means the achievement of national independence, while in the US context, it means being admitted as a state of the Union. Likewise, in international law, *annexation* refers to the integration of one territory by another.

[24] Ponsa-Kraus (n 17) 2452.

autonomy, self-determination in this context is a collective political right that belongs to the peoples of dependent territories that have not been fully integrated into the dominant political unit as an equal component and have also not acquired total self-government. In other words, international law requires territories that are still subject to colonial control to have the right to determine their own destiny.

Furthermore, current international law considers colonialism as utterly unacceptable. Regardless of the *individual* situation of the inhabitants of Puerto Rico – mostly Puerto Ricans who identify with that nationality – in terms of their civil rights, there is an additional *collective* component that should also be taken into consideration for purposes of determining the current state of constitutionalism on the island. Chapter 7 revisits this issue in the context of analysing the substantive and procedural alternatives to address and transcend the current colonial situation of Puerto Rico.

Although the Jones Act was an improvement over the Foraker Act, it did not eliminate the universally repudiated and wholly unacceptable stench of colonialism. If anything, it was a reminder of how colonialism was still the underlying principle of the US-Puerto Rico relationship. While Puerto Ricans disagreed – and still do – as to what the future relation to the US should be, with some advocating annexation and others some sort of independence, during the first decades of US occupation there was a generalised consensus that the current territorial condition was unacceptable. This included the development of a militant independence movement that resorted to armed struggle in an attempt to destroy the colonial relationship and establish an independent republic.

In 1947, US Congress approved a statute that allowed Puerto Ricans to elect their own Governor. In 1950, Congress also adopted Public Law 600, which allowed Puerto Ricans to write their own constitution. This led to an island-wide referendum in which the People of Puerto Rico accepted Congress's offer. As a result, in 1951 elections were held for a Constitutional Convention that would draft Puerto Rico's first autochthonous Constitution.

But the 1952 constitutional process did not substantially alter Puerto Rico's condition as an unincorporated territory of the US. It is worth noting that important parts of the population believed, or allowed themselves to believe, that the 1952 constitutional process was the result of a true exercise of sovereignty by the Puerto Rican People. The US government furthered that narrative, particularly to avoid international embarrassment as the Cold War started heating up. That included an official statement given to the United Nations, indicating that Puerto Rico had exercised self-determination and achieved sufficient self-government. As a result, the US government succeeded in erasing Puerto Rico from the UN's list of colonial territories.

Not all were convinced, however. For example, the Puerto Rican Independence Party, then the second electoral force in the island, boycotted the 1952 Convention. But, for our purposes here, the key element is that it appeared that the calling of a Constitutional Convention in order for Puerto Ricans to democratically enact their own constitution was – or could have been at the very least – a significant move away from colonialism.

Because the legal question as to whether Public Law 600 or the enactment of the 1952 Constitution had, in fact, changed Puerto Rico's colonial and territorial condition would not to be settled for several decades, an analysis of the colonial nature of the 1952 requires other factors to be examined. The next chapter focuses on those that had a direct impact on the process that generated the 1952 Constitution, its substantive content, political structure, and mechanisms for future amendment.

III. THE UNFULFILLED POTENTIAL OF PUERTO RICO'S QUEST FOR SOCIAL JUSTICE

Puerto Rican history is replete with systems that produced social injustice and exploitation. It is also a history full of frustrated and sabotaged attempts to transform society and overcome inequality. This contradiction has characterised the island for centuries.

Since the early stages of the Spanish conquest, systems of economic exploitation have been implemented. These, in turn, have generated resistance and opposition, mostly unsuccessful. For example, the Spanish instituted a harsh system to subordinate and exploit the island's indigenous population that, while legally distinct from slavery, was from a practical perspective hardly distinguishable.

That *encomienda* system generated strong opposition from a minoritarian sector within the clergy, which objected to the harsh treatment of the *taínos*. While those objections helped pave the way for legislation that nominally protected the indigenous population, these mild attempts at reform were not enough to impede the annihilation of Puerto Rico's *taíno* population.

As noted above, something similar happened with attempts at democratising – or even mildly liberalising – the colonial economic structure, as the San Germán example demonstrates. The movement for the abolition of slavery was also constantly foiled by the ruling classes, including the crushing of the *Grito de Lares* in 1868, until the institution finally died out in 1873.

The US military government's move to legalise labour unions shortly after the end of the Spanish-American War, coupled with the island's rapid industrialisation during the early decades of the twentieth century led by American capital, created both a wholly unequal economic system and a militant labour movement committed to reforming it. The labour movement was eventually able to push for the adoption of progressive labour legislation, some of which was even constitutionalised in 1952.

As mentioned above, one of the first decrees of the military government after the US occupied Puerto Rico was the legalisation of labour unions. Prior to that, Spain had banned labour organisations, although economic transformations at the end of the eighteenth century meant the rise of a mass of labourers that started to act collectively.

The first labour union founded in Puerto Rico was the *Federación Libre de Trabajadores* (FLT), established in 1899.[25] In turn, the FLT – later affiliated with the US-based American Federation of Labour – created a political arm called the Socialist Labour Party (*Partido Obrero Socialista*, POS). This signalled a significant shift in Puerto Rican politics and society. Reorganised in 1915 as the Socialist Party (PS), this organisation, in conjunction with the FLT, contributed to the creation of a strong and militant labour movement that made its presence felt in Puerto Rico, particularly during the 1920s and 1930s. This period also saw the creation of the first Communist Party in the island.

In addition to significant industrial actions, the PS-FLT also engaged in education campaigns – including initiatives where union members literally read to workers during their shifts, including literary fiction, science, and history[26] – meant to organise, politicise, and mobilise workers. This combination of trade unionism, electoral participation, and social projects made the PS-FLT a significant force in Puerto Rican politics and society. Part of its legacy was the adoption of a series of progressive class legislation that, eventually, would find itself embedded in the constitutional text several decades later.

The main class antagonists of the labour movement in the twentieth century were the sugar and tobacco corporations that owned considerable tracts of land and employed a substantial number of workers on substandard wages and conditions. This marked the wholesale takeover of Puerto Rico's nascent capitalist economy by US corporate interests. At the same time, there were massive strikes in these sectors, which signalled the emergence of a militant labour movement that, while not strong enough to defeat their class antagonists, was able to keep them at bay.

As Kenneth Lugo explains, '[b]etween 1918 and 1932, more than 130 labour unions were organised [in Puerto Rico] with a membership of more than 40,000. There was practically no important sector of the economy where the labour unions had not successfully penetrated'.[27] These unions were considerable politicised and adopted socialism as their guiding principle. Although considerably weakened by 1951–52, there was still a generally pro-union culture in Puerto Rico that allowed their agenda to be included during the deliberations of the Constitutional Convention.

[25] This includes the short-lived *Federación Regional de Trabajadores de Puerto Rico* that same year. See K Lugo del Toro, *Nacimiento y Auge de la Confederación General de Trabajadores 1940–1945* (Universidad Interamericana de Puerto Rico, 2013) 27. The historical leader of both the PS and the FLT was the Spanish-born Santiago Iglesias Pantín, whose name was constantly invoked during the deliberations of the Constitutional Convention.

[26] See M del Carmen Baerga Santini, '"¡A la Organización, a Unirnos Como un Solo Hombre!": La Federación Libre de Trabajadores y el Mundo Masculino del Trabajo' in E Pérez Velazco (ed), *100 Años de Sindicalismo Puertorriqueño* (Ediciones Callejón, 2007) 149.

[27] Lugo del Toro (n 25) 69 (author's translation).

3

The Constitutional Creation Process

I. IN THE SHADOW OF COLONIALISM

Recent US Supreme Court rulings, which are discussed in greater detail in Chapter 7, have made it clear that the 1952 Constitution did not substantially alter Puerto Rico's status as an unincorporated territory of the US. In fact, the Court has held that what happened in 1952 was merely a delegation of congressional power under Article IV of the Constitution. As a result, Congress did not, and has not, relinquished its sovereignty or plenary powers over Puerto Rico and still acts as the ultimate constitutional source of authority on the island. That holding was not a harmless legal statement: it served as the normative basis for US Congress's passing of the PROMESA statute,[1] which basically reverted Puerto Rico to its pre-1952 state, where federal appointees held ultimate power over the island and its affairs.

While this would be made obvious decades later, an analysis of the 1952 process and the content of the constitutional text and structure itself makes abundantly clear that Puerto Rico's 1952 Constitution is colonial in nature. In that sense, colonialism can be found both in its process of creation, as well as its content. In this chapter, we begin with an analysis of the process that resulted in its adoption.

In 1952, some in Puerto Rico believed that the constitution that was about to be adopted would constitute a binding bilateral covenant between Puerto Rico and the US as equals. This view was fervently defended by the majority party at the time, the Popular Democratic Party (PPD). The PPD was then made up of mostly ex-independence supporters who wished to expand Puerto Rican autonomy while preserving some sort of permanent union with the US. The possibility of a political arrangement that combined association with maximum self-government was the main goal of the PPD. The remaining question was whether this arrangement would still be considered territorial or colonial in nature. At least publicly, colonialism continued to be an unacceptable prospect.

[1] Puerto Rico Oversight, Management, and Economic Stability Act (PROMESA), Public Law No 114-187 (2016).

The so-called theory of the 'pact' or 'covenant' meant that because it was an agreement amongst equals, Puerto Rico had ceased to be a colony – unincorporated territory, in US domestic law parlance – and became a truly autonomous and self-governing political entity that had entered into a covenant with the US; a pact that could only be modified through mutual agreement. At least, that was the hope of the PPD, which was the dominant political force at the time and represented a substantial portion of the Puerto Rican population.

However, the US Supreme Court has recently held that Public Law 600 references to a bilateral covenant merely meant that the Puerto Rican People had accepted Congress's offer to delegate some of its powers over Puerto Rico to its People with the specific and limited objective of drafting a local constitution. It was neither an agreement among equals nor a covenant that required mutual consent to alter. Congress still held the last word over Puerto Rican matters. The colonial condition was not materially altered in 1952. It only appeared that way to some. Whether this was the result of self-delusion or intellectual dishonesty is still an open question.

In other words, Congress, through Public Law 600, chose a different path from the Foraker Act and the Jones Act. Instead of directly organising Puerto Rico's local government by way of unilateral statutory enactment and presidential appointment of its main officers, through Public Law 600 Congress chose to delegate that specific design task to the Puerto Rican People themselves.

But that exercise did not constitute a congressional abdication of its plenary powers under Article IV of the federal Constitution. Instead, it was a practical decision to delegate some of its powers, so that the People of Puerto Rico could design their own structures of local self-government and, eventually, select their own governmental officers. Ultimate sovereignty over Puerto Rico would still be in the hands of the federal Congress, which held on to the right to intervene at any time, if it chose to do so.

But the colonial nature of the Puerto Rican constitutional project – and particularly, its colonial origin – was evident to many from the start. As such, we must start our analysis with Public Law 600, which served as its legal starting point.

This statute approved the holding of a referendum on the island to gauge the Puerto Rican People's response to Congress's offer to delegate some of its power, so as to adopt a local constitution. Although Public Law 600 was met with some resistance and scepticism on the island, the People by and large accepted Congress's offer by way of referendum. If nothing else, it seemed like the end of the widely repudiated Jones Act regime.

The antecedent description of the colonial condition of Puerto Rico was wholly present during the 1952 process. But colonialism was not relegated to a mere background feature. Colonialism was at the essence of Public Law 600 and the legal regime it created. In that sense, the 1952 process cannot be characterised as an actual move towards decolonisation. On the contrary; it was premised on the legality of the US presence in Puerto Rico and of the continued territorial status of the island.

By 1952, Puerto Rico had been directly governed by the US for over half a century and its economy was now fully in the hands of American capital and corporations. This is hardly what the United Nations thought of as a decolonisation process after World War II. Still, the US government, then at the height of Cold War geopolitics, did not want to publicly admit that it engaged in naked colonialism. As such, the 1952 process allowed the US to hide its colonial exercises, by claiming that Puerto Rico had achieved sufficient self-government so as to not be regarded as still a colonial possession under international law. This would later prove to be a sham or even a fraud on the international community.

When Puerto Rico accepted Congress's offer to draft its own constitution, it also accepted the procedural and substantive conditions that came with it. Further below, we analyse the substantive conditions. For now, we focus on the procedural ones.

The most important procedural limitation was that the final draft of the constitution, once approved by the Constitutional Convention and by the People of Puerto Rico in a referendum, would still need to be considered by Congress, which held the ultimate authority to modify and accept the constitutional text. And, as we will see, Congress did in fact use this power to alter the text drafted by the elected representatives of the Puerto Rican People. While the final text accepted by Congress would return to the Puerto Rican People for their consideration in another referendum, this series of events made it abundantly clear that Congress held, and still holds, ultimate power over the island.

The Constitutional Convention that met in San Juan from 1951 to 1952 was selected through a very democratic and participatory process. That partially explains its continued legitimacy in the eyes of the public, at least in terms of its substantive content.

But its nature was still colonial, as the legal authority of the Convention did not originate from the Puerto Rican People, but from an Act of Congress – a Congress where the Puerto Rican People had no voting rights. This colonial stain on the constitutional process has hampered its claim to a higher level of validity and legitimacy. The boycott by the Puerto Rican Independence Party also served as a reminder of the process's colonial blind spots. This accounts for the Puerto Rican People's ambivalent relationship with their Constitution: democratic legitimacy and substantive agreement, coupled with colonial illegitimacy and structural deficiencies.

During the deliberations of the Constitutional Convention, there was little *direct* official interference by Congress, although individual members of Congress did send remarks to the delegates during their sessions.[2] In that sense,

[2] For example, Representative Eva Beck Bone of Utah actually visited the Convention and spoke to the delegates. When introducing her to the delegates, the President of the Constitutional Convention, Dr Antonio Fernós-Isern remarked that '[s]he will be one of those who will pass upon our constitution'. On another occasion, Senator Brian McMahon of Connecticut, chairman of the Joint Congressional Committee on Atomic Energy, also spoke directly to the delegates.

Congress's direct control of the 1952 process was exercised at the edges: (1) the authorising statute that began – and conditioned – the process; and (2) the power to have the real final say as to the text itself. This allowed Congress to maintain a firm grip over the constitutional process without the need to be visibly present during its drafting stage.

As noted above, through Public Law 600, Congress merely *authorised* Puerto Ricans to draft their own local constitution if they chose to accept its offer: hardly the stuff of the exercise of constituent power, sovereign self-government, or effective decolonisation. The Act provided that the offer contained in the Act itself would be submitted to the Puerto Rican People in a referendum.

Of course, this did not mean that Puerto Ricans got to decide on the existence of Public Law 600, but that they would be asked to accept its offer 'in the nature of a compact'.[3] This language did not constitute a binding treaty between Puerto Rico and the US. On the contrary, the 'compact' would merely reflect the fact that the Puerto Rican People accepted Congress's offer to start a local constitutional drafting process. Accepting an offer does not mean that the agreement was made between equal, independent parties; nor does it mean that one of the parties does not maintain ultimate control over the relationship itself.

The Act laid out the specific procedure for the implementation of its offer to the People of Puerto Rico. First, an island-wide referendum would take place, where qualified voters would be able to accept or reject Congress's offer to start a local constitutional process. If approved, Congress authorised the Puerto Rican Legislature to 'call a constitutional convention to draft a constitution for the said island of Puerto Rico'.[4] Again, the compact merely meant that Puerto Rico was consenting to the process laid out by Congress. Had the Puerto Rican People rejected the offer established in Public Law 600, then the Jones Act would have continued to operate, and it would be up to Congress, in the exercise of its plenary powers under Article IV, to consider other design alternatives, if any.

From the beginning, Congress established the substantive boundaries regarding what the Puerto Rico Constitutional Convention could do and established a substantive minimum. For example, Public Law 600 required the Convention to 'provide a republican form of government' and to 'include a bill of rights'.[5] This severely limited its constituent authority.

But Congress was not yet finished. Public Law 600 also laid out the procedural steps that would take place after the Convention drafted a complete text. First, the draft would be subjected to another island-wide referendum to approve

[3] Puerto Rico Federal Relations Act of 1950, Public Law No 81-600, § 1 (1950).
[4] Puerto Rico Federal Relations Act of 1950, Public Law No 81-600, § 2 (1950).
[5] ibid.

or reject the proposed text. In ordinary circumstances, this would be the final step of a true constituent process where the People have the last word.

But in the case of Puerto Rico, its People would not have the final say. The President of the US would then send the proposed constitution to Congress for its final approval. According to Public Law 600, '[u]pon approval by the Congress the constitution shall become effective in accordance with its terms'.[6] The second referendum to accept any changes to the text made by Congress would be purely pro forma.

This language was not just symbolic, seemingly harmless imperialism. Congress did, fact, exercise its plenary powers and modified some of the text that had already been approved by the Constitutional Convention and accepted by the people in a first ratification referendum. That Congress still exercised its powers after these two events clearly demonstrates two things: (1) that the US Congress exercised ultimate sovereignty over Puerto Rico, above its constitutional delegates and People; and (2) that Congress did not feel inhibited at all in exercising that power.

Congress both required the inclusion of additional text and expressly vetoed an entire section of the proposed Bill of Rights. Through a joint resolution, Congress withheld final approval of the Constitution until the government of Puerto Rico activated the Constitution's Article VII amendment procedures and adopted Congress's changes.

One of the required changes was an amendment to Section 5 of Article II (Bill of Rights). That provision dealt with the general right to education. The Puerto Rican Constitutional Convention had adopted language making it a requirement that all children attend elementary school. Congress demanded that the provision make clear that parents could fulfil this obligation by sending their children to private schools. While not in direct opposition with the will of the Puerto Rican framers, it was still a direct modification of the constitutional text.

Congress also demanded that Section 20 of the Bill of Rights be eliminated completely. Section 20 recognised a series of important human rights as a matter of general public policy. It included many of the socio-economic rights found in the Universal Declaration of Human Rights, including housing, healthcare, employment, and nutrition. It was supposed to be the cornerstone of Puerto Rico's commitment to a more just and equal society. Even though the Convention made it abundantly clear that Section 20 would not be directly justiciable, Congress would not have it; it smelled like socialism, which was out of the question in 1952. This requires further analysis, which is offered below. As relevant here, it exemplifies how Congress preserved and exercised control over the 1952 process.

[6] Puerto Rico Federal Relations Act of 1950, Public Law No 81-600, § 3 (1950).

Finally, Congress demanded that Article VII of the Constitution, which dealt with the amendment procedure, include a substantive limitation on the power of the Puerto Rican Legislature and People to amend *their own* constitution. Congress's language established that '[a]ny amendment or revision of this constitution shall be consistent with the resolution enacted by the Congress of the US approving this constitution, with the applicable provisions of the Constitution of the US, with the Puerto Rican Federal Relations Act, and with Public Law 600, Eighty-first Congress, adopted in the nature of a compact'.[7] This limitation is revisited and discussed in more detail in Chapter 5.

In the end, all the changes made by Congress *were agreed to* by the Puerto Rican People and they became part of the official text of the Constitution of Puerto Rico. These events cement the colonial nature of the constitutional making process of 1951–52, one which still exists today. This is consistent with Colón-Ríos and Hevia's characterisation that 'Puerto Rico is a colony that formally consented to colonial rule'.[8]

II. DEMOCRATIC MECHANISMS AND MAJORITARIAN PREFERENCES

The previous discussion explained the colonial nature of the process that culminated in the adoption of the 1952 Constitution. Paradoxically, that process was also substantially – though not entirely – internally democratic. This would coincide with Andre Arato's suggestion that 'non-democratic procedures of constitution making cannot be justified today'.[9] The same was true then.

The cross-party consensus as to the unacceptable nature of the Jones Act and the island's palpable lack of truly self-governing institutions paved the way for a tentative agreement regarding the desirability of drafting a local constitution through democratic mechanisms. Yet, for some important political sectors on the island, particularly the pro-independence movement, any constitutional process carried out under the shadow of colonialism would be illegitimate from the start. As such, the main opposition party at the time, the Puerto Rican Independence Part (PIP), boycotted the elections for the Constitutional Convention. The active opposition by the PIP threatened the legitimacy of the entire constitutional process.

It should be noted, as a further contradictory feature of the Puerto Rican constitutional project, that, while there were important democratic mechanisms used during the framing process, this was accompanied by a significant wave of political repression against the independence movement, particularly its more

[7] Public Law No 82-447 (Joint Resolution) (1952).

[8] J Colón-Ríos and M Hevia, 'The Legal Status of Puerto Rico and the Institutional Requirements of Republicanism' (2011) 17 *Texas Hispanic Journal of Law and Policy* 1, 2.

[9] A Arato, 'Forms of Constitution Making and Theories of Democracy' (1995) 17 *Cardozo Law Review* 191, 192.

militant nationalist current, which undermined its general democratic credentials and legitimacy. Some believe this may be sufficient to deny the constituent process the characterisation of being democratic.[10]

As might be expected, there was resistance to the US presence in Puerto Rico from the very beginning. Even important sectors that initially welcomed the US invasion had joined this resistance, once it became obvious that the new imperialist power's designs on Puerto Rico were of a clearly colonial nature.

Historically, the independence movement in Puerto Rico, prior to 1952,[11] was mainly divided between reformist and radical factions. This dichotomy refers, mostly, to matters of tactics, use of violence, and participation in colonial institutions, including elected ones. In general terms, significant parts the independence movement during the first decades of the twentieth century were mostly liberal in character and did not challenge the economic underpinnings of the capitalist economy. It was after the advent of the Cold War and the triumph of the Cuban Revolution that the Puerto Rican independence movement shifted significantly to the Left ideologically.

During the 1930s, the Nationalist Party of Puerto Rico became the main conduit for armed resistance to the US occupation and its colonial allies. This included a significant set of armed clashes between Nationalist cadre and military and police forces. Chief among them was the Ponce Massacre of 1937.

Yet, the most momentous actions of the Nationalist Party were carried out at the very beginning of the 1950s. In other words, immediately before the constitutional drafting process began. This has important significance with regard to that process.

First, the breadth of the Nationalists' actions created a difficult political situation for the US, particularly in the international arena. This pushed Congress to address the colonial situation and, at the very least, attempt to reform the current situation in a direction of decreased colonial egregiousness. Cold-War politics made it hard for the US to admit to the world that it still had colonial possessions.

Second, the governmental reaction to Nationalist operations was characterised by severe repression. This included not just the jailing of a great number of Nationalist members and sympathisers, but also of the Puerto Rican Independence Party (PIP) which was, at the beginning of the decade, the second

[10] See PA Malavet, *America's Colony: The Political and Cultural Conflict Between the United States and Puerto Rico* (New York University Press, 2007) 71.

[11] The wave of Latin American revolutionary movements during the 1960s and 1970s ushered a new paradigm with regard to the Puerto Rican independence movement. First of all, the emergence of a strong socialist ideology and the development of an organic connection between the independence movement and an important, although relatively small, segment of the working class. Second, the creation of revolutionary organisations that combined independence with socialism, many of which turned to the armed struggle similar to the urban guerrilla experiences of Latin America. During the Cold War, independence meant Left and annexation tilted Right. This was not the political situation prior to 1952.

largest electoral force on the island. This constitutes a black eye in the attempts of the 1952 process to obtain democratic legitimacy.

The main Nationalist action immediately preceding the 1952 drafting process was the Nationalist Insurrection of 1950. This included revolts in many Puerto Rican towns, as well as assassination attempts made against US President Harry Truman at the Blair House in Washington DC and against Puerto Rico Governor Luis Muñoz Marín in San Juan.

The Insurrection began on 30 October 1950. A few days later, following the mobilisation of the National Guard and the imposition of martial law, the Insurrection had been snuffed out. The post-revolt repression was relentless. Ironically, one of the by-products of the Nationalist Insurrection was that the US was forced to initiate some sort of self-determination mechanism that, at the very least, established basic or minimal democratic home rule over local affairs.[12]

It should also be noted that Nationalist leader Pedro Albizu Campos was tried for sedition during the campaign to elect the members of the Constitutional Convention in 1951. As a curious note, one of the leading Socialist members of the Convention, Antonio Reyes Delgado, although a supporter of Puerto Rico's annexation as a state of the Union, actually defended many Nationalist defendants in their criminal trials. This is just one example of the contradictory and complex nature of Puerto Rican politics.

With this important historical context in mind, we can proceed to analyse the concrete steps that initiated the constitutional drafting process itself. First of all, Congress's Public Law 600 required that the Puerto Rican people accept the invitation to initiate the constitutional process.

An election as to that issue was held on 4 June 1951. A total of 65 per cent of qualified voters participated, of which 76.5 per cent voted in favour and 23.5 per cent voted against.[13] While the PIP called for a 'No' vote, all other main political parties called on their supporters to vote in the affirmative. The generalised rejection of the Jones Act regime and the promise of even a limited constituent process persuaded the majority of the political class and the electorate to accept Congress's offer, regardless of their reservations as to the content of the offer itself.

The boycott by the Puerto Rican Independence Party left only the governing Popular Democratic Party (PPD) and the minority Republican Statehood Party (PER) and Socialist Party (PS) as possible participants in the Convention. On the one hand, the electoral might of the PPD in 1951 was impressive and

[12] The Nationalists were not yet done. In March 1954, members of the Nationalist Party attacked the US Congress with firearms, denouncing the continued colonial status of Puerto Rico, even after the 1952 process had culminated.

[13] A Fernós-Isern, *Original Intent in the Constitution of Puerto Rico: Notes and Comments Submitted to the Congress of the United States* (LexisNexis, 2002) 21. For his part, Pedro Malavet characterised the vote as 'marked by controversy and low voter turnout': Malavet (n 10) 71.

sufficient to comply with basic democratic requirements in terms of reflecting the general policy preferences of the population: it easily managed to garner over 60 per cent support during electoral events. On the other hand, the PPD needed to make sure that the document that would emerge from the Convention would not be seen as a strictly partisan constitution. In other words, the governing PPD craved cross-party support for the constitution, in order to ensure its acceptance by the general population, particularly given the rejection by pro-independence forces.

As a result, while they would not relinquish overall political control over the process, the PPD sought to design an electoral system for the Convention that would be acceptable to both the PER and the PS.[14] In that sense, it was a process aggressively controlled by the PPD, with the sometimes lukewarm support of the other two participating parties. This control manifested more clearly during the cross-party talks regarding the structure of the Convention and the election of its members.

Each party proposed a different mechanism for the selection of the delegates to the Convention, directed at maximising their electoral prospects. For example, the Socialist Party insisted on a guaranteed minimum delegation quota for each party. Evidently, it was well aware of its declining electoral fortunes. Once a party that was able to muster more than 25 per cent of the overall vote in 1936, by 1950 it was a mere shadow of its former self. For its part, the Republican Statehood Party proposed an at-large, proportional election. The PPD proposed a mixed system of at-large and district seats, which it was sure to dominate.

In the end, a compromise was struck, one which still favoured the PPD, but guaranteed sufficient benefits to the opposition so as to acquire their acceptance.

First, there were the at-large delegates, of which a total of 20 would be elected.[15] No party could nominate more than 14 candidates, assuring that the remainder would be distributed among the minority parties. This accommodated the PER's request for some sort of proportionality element. A further political agreement was reached which guaranteed each party at least a basic quota of three at-large delegates. This placated the PS's concerns.

Second, the remaining delegates would be selected in eight individual districts. Each district would elect nine delegates and no party could nominate more than seven, which meant that, in each district, there would be, at least, two minority delegates. This general scheme overwhelmingly favoured the PPD but

[14] The PPD also made sure that the minorities had relatively greater substantive influence during the deliberations than their actual numbers would have produced. Of course, this influence would be exercised at the edges. The main structure of the constitutional project would be supplied by the PPD.

[15] The original number was 23, but this included a minimum quota of three delegates per party. Since the PIP boycotted the process, its share of seats was subtracted.

left sufficient space for a quasi-proportional mechanism through which minorities would be able, at least marginally, to enlarge their delegations.

The election to the Constitutional Convention was preceded by intense campaigning by the political parties. Most of them shared their constitutional proposals with the public. Individual rights in general, and labour rights in particular, dominated the national discussion regarding the potential content of the constitutional text. The political relationship between Puerto Rico and the US was also a hot topic.

Socioeconomic issues were at the top of the list. In addition to the general progressive and reformist atmosphere of Puerto Rican politics at the time, this situation was due to the enormous challenges facing Puerto Rican society. Several issues stood out:

- First, the existence of discriminatory institutions and practices, particularly with regard to class, sex, and race. Also, the unjust prejudice against children of unwed parents, who were treated by the legal system as inferior to those whose parents were married.
- Second, the important task of transferring thousands of children from the factories and the work fields into schools. This required, for example, the enforcement of child labour laws and the strengthening of the public education system, including establishing the right to a cost-free primary and secondary education, as well as imposing on parents the legal duty to send their children to school.
- Third, the pressing labour issues facing Puerto Rican society as a result of its rapid industrialisation and the emergence of a growing working class, alongside the substantial numbers of land workers. These forces would be in constant tension with powerful economic interests, particularly land-owning corporations, as well as commercial and industrial entities. This set the stage for policy proposals that were discussed during the campaign and which found their way into the constitutional text, including important provisions dealing with employment conditions and benefits – such as a reasonable minimum wage and overtime pay – as well as with collective rights such as unionisation and collective bargaining. Furthermore, it included the entrenchment of statutory limitations on the power of private corporations to own substantial amounts of land in Puerto Rico.

While originally founded as a reformist and populist party by disaffected members of the Liberal Party who believed that the old party had abandoned its pro-independence stance, by the 1950s the PPD had mostly become an autonomist party that championed some sort of association with the US, while nominally rejecting the territorial or colonial label. As such, much of the energy that the PPD leadership employed during the campaign for the Constitutional Convention focused on the status question, specifically, the development of a structural arrangement that maximised self-government, while cementing Puerto Rico's relationship with the US.

But the PPD still possessed some of the traits of a social reformist party; in this case, one that still commanded great deal of support from the urban and, especially, the rural working class. Therefore, the PPD's programme for the Convention elections also reflected some of these class-based social policies. For example, its platform expressly adopted several principles and provisions taken from the Universal Declaration of Human Rights, as well as the American Declaration of the Rights and Duties of Man. This included, sometimes general, references to a just distribution of wealth, the establishment of basic material conditions for the inhabitants of Puerto Rico that guaranteed a dignified life, as well as other progressive social measures.

As to substantive proposals, the PPD focused on the right of workers to form unions and bargain collectively, as well as the inclusion of specific and assertive provisions banning discrimination on several accounts. It also proposed the entrenchment in the constitutional text of the statutory scheme that existed at the time regarding the limitations placed on corporations pertaining to land ownership. Yet, the PPD's programme was very general and somewhat vague. This was mostly due to the party's commanding electoral force, which meant it could adopt most of its policy preferences through ordinary legislation, with no need to embed them in the Constitution.

With regard to their proposal for the *governmental* structure that would be adopted by the Constitution in the case of a PPD victory, the party's electoral programme was notably scarce. This was odd indeed, given the almost inevitable landslide the PPD would receive and the overshadowing presence of Luis Muñoz Marín as party president and paramount leader, as well as Puerto Rico's first elected Governor.

While the PPD constituted the main ideological and electoral engine of the constitution-making process, it was by no means the only one. The Socialist Party, founded originally in 1899 as the electoral arm of the labour movement and one of the main political forces in the island during the 1930s, substantially invested itself in the constitutional project. Why?

Before the Cold War set in and the revolutionary wave of the 1960s arrived in Latin America, Puerto Rico's statehood movement had two separate ideological articulations. One comprised the business class, and adopted classic Republican worldviews. This current was organised as the PER during the constitutional creation process.

The other was born of the labour movement, which saw in Puerto Rico's relationship with the US the historical vehicle for the adoption of pro-worker measures and for radical social transformation. The experiences of the New Deal strengthened that ideological commitment, particularly regarding the possibility of overcoming the exploitative nature of the capitalist system.

Originally, the Socialist Party was first and foremost a left-wing organisation committed to the development of a radical working-class project. While its leadership mostly favoured annexation, the party itself was agnostic on that issue, except for a generalised rejection of the colonial condition. But, during the 1930s, its political leadership committed the capital sin of allying with the PER, their class adversaries. The main reason for the joining of this odd couple was their leadership's shared commitment to the cause of statehood.

In the short term, this Coalition, as their alliance was known, was successful: it produced eight years of Socialist-Republican rule between 1932 and 1940, during which time some modest pro-labour statutes and programs were adopted. But it proved to be fatal to the Socialist Party in the long run.

The larger Republicans were able to dilute the more radical and progressive measures proposed by the Socialists, leading to much disenchantment on the part of the Socialist rank-and-file, who felt that their leadership had betrayed their class positions in order to placate their pro-annexation allies. This had catastrophic consequences for the Socialist Party. After obtaining its greatest electoral performance ever in 1936 with nearly 27 per cent of the vote, the party suffered a crushing defeat in 1940, from which it would never recover.

While the PER was able to profit from the Socialists' electoral calamity, admitting into their ranks a vast section of the pro-statehood faction of the party, it was the PPD which benefited most from the Socialist downfall. The mostly working-class base of the Socialist Party saw in the PPD, which by the early 1940s had adopted a modest reformist and populist platform, their only real alternative.

By 1951–52, the Socialist Party was a shadow of its former self. After its historic 27 per cent of the vote merely 15 years earlier, the Party only managed to poll a little over 5 per cent of the vote for the elections to the Constitutional Convention. This meager result was no surprise to the Socialist Party leadership.

As a result, the Socialist leaders very early on identified their main goal for the constitutional drafting process: to entrench as much of their existing legislative victories of the labour movement as possible, so that they would be protected in a future where there would be no real socialist presence in the Legislature. In other words, to avoid the scenario where a future, more conservative Legislature could overturn the statutory achievements of the working class, particularly when those measures still garnered substantial popular support.

This reality explains why the Socialist Party was so active during the election campaign for delegates to the Constitutional Convention. In a last-ditch, desperate attempt to prove their relevance as a political entity, the Socialists wanted social justice issues in general, and labour issues in particular, to be central in the public debate regarding the content of the future constitution.

As is discussed in greater detail below in this chapter, the 1952 Constitution was written in a period of substantial class tensions and class consciousness. It is no wonder, then, that a great many of the rights included in the constitution deal with labour and economic issues. For now, it is important to know that the Socialists aggressively campaigned on two related issues: (1) their specific proposals regarding labour rights; and (2) their insistence to the electorate that they needed to pick Socialist delegates to make sure that these rights were adequately defended in the Convention, particularly, by pressuring the PPD from the Left to make sure it did not balk with regard to these matters.

Among the Socialist proposals made during the campaign were the recognition of important labour rights, such as the right to strike and establish picket lines. They also proposed that the Constitution devote an entire part to a Labour Bill of Rights that would complement the more general Bill of Rights.

For its part, the PER also campaigned for the Convention, focusing almost entirely on the status question, with one of its primary objectives being to make sure that the Constitution would not block any future movement to incorporate Puerto Rico as a state of the US. Although the PER was a pro-business conservative party, it mostly concentrated its energy on advancing its statehood agenda. This mostly manifested itself in the language used in the Preamble and Article I of the Constitution, both of which address Puerto Rico's relations with the US.

The vote for the Constitutional Convention was held on 27 August 1951.[16] In the end, the PPD had a total of 70 delegates elected,[17] the PER 15, and the PS 7.[18] With regard to the at-large column, the PPD had 14 delegates elected – the maximum allowed – while the PER and PS each received the minimum at-large quota of three delegates for each party. As to district delegates, the PPD had all seven members elected in each of the eight individual districts, for a total of 56. The PER had 12, while the PS had four elected.

The social composition of the Convention also speaks to its democratic credentials and social character. In addition to the very large number of lawyers – 32 in total – there were 13 farmers or land workers (*campesinos*), 9 labour leaders, 6 teachers, 6 merchants, 5 industrialists, 4 doctors and 3 journalists, among others.[19] The combination of farmers and labour leaders reflects the social composition of the island in 1951–52, mostly made up of agricultural and industrial workers. The social composition of the Convention directly impacted the substantive policy content of the constitutional text, which accounts for much of its progressive orientation.

The Constitutional Convention met continuously from September 1951 until February 1952. Its deliberations were public and accessible to the general population. Because of the historic nature of the constitution-making process, the deliberations of the Convention generated great public interest. The Puerto Rican news entities also followed its progress, supplying constant information to the general population.

[16] Again, Malavet shares his view that 'the turnout was rather low': Malavet (n 10) 71. The turnout was approximately 55%. As noted above, this takes into account the boycott by the PIP, then a significant electoral force.

[17] This was the maximum that any party could hope to elect. In other words, the PPD had all of its candidates elected to the Convention.

[18] Percentagewise, the PPD obtained 83% of the total votes cast; the PER 12% and the PS just 5%. It should be remembered that the then-second largest party, the PIP, boycotted the election, which would explain the lopsided result in favour of the PPD.

[19] See Fernós-Isern (n 13) 25.

In addition, multiple public hearings were held by the different committees of the Convention.[20] As the President of the Constitutional Convention later explained, '[a]ll these hearings were held in the Capitol Building and testimony was received from civil organisations, university professors[,] and citizens in general'.[21] These public committee meetings and hearings facilitated the creation of consensus and the identification of widely held policy beliefs that could be incorporated as constitutional text. Although, as with any process of this nature, there would be the inevitable backroom dealing, the public nature of the committee deliberations also strengthened the Convention's democratic credentials by encouraging transparency, participation, and public discussions.

Public participation also found its way into the actual deliberations of the Convention. Individual citizens and social groups were encouraged to send specific petitions. The Convention received dozens of such petitions, many of which were, directly or indirectly, included in the constitutional text. This should be seen as an example of direct popular participation in the drafting process itself, which further enhanced its democratic credentials.

Let us briefly analyse a few examples of this type of direct public involvement with regard to the drafting of the constitutional text. It should not be surprising to learn that the three main sources of petitions to the Constitutional Convention came, in order, from private citizens, religious organisations, and labour unions. Other groups that sent petitions included women's groups, civic organisations, and business entities. Also not surprisingly, the main focus of the petitions made by religious organisations was with regard to religious liberty and, more importantly, *the separation of church and state*. We should note that the vast majority of these organisations were protestant, which were naturally worried about the substantial power and influence that the Catholic Church had, and could continue to have, over the government and society as a whole.

These petitions found their way into Section 3 of the Bill of Rights. This provision recognises the right to the free exercise of religious worship and prohibits the establishment of an official religion – as does the First Amendment to the US Constitution. It also explicitly requires the 'absolute' separation of church and state. It is a categorical rule that is entrenched in the constitutional text. In other words, the constitutionally required strict separation between church and state was, in part, due to public pressure exercised by protestant religious organisations that, in order to avoid too much Catholic influence over government policy, decided to insist on the secular nature of the state.

With regard to labour unions, their main demands were a constitutional requirement that all employers share part of their profits with their workers,

[20] For example, there was a Committee of the Bill of Rights, Committee for the Legislative Branch, and so on.

[21] Fernós-Isern (n 13) 29.

and the entrenchment of basic collective labour rights, such as the right to form unions, bargain collectively, and engage in strike actions and other concerted activities. While the former would not be included in the constitutional text, the latter was: Sections 17 and 18 of the Bill of Rights guarantee to every worker employed by a private enterprise or by a state-owned corporation that operates as a private enterprise, the right to form unions, to bargain collectively with their employer, and to engage in strikes, pickets, and other concerted activities.

Other petitions were also constitutionalised. For example, proposals regarding the establishment of a tuition-free, secular public school system (Section 5), the abolition of the death penalty (Section 7), the right to work (Section 20), prohibition against discrimination (Section 1), the right to freely choose one's own profession (Section 16), the right to housing (Section 20), and basic civil rights. While not substantial in number, these petitions reflected popular consensus regarding important policy issues. They were not sent in randomly; it was part of a concerted effort by important sectors of society to make sure that basic policy preferences were adopted in the constitutional text.

The constitutional text was eventually adopted by a vote of 88–3, which meant that even the vast majority of the minority delegates voted in favour of the new constitution. Notwithstanding the opposition from three delegates and the absence of a fourth, '[a]ll the remaining ninety-one delegates signed the enrolled text of the Constitution'.[22] This could be seen as evidence of the fact that, as to the basic constitutional project – excluding the status question – there was widespread consensus. The 1952 Constitution was considered, particularly as to its governmental structure and social content, as a significant improvement over the Jones Act. At the very least, it was – unlike all previous experiences – a Puerto Rican product.

After the text was adopted by the Convention, it was submitted to a popular referendum, where almost 82 per cent of the voters that participated approved it. This substantially broad margin was similar to the final vote at the Convention and was an indication that the public felt the Convention had adequately reflected its aspirations and beliefs, at least at a general level. With 82 per cent approval, it was difficult to argue that 'We the People' were not in agreement with the text that was drafted in their name.

It was next sent to the US Congress for its final approval, as required by Public Law 600. But Congress was not yet finished. As discussed above, Congress demanded several modifications to the text before giving it its approval, which were eventually accepted by the Convention and then incorporated using the Constitution's Article VII amendment mechanisms. But before that was done, the Constitution came into effect on 25 July 1952, 54 years to the day after the US invaded Puerto Rico during the Spanish-American War – an irony that has not been lost on Puerto Ricans.

[22] ibid 29.

III. AN EXERCISE IN, SOMETIMES, RADICAL POLITICS

As discussed further in Chapter 5, Puerto Rico's 1952 Constitution is full of progressive content, ranging from a comprehensive list of individual and collective labour rights to an assertive policy on public education and the eradication of discrimination. But that this would be the case was not a foregone conclusion.

Entities such as the Socialist Party and the broader trade union movement, as noted above, aggressively championed for a social and labour Constitution, fearing that the governing PPD would either water down many of their proposals or would opt to omit them altogether from the constitutional text, relying on their legislative majorities to enact them through ordinary statutes.

But there were important historical, ideological, and international considerations that impacted on both the approach to constitution-making and the actual content of the Constitution itself. Even though the Cold War was heating up, there was still a post-war progressive atmosphere that influenced the leadership of the Constitutional Convention and made its way into the content of the constitutional text.

Puerto Rican politics, starting in the 1920s, included a visible radical strain, particularly with regard to socioeconomic and labour matters. Class conflict generated class politics which in turn produced class-conscious legislation. While socialism did not acquire majoritarian status on the island, progressive politics did. And although there was a visible retreat that started at the beginning of the 1950s, there was still enough of it to have an impact on the content of the Constitution. In that sense, the combination of socialism and liberalism produced a moderate reformist, but at least generally transformational, progressivism that was meant to usher in a more equal and just society.[23]

The social and ideological composition of the Constitutional Convention somewhat mirrored the more general trends existing in Puerto Rican society during the early 1950s. In particular, there was significant working class and trade unionist representation in the Convention, which was wholly aware of the need to address economic inequalities through the constitutional text.

As discussed above, labour issues, education, discrimination, corporate power, and the creation of an interventionist state were at the forefront of the Convention's social agenda. Though the final text was hardly revolutionary, it reflected the general progressive and reformist currents that were dominant in early 1950s Puerto Rico.

[23] It should also be noted that, during the 1940s, there was a significant shift of allegiances within the labour movement. After what many saw as the betrayal of the PS-FLT leadership during the Coalition with the Republicans, many trade unionists and rank-and-file members flocked to the PPD. This also included the PPD's takeover of the General Workers' Confederation (CGT) during that time. See K Lugo del Toro, *Nacimiento y Auge de la Confederación General de Trabajadores 1940–1945* (Universidad Interamericana de Puerto Rico, 2013).

The Socialist Party, the most left-leaning of the parties present at the Constitutional Convention, voted in favour of the constitutional text. As might be expected, there were contradictory reasons for this. On the one hand, there were, in fact, several progressive provisions which reflected the PS's consistent moves to pressure the PPD from the Left. On the other hand, the PS's precarious electoral position meant that its leadership was desperate for a political victory, even if it meant supporting a socially moderate and mild constitution. The truth is probably somewhere in the middle: the 1952 Constitution is neither revolutionary nor classically liberal. Whether it has been seen as closer to one or the has other depended on social events and the attitude of institutional actors, and this is unlikely to change in the future.

The PER had little riding on the outcome of the drafting process, except to guarantee that the 1952 Constitution would not become a legal or structural obstacle to its pro-annexation designs. As to that goal, the PPD obliged. That was the price for receiving the PER's support, which was essential to the PPD's objective of having cross-party support for the new constitution.

Although there were twice as many PER delegates as Socialists, the latter were able to exert much more influence with regard to the content of the constitutional text than the former. There were several reasons for this. First, there was more ideological proximity between the PPD and the PS regarding social and labour issues. Most of the Convention's labour leaders heralded from these two parties. And second, the Socialists were more welcoming of the constitutional process than the Republicans. This attitude was rewarded by the PPD.

The end result was a constitution that addressed several important social issues, such as a robust right to education and the granting of constitutional status to the public education system, limits on corporate ownership of land, individual and collective labour rights, strong anti-discrimination language, and the granting of substantial police powers to the Legislature. The actual content of these provisions requires further analysis, but we begin first with the governmental structure that emanated from the Constitutional Convention.

4

The 1952 Constitution (Structure)

I. A COLONIAL CONSTITUTION

A. General Overview

THE DRAFTERS OF the 1952 Constitution were native Puerto Ricans. Most favoured a non-colonial association with the US, though they did little to test the limits of the territorial condition; more self-government and autonomy were their immediate objectives. A minority favoured annexation.

The pro-independence forces were absent as a result of their boycott. As such, and even though there was a consensus within the Convention that the Constitution needed to be a Puerto Rican product, there was no denying that the US system would be highly influential. Colonialism would make its mark in the 1952 Constitution, particularly with regard to the governmental structure and its amendment processes.

While Puerto Rico's 1952 Constitution is not a reproduction of the federal Constitution by any means, the influences are obvious. Various state constitutions also served as models. But before diving into an analysis of the influences of colonialism on the structure of the Puerto Rican Constitution, it is worth noting that there are, in fact, important differences between the text adopted in 1952 and its federal counterpart.

For example, the Puerto Rican and US Constitutions share a similar starting point in terms of individual rights and, most importantly, governmental structure. As to the latter, Puerto Rico's political system is more similar to the federal structure than to other states of the Union. With regard to rights, Puerto Rico's Article II (Bill of Rights) includes almost all of the individual political rights that are found in the federal text.[1] But this merely represented the adoption of a rights floor that was meant to be built upon.

[1] An interesting exception is the right to bear arms. It is one of the few instances where a federally recognised constitutional right has no Puerto Rican counterpart. This is not the result of happenstance. While the Puerto Rican framers made great effort to, at the very least, include all the rights contained in the US Constitution, they explicitly rejected adopting a Puerto Rican version of the Second Amendment. The reasons for this decision are historical. During the 1950s, Puerto Rican nationalism had resulted in violent actions against US and colonial institutions. This weighed heavily on the majority delegation of the Constitutional Convention, the governing PPD. It saw pro-independence nationalist militancy as a threat. The notion of a constitutionally guaranteed

As is discussed in greater detail in Chapter 5, this has two effects. First, the Puerto Rican Constitutional Convention adopted an expansive version of those classic political rights. This includes, inter alia, the inclusion of explicit provisions such as a ban on the death penalty, a clear exclusionary rule, a non-exhaustive list of prohibited classifications in terms of discrimination. Second, the Convention made an intentional decision not to limit the Bill of Rights to classic, individual political rights. The Constitutional Convention also decided to incorporate new generation socio-economic rights, most of which were meant to be wholly enforceable in judicial proceedings.

This means that, while the Puerto Rican and US Constitutions start out similarly with regard to rights, they eventually part ways through expansion and addition. Puerto Rico's 1952 Constitution is a modern document that avoids some of the abstractions and shortcomings of its federal counterpart. This reflects a conscious choice on the part of the Puerto Rican Constitutional Convention.

Other documents and sources were also highly influential with regard to the content of the Puerto Rican Constitution, particularly the Bill of Rights and its related provisions. Chief among these were the Universal Declaration of Human Rights, the American Declaration of the Rights and Duties of Man, and the Charter of the United Nations. We must bear in mind that the memory of World War II and the emergence of an international human rights regime were fresh in the minds of the framers. The primary effects of that influence can be found in the substantive provisions of the Bill of Rights, particularly as to socioeconomic rights. This analysis continues in greater detail in Chapter 5.

For its part, the federal Constitution was mostly influential as to civil and political rights, and the basic structure of government. State constitutions were used mostly for specific rights provisions and particular issues related to structure, most notably the Judiciary.[2]

B. Legal Importation

The 1952 Constitution is a mixed bag of imported content and autochthonous creativity. As noted, some of that importation can actually be seen as contrary to colonialism: the Puerto Rican framers looked to international instruments and even some foreign countries as inspiration for their constitutional text. In that sense, importation was not just an expression of colonialism. The Constitutional Convention also incorporated the most advanced notions of

right to gun ownership was unacceptable to the ruling party. Thus, a proposal made by the PER to include even an individual right to keep arms in the home was soundly rejected by the Constitutional Convention. Puerto Rico's constitutional right to bear arms exists only at the federal level.

[2] For example, the New Jersey Constitution served as a model for the administrative structure of the Puerto Rican Judiciary.

modern constitutionalism, whether they were found in international instruments or even foreign constitutions. A clear example of this is the inclusion of 'human dignity' as the main conceptual foundation of the constitutional project. This concept is mentioned both in the Charter of the United Nations and in the (then) West German Basic Law.

This intentional borrowing from international and foreign sources was a sign of the times – the result of the post-World War II wave of modern constitutionalism that emphasised individual dignity and the need for the inclusion of socioeconomic rights and other substantive provisions in the constitutional text. Puerto Rico's framers affirmatively chose to put their constitution in the column of modern constitutionalism.

Unfortunately, as discussed further in Chapter 5, the Puerto Rican framers would frustrate their own achievements by deliberately underselling their foreign importation in a colonialist effort to gain congressional approval. In other words, the Constitutional Convention would considerably underplay to Congress what was hailed during the deliberation process in Puerto Rico: the incorporation of the most advanced theories of constitutionalism in the world at that time, which would make the 1952 Constitution an undisputed trailblazer.[3]

But even during the deliberations of the Constitutional Convention there were conscious efforts to, at least partially, mimic the federal constitutional framework. Part of this approach was based on the fact that the 1917 Jones Act already provided the basic structure of the Puerto Rican government and the island's first bill of rights. In that sense, several provisions of the 1952 text either copied the Act's language – some of it, in turn, based on several aspects of the federal Constitution – further elaborated on its content, or simply opted for a separate, purely autochthonous path. That could be explained by the Convention's goal of convincing Congress that the governmental structure would be somewhat similar to the existing system under the Jones Act, while the approach to rights mirrored other states of the Union.

Because of the influence of the Jones Act and the general colonial background at play, important parts of the 1952 Constitution track their federal counterparts. In terms of governmental structure, Puerto Rico adopted a bicameral Legislature, a Judiciary appointed by the Chief Executive with senatorial

[3] See A Fernós-Isern, *Original Intent in the Constitution of Puerto Rico: Notes and Comments Submitted to the Congress of the United States* (LexisNexis, 2002). Fernós-Isern was, simultaneously, President of the Puerto Rican Constitutional Convention and the elected, non-voting Resident Commissioner for Puerto Rico in the House of Representatives. Fernós-Isern's report to Congress systematically downplayed the influence of international and foreign sources on the constitutional text, in an apparent effort to avoid congressional skepticism as to the substantive content of the 1952 Constitution which, as discussed in Ch 5, was remarkably radical and left-wing. Instead, Fernós-Isern apparently opted for a less confrontational strategy: to emphasise the similarity between the 1952 Constitution's most radical elements and other US state constitutions existing at the time.

confirmation, and a unitary Executive Branch headed by a Governor as its only elected member. As to individual political rights, the 1952 text includes clauses related to free speech, religious liberty, due process, the rights of criminal defendants and even a prohibition concerning titles of nobility.

It should be noted that, starting with the Jones Act, the Puerto Rico Supreme Court embarked on an independent and expanded reading of constitutional rights, even those that were directly copied from the federal constitutional text. In other words, the Court resisted adopting a strict, lockstep approach to interpretation with regard to federal constitutional rights, whether through its concurrent jurisdiction or the analysis of the rights contained in the Jones Act's Bill of Rights which were, for the most part, repetitions of the federal text. This practice of independent and liberal interpretation would continue after the adoption of the 1952 Constitution, especially with regard to those constitutional rights that were mostly autochthonous in nature.

While several state constitutions were also considered during the drafting process, particularly with regard to socioeconomic rights which are evidently absent from the federal text, the US Constitution, both directly and indirectly through the Jones Act, was the main American source that inspired the Puerto Rican document, especially as it pertains to governmental structure and the minimum content of individual political rights.

C. Cautious Creativity

The 1952 Constitution has important substantive differences from its US counterpart. Most of these differences are related to rights provisions, which are discussed in greater detail in Chapter 5. Sometimes, the devil is in the detail.

Even when it came to basic political rights such as free speech and due process, the Puerto Rican drafters added important and significant local touches. For example, the Establishment Clause includes an express reference to the 'absolute' separation between church and state.[4] As to cruel and unusual punishment, the text also includes a categorical ban on capital punishment.[5] Another example is the textual articulation of the exclusionary rule in instances of unreasonable searches and seizures.[6]

In that sense, the Puerto Rico Constitution builds on a federal floor, even with regard to classic, first generation individual political rights. The formula used by the framers was the inclusion of the basic language of the federal text followed by further detail or expansion. Another example of this phenomenon

[4] See Puerto Rico Constitution, Art II, § 2.

[5] Compare Art II, § 7 (explicit ban on the death penalty) with Art II, § 12 (general prohibition against cruel and unusual punishments) of the Constitution of Puerto Rico.

[6] See Puerto Rico Constitution, Art II, § 10.

is the inclusion of both a general equal protection clause and a specific list of prohibited classifications such as sex, race, colour, religious or political beliefs, and birth, among others.

This model has two main consequences. First, it establishes a clear minimum protection that is not susceptible to judicial under-enforcement through excessively narrow interpretation. Second, it pushes courts to actually expand the scope of rights protection on top of that minimum.

A good example of this phenomenon is Section 19 of the Puerto Rican Bill of Rights. This provision partially tracks parts of the US Constitution that deal with unenumerated rights and reserved powers.[7] Section 19 is much clearer, more precise, and more empowering than the federal text.

Section 19 specifically establishes: (1) that the list of rights contained in Article II is non-exhaustive; and (2) that courts are required to interpret both sets of rights – enumerated and unenumerated – in an expansive and liberal fashion. This combination has huge normative implications.

As to the first issue, Section 19 explicitly states: 'The enumeration of the previous rights [in Article II] … does not suppose the exclusion of other rights belonging to the People in a democracy and not specifically mentioned'. Note that Section 19 expressly addresses the existence of unenumerated rights, and, in turn, that these are characterised as inherently *democratic* in their nature. As to the second issue, Section 19 states that the rights explicitly mentioned in Article II 'shall not be understood [interpreted] in a restrictive manner'. Thus, there is an express constitutional command that constitutional rights must be interpreted by courts in an expansive, as opposed to restrictive, manner. This text is reinforced by the clear intent of the framers, which is explicitly recorded in the Report of the Bill of Rights Committee and the exchanges during the deliberations of the Constitutional Convention.[8]

But the Puerto Rican Bill of Rights did not stop at classic, first-generation political rights. As explained in greater detail in Chapter 5, these substantive rights include matters related to labour conditions and relations, education, and environmental protection. As relevant here, it is worth mentioning that, although international documents such as the American Declaration of the Duties and Rights of Man and the Universal Declaration of Human Rights were the main sources for these second-generation rights, the Puerto Rican framers attempted to conciliate these international provisions with US state constitutions, in order to lessen potential objections by a conservative federal Congress, which could be reluctant to accept such transnational influences.

As noted above, Fernós-Isern's report to Congress emphasised that the social rights contained in the 1952 Constitution were very similar to several state constitutional clauses that existed at that time. This was mostly a post

[7] See United States Constitution, amendments IX–X.
[8] These deliberations are recorded in an official transcript of more than 3,500 pages.

hoc justification to avoid congressional rejection of the Constitution's progressive provisions by characterising them as compatible with the US constitutional order. After all, if similar provisions could be found in established state constitutions, there should be no problem with Puerto Rico adopting them in its own constitutional text.

This strategy was partially successful, yet would not be enough to save Section 20 of the Bill of Rights, the crown jewel of the 1952 Constitution's progressive nature, from ending up on the cutting-room floor.[9]

D. Legalised Subordination

Puerto Rico's colonial situation can also be found explicitly in the text itself. The island's political subordination to the US finds express constitutional articulation in the Preamble, Article I, and Article VII. Since the amendment mechanisms laid out in Article VII are discussed separately below, the prime focus of this section is the colonial content of the first two provisions.

With regard to the 1952 Constitution's Preamble, two clauses stand out. First, the Preamble begins:

> We, the people of Puerto Rico, in order to organize ourselves politically on a fully democratic basis, to promote the general welfare, and to secure for ourselves and our posterity the complete enjoyment of human rights, placing our trust in Almighty God, do ordain and establish this Constitution for the commonwealth which, in the exercise of our natural rights, we now create *within our union with the United States of America*. (emphasis added)

What is curious about this part of the Preamble is that it identifies Puerto Rico's 'union with the United States' as an apparent constitutive element of Puerto Rican society. It should be noted that this 'union' is more semantic than real. As discussed in detail in Chapter 7, Puerto Rico remains a territory of the US that, as both the *Insular Cases* and *Balzac v Porto Rico* plainly establish, belongs to, but is not a part of, the metropolitan power. Here, 'union' could be code for consented colonialism and permanent subordination. At best, it attempts to characterise the relationship as an agreement among equals, regardless of the legal and material reality.

This phrase also signals the influence that the pro-annexation forces were able to exercise during the Constitutional Convention, particularly given the absence of pro-independence voices. For these forces, the reference to 'union' also signifies the possibility of the future incorporation of Puerto Rico as a state of the Union. 'Union' was also meant to provide a constitutional obstacle to independence.

[9] See ch 5, s XVIII.

The Preamble's reference to Puerto Rico's political status with the US has two direct consequences: (1) that the creation of the Constitution itself must be seen in the context of the island's political subordinate relationship with the US. Note the use of the word 'within'. This severely limits the constituent credentials of the Puerto Rican Constitution and its claim to be an original exercise of true sovereign power; (2) that the Constitution seems to perpetuate that relationship through explicit entrenchment in the text. In other words, this part of the Preamble can be seen as a constitutional endorsement of Puerto Rico's colonial status, even if partially meant to placate pro-annexation forces that participated in the Constitutional Convention.

But there is more. The second part of the Preamble declares: 'We consider as *determining factors* in our life our *citizenship of the United States of America* and our aspiration continually to enrich our democratic heritage in the individual and collective enjoyment of its rights and privileges; *our loyalty to the principles of the Federal Constitution*; the co-existence in Puerto Rico of the two great cultures of the American Hemisphere'.[10]

Once again, Puerto Rico's relationship with the US is characterised as a constitutive part of its very existence as a political community. References to 'determining factors' and 'loyalty' stress a constitutional commitment to a particular political situation, namely, the island's colonial status with the US. This subordinate-sounding language reinforces the view that the Preamble's first reference to 'union' is but a euphemism for submission. It also indicates that even pro-annexation forces, who wish to turn Puerto Rico into a state of the Union on equal terms, see Puerto Rico as a dependent political unit that is subordinate to a larger national entity which holds ultimate sovereignty.

One could be forgiven for dismissing the Preamble as a symbolic statement with little normative power. But Article I of the Constitution dispels that notion and makes clear that the Preamble's statements are not just isolated symbolism. Section 1 of Article I states that:

> [t]he Commonwealth of Puerto Rico is hereby constituted. Its political power emanates from the people and shall be exercised in accordance with their will, within the terms of the compact agreed upon between the people of Puerto Rico and the United States of America.

The word 'within' creeps in again. More importantly, it signals an important limitation on the first phrase. In other words, the will of the people ('from the people' and 'their will') is subject ('within') to the legal norms that stem from Puerto Rico's subordinate relationship with the US.

[10] Note the use of the phrase 'the two great cultures of the American Hemisphere', in an explicit reference to the US and Spain. This is a very European-centered view of the American – in terms of the Americas more broadly – experience, which omits the evident role of the indigenous populations and the descendants of African slaves. It is likely that this language was adopted solely to placate a US audience, combined with a romantic view of the Spanish heritage.

As we saw previously, the so-called 'compact' merely reflects the Puerto Rican people's acceptance of Congress's offer to write a constitution, as authorised by Congress through Public Law 600.[11] It was not an agreement among sovereign equals and nor was it a Treaty under the auspices of Article II of the US Constitution. As a result, the so-called compact is still an element within a congressional statute.

It is plainly clear from the text of Article I of Puerto Rico's Constitution that the supposed exercise of popular sovereignty carried out in 1952 was wholly subject and beholden to its relationship with the US. This language serves as a sort of reverse Supremacy Clause: the Puerto Rican Constitution acknowledges the hierarchical superiority of the US.

This leads to the conclusion that when 'We the People' wrote a constitution, it was not truly the exercise of constituent power, but the manifestation of constituted power, and limited constituent authority. In this case, this constituted power is not subject to a previous legal order within the same political unit, but to a superior, external power that maintains ultimate sovereignty. It is a form of colonial constituted power.

This merits a quick explanation of the differences between the 1952 process and other state constitutional systems. State constitutions have a very interesting dual nature. On the one hand, they can be characterised as exercises in constituent power. After all, the US is a *federation* of *sovereign* entities. On the other hand, entry into the Union requires legal recognition of the supremacy of the US Constitution and that Congress gives its consent to such integration by a new member state. In this situation, a state constitution must be compatible with its federal counterpart and Congress may condition statehood on the adoption of modifications to the state constitutional text.

But once a state has been formally incorporated into the Union, the relationship between the state and the federal government, particularly Congress, changes significantly. In this new paradigm, both the state and the federal government are the recipient of original sovereignty. Even in the case of states that were admitted after independence was obtained in the eighteenth century, there is a legal fiction that their sovereignty is pre-existent and separate from the federal government. As such, it can be said that the adoption of a state constitution is a form of *limited* constituent power that, voluntarily, accepts the supremacy of a higher level of political governance. Such is not the case with the territories, including Puerto Rico.

Finally, Article VII states that:

> [a]ny amendment or revision of this constitution shall be *consistent* with the resolution enacted by the Congress of the US approving this constitution, with the applicable provisions of the Constitution of the US, with the Puerto Rican Federal Relations Act, and with Public Law 600, Eighty-first Congress, adopted in the nature of a compact. (emphasis added)

[11] This view was recently confirmed by the US Supreme Court. See Ch 7.

This requirement of *consistency* reflects a simple reality: all of the sources that are mentioned in Article VII are *superior* in normative power than the entire text of the 1952 Constitution.

As can be appreciated, these instances are all *federal* sources, from the US Constitution to congressional statutes. It goes well beyond the normal operation of Supremacy Clause considerations. The text of Article VII reinforces Article I's reference to the 'compact' with the US as a normatively superior source to which both the constitution and popular will must conform. The implications of this textualised subordination to specific federal sources is discussed further below.

II. THE DIRECT IMPACT OF COLONIALISM ON THE POLITICAL STRUCTURE AND AMENDMENT MECHANISMS

As explained above, Puerto Rico's governmental structure is a cross between its state and federal counterparts. Congress required that the political system created through the 1952 Constitution mirror a republican form of government.[12] Puerto Rico's political structure was also directly influenced by the existing system created by the Jones Act which, in turn, also mirrored the federal experience.

Puerto Rico's government is made up of the usual three branches, under a classic separation of powers model. Even the 1952 Constitution tracked the same branch sequence of the US document: legislative, executive, and judicial. This requires a closer analysis in terms of the structure's colonial and (un)democratic characteristics.

Article III of the 1952 Constitution established a bicameral Legislative Assembly, made up of a House of Representatives and a Senate. Bicameralism in Puerto Rico is a direct federal influence, since the island does not have provinces, counties or similar regional divisions that require separate representation from the population at large. The only existing political sub-units are municipalities, currently numbering 78. As such, there is very little difference as to the relation between House and Senate districts and the type of populations they

[12] Whether a parliamentary system is out of reach remains an open question. On the one hand, it seems that the requirement for a republican form of government is simply an extension of the 'Republican Guarantee Clause' found in the US Constitution. If this is the case, that clause serves more as a deterrent against monarchy and tyrannical government, and less a requirement for a tripartite structure of government based on a separation of powers and a strong, independent executive. In such circumstances, there is no inherent bar against a parliamentary government for Puerto Rico in the future, unless Congress expressly denies that possibility. On the other hand, it does seem that Congress was not just mimicking the federal constitutional clause. It could be argued that the republican requirement for the Puerto Rican government was a deliberate move on Congress's part to precisely require a tripartite governmental structure similar to the federal sphere. As examined in Ch 7, it is still a mystery where the Fiscal Control Board (created by the PROMESA statute adopted by the US Congress in 2016) fits into the tripartite structure that was created by the 1952 Constitution – the paradoxes of colonialism at their finest.

represent. Because the House has a baseline of 51 members, while the Senate has 27, House districts tend to be smaller than their Senate counterparts. But both are drawn proportionally in terms of equal population, and both are elected simultaneously for a four-year term.

Article IV established the Executive Branch, headed by an elected Governor, who serves a four-year term. There are no term limits in Puerto Rico for any elected position. The Governor is the only elected member of the Executive, mirroring the federal practice. Similarly, the Chief Executive appoints all members of the Cabinet, subject to Senate confirmation.

However, unlike the US model, there is no Lieutenant Governor. This is an example of local considerations outweighing American influence. But those local considerations were hardly radical or democratic. On the contrary, it was the result of an effort to consolidate the power of the governorship in general, and a specific Governor in particular. With regard to this issue, it seems that undemocratic partisan interests outweighed colonial influence.

In 1948, Puerto Rico elected it first Governor. From 1900 to 1948, all the Governors were appointed by the President of the US. The first elected Chief Executive was Luis Muñoz Marín, who was, by far, the dominant political figure of the time. As with George Washington, the constitutional drafters could not erase from their mind that the office they were creating was to be held by this towering figure. A majority of the delegates to the Constitutional Convention felt that a 'Vice-Governor' would either eclipse or be eclipsed by Muñoz Marín. In either case, there was no need for the post. The proposal to create the office was rejected. The Secretary of State would be the first in line in terms of succession. And because the Secretary would be appointed by the Governor, it strengthened his dominance over the entire branch.

Finally, Article V establishes the Judicial Branch, headed by a Supreme Court. The Justices that make up the Court are appointed by the Executive, subject to Senate confirmation, as is the case in the federal sphere. Lower courts are established by statute and all judges are also appointed by the Governor with Senate approval.

A proposal for an elected Judiciary was rejected. As to that issue, the colonial and un-democratic aspects of the 1952 Constitution converged and displaced its progressive instinct. However, it should be noted that, unlike their federal counterparts, members of the Puerto Rican Judiciary, including the Supreme Court, are not appointed for life terms. On the contrary, its members must retire at age 70, among them the Justices of the Supreme Court. This limitation is, curiously, an indirect consequence of the *Lochner* experience in the US.[13] The Puerto Rican drafters did not want to turn the Judiciary into an exclusive club made up of old men of European descent that looked notably different from

[13] *Lochner v New York* 198 US 45 (1905).

the rest of the country. An age limit was seen as a stopgap method of preventing this undesired outcome. Here, the progressive instinct of the Constitution prevailed over its colonial and undemocratic impulses.

The naked textual colonialism found in the Puerto Rican Constitution mostly lives at two extreme points: the beginning (Preamble and Article I) and at the end (Article VII). In between, colonialism operates silently, through influence and voluntary importation. We now turn to the last piece of the puzzle: the amendment process laid out in Article VII.

The (un)democratic characteristic of the procedural aspects of Article VII are examined in more detail below. We focus first on the colonial characteristic of the substantive limits of Article VII. As is discuss in greater detail below, there are two main amendment mechanisms in the 1952 Constitution: (1) specific, individual amendments and (2) a general – or possibly partial – revision through a constitutional convention.

Article VII imposes a critical substantive limit on either mechanism:

> Any amendment or revision of this constitution shall be consistent with the resolution enacted by the Congress of the United States approving this constitution, with the applicable provisions of the Constitution of the United States, with the Puerto Rican Federal Relations Act, and with Public Law 600, Eighty-first Congress, adopted in the nature of a compact.

It should be noted that this language was *imposed* by Congress in 1952, with the eventual acquiescence of the Puerto Rico Constitutional Convention.

In that sense, this part of Article VII has two distinct colonial characteristics. First, that it was the direct result of Congress's exercise of its power over the constitutional process itself. Even though the 1952 Constitution was written by 'We the People of Puerto Rico', the US Congress still exercised ultimate sovereign power. And in this case, Congress decided to use that power fully by imposing direct language on the 1952 Constitution that was not originally drafted by the elected Constitutional Convention. Second, that the actual substantive content of this part of Article VII reveals an inherent colonial nature. Note that this provision *subordinates* the will of the Puerto Rican People to a whole host of federal legal sources: (1) the Constitution; (2) the Federal Relations Act; (3) Public Law 600; and (4) Public Law 447 (Joint Resolution) (3 July 1952), which finally approved the Puerto Rican Constitution.

Of course, no US state constitution can directly violate either the federal Constitution or any other federal statute that is part of the law of the land, by virtue of the Supremacy Clause. But this does not require the sort of strict, *textual* limitation imposed on Puerto Rico. As such, not only is Puerto Rico's Constitution forbidden to violate these federal sources as a matter of basic federal constitutional law, but its actual text also conveys that requirement. That is a step further than is currently imposed on states. In addition, of course, those states possess Senators and Representatives, who participate in the drafting and adoption of federal statutes which the state constitution cannot violate.

But note also what these federal legal sources all have in common: they are the foundation of Puerto Rico's colonial condition. This means that Article VII categorically prevents the Puerto Rican People from attempting to modify their colonial situation through constitutional modification. In other words, colonialism is not subject to constitutional alteration by way of popular will. It is as if colonialism was a bedrock element of Puerto Rico's existence.

Of course, Puerto Rico's colonial situation has been the subject of ample debate and interaction. But the forums that have been used have been outside of Puerto Rico's internal constitutional structure. Whether it has been through litigation in federal courts under the US Constitution, or political lobbying in the federal Congress or in the United Nations, Puerto Rico's colonial condition – probably its main existential challenge – has simply and totally been excluded from consideration by way of constitutional modification. Article VII explains why this is so.

This sort of arrangement has dangerous implications. First, it creates a constitutional culture where colonialism is an unreachable issue, thus elevating colonialism to near super-constitutional status. Second, it prevents the People from using the formal mechanisms designed to channel popular will to address the colonial problem. Third, it reinforces the notion that colonialism is a permanent and seemingly inherent feature of Puerto Rican politics and that the 1952 Constitution can never be characterised as the ultimate exercise of the sovereignty of We the People of Puerto Rico.

III. DEMOCRATIC DEFICITS: THE POLITICAL STRUCTURE OF THE 1952 CONSTITUTION

Puerto Rico's current political system is based on an aggressive belief in representative democracy, as opposed to direct democracy. While the 1952 process used formal and informal vehicles of popular participation, the political structure adopted in the Constitution itself leaves very little room for this type of direct democratic action. In other words, while popular forces were an active element of the 1952 process, they would be relegated to passive status in terms of the governmental system that would follow.

In turn, the type of representative democracy chosen by the framers was designed to accommodate single-party rule – or majority – governments within a de facto two-party system. This has historical explanations.

First, it is the result of extensive borrowing from the federal constitutional structure: a strong and unitary Executive Branch headed by an elected Governor under a plurality system and a mostly first-past-the-post model for legislators. This combination of plurality and first-past-the-post is a safe bet in favour of generating single-party governments, regardless of their ability to muster a convincing majority of the electorate.

Second, in 1951–52, the Popular Democratic Party (PPD) was unquestionably the dominant electoral force of the day. For example, in 1952, it obtained nearly 65 per cent of the vote. In 1956, its share was 60 per cent, while in 1960 it fell to a still commanding 58 per cent, which is explained by the fact that three other parties participated in that election. This electoral reality made its way into the constitutional text. Although no single political party has been able to enjoy this type of majoritarian support in recent decades, the current political system is substantially premised on the electoral situation in 1952. This historical disconnect compounds the system's severe democratic deficits.

Recent developments highlight this problem. Section 4 of Article VI of the Constitution states that for all elected offices, the winner shall be the candidate who receives the most votes, even if they fail to obtain a majority. This is the plurality principle in its purest form. While the *losing* candidate in 2008 received 41.29 per cent of the vote, the *winning* candidate in 2020 only obtained 33.24 per cent of vote. This has led to renewed calls for a two-round model or a ranked vote system which guarantees that the winner receives a clear majority of the vote or something that resembles it.

A. Legislative Branch

Puerto Rico's Legislature is the main protagonist of its governmental structure. This role is not only the result of its relative position in contrast to its counterparts, but the product of a widely held belief in the need for an active and strong legislative body that would tackle the pressing social and economic needs of the population. This approach generated a robust articulation of the police power and a positive view of public intervention in general. The social consensus at the time favoured direct and aggressive government participation in social and economic affairs. This required an empowered Legislature.

As noted above, Puerto Rico's Legislature is bicameral and is mostly selected through a first-past-the-post system in district constituencies. This has enabled the creation of a two-party system which has dominated Puerto Rico's political life for more than 60 years, although there are recent signs that the two-party system has weakened considerably in terms of overall electoral and popular support.

The House of Representatives is ordinarily made up of 51 members: 40 selected in single-member, territorial districts and 11 selected at-large on an island-wide basis. In turn, the Senate is ordinarily made up 27 members: 16 selected in two-member, territorial districts and 11 selected at-large on an island-wide basis.

As to the individual house districts, each political party is entitled to nominate a particular candidate. This means that, theoretically, a single party can win all 40 single-member seats, even if it cannot muster an outright electoral majority. This is due to Puerto Rico's electoral system being based on the plurality principle. As to the individual senate districts, each party is entitled to nominate two candidates, while voters can vote for up to two as well. This means that a single political party can win all 16 seats without an actual electoral majority, still less a supermajority.

This approach tends to favour a two-party system, since it is close to impossible for a smaller third-party to come first in any individual district. This creates a vicious cycle: people may not vote for third parties because they think they cannot win, thus guaranteeing that they never will, which in turn strengthens the initial inclination to not vote for them. Unlike other representative democracies, Puerto Rico's political landscape is not based on substantial regional disparities among the political forces. While third parties have been, historically, stronger in urban areas, this has not been enough for them to come even close to first in any legislative district. However, as discussed below and further in Chapter 7, Puerto Rico is now as close as it has ever been to a true multi-party democracy, with as many as five political parties obtaining legislative representation. Yet, to this day, no third party has ever won a first-past-the-post district.

The only remaining direct route for smaller parties to enter the Legislature at all is through the at-large seats. As outlined above, there are 11 at-large seats up for grabs in each house. The current statutory scheme only allows each party the right to nominate up to six at-large candidates per legislative chamber. While two strong parties could run the table – each with 6 candidates, totalling 12 between them – the practice in recent decades has been that at least one, but no more than two, candidates from outside the two main parties has been able to be directly elected to an at-large seat.

In 2016, the two-party system began to crack. In 2020, the crack became a schism. During the 2020 election, the *winning* party – in terms of most overall votes under the party column – obtained only 33 per cent of the vote. That is hardly the level of support envisioned by the constitutional system. In two single-member districts for the House of Representatives, a new, third party came in second. In one of them, the third-party candidate lost by a little more than 100 votes.

But there are 40 representative districts in Puerto Rico, which means that third parties still have a long way to go. There are two distinct possibilities that could emerge from the current political shift: (1) that a third party becomes the second party, thus maintaining the two-party system, just with different players; or (2) that a realignment occurs, and more than two parties are able to elect a substantial number of single-member districts. Time will tell.

But the most striking aspect of the 2020 election was the entry of *five* political parties to the Legislative Assembly. In the Senate, these five parties are accompanied by a re-elected independent candidate. *All* of the third parties managed to elect their candidates through the at-large mechanism. In fact, they did better, accumulatively, than the two main parties. For example, in the Senate, of the 11 elected at-large seats, five were obtained by third parties or independent candidacies.

In that sense, while the at-large seats make it relatively easier for a third party to enter the Legislature with at least a seat or two in each house, it also makes it almost impossible to elect more than that, bar some substantial change in the electoral balance. As a result, the system is designed to perpetuate the minority status of third parties, even if they manage to garner substantial electoral support.

More importantly, it seems highly likely that the two main parties in Puerto Rico, for the first time in modern history, will actually not even nominate the statutorily allowed maximum of six candidates to the at-large seats in each house, in an attempt to regain some of the seats from the emerging parties. Even if this strategy is ultimately successful, it signals a substantial adjustment by the main parties that was unthinkable only ten years ago.

In fact, most third parties decided to nominate few candidates, or even only one, in order to avoid vote splitting. The result is that a single candidate can amass sufficient votes that, if evenly divided with another candidate from the same party, would allow for the election of two representatives. Still, most third parties are hesitant to attempt this risky strategy, since the opposite could also be true: a party could nominate two candidates, resulting in both being unable to win, but their combined votes could have been enough to elect one of them. In 2020, while the PIP and the new, right-wing party Dignity Project nominated and elected a single member to each house through the at-large mechanism, the progressive Citizen's Victory Movement took a risk and nominated two candidates for each house. The gamble paid off and the party managed to elect them both.

The House of Representatives, as mentioned above, is *ordinarily* made up of 51 members, while the Senate is *ordinarily* composed of 27. The use of the word 'ordinarily' is intentional: the Constitution itself allows for a limited enlargement of those numbers in particular situations.

The 1952 Constitution does not allow a single political party to control more than two-thirds of the seats in either of the two legislative houses. If a single party wins more than this number, the Constitution requires that additional seats be created and allotted to the minority forces, up to a maximum of a third of the total number of seats in the particular chamber.

This peculiar mechanism presents a great contradiction. First, it still allows a party that receives a bare plurality of the votes to control up to 66 per cent of the legislative chambers. Second, it prohibits a party that receives more than 66 per cent of the vote from obtaining more than 66 per cent of the seats. In other words, it artificially inflates or deflates actual popular support.

Another element of Article III deserves mention. Section 7 established the mechanisms for the enlargement of either of the legislative houses to accommodate the one-third of seats guaranteed to minority parties. The curious thing is that this provision distinguishes between two scenarios. The first applies when the winning party obtains more than two-thirds of the vote for Governor. The second applies when it obtains less than that number.

As can be appreciated, this provision was designed at a time when the governing party, the PPD, could and did achieve vote totals that surpassed the two-thirds threshold. In that sense, the Convention was legislating for a very contemporaneous reality instead of for the future, unless the PPD was arrogant enough to think that their massive vote tallies would last indefinitely. Since the PPD lost its electoral might during the 1960s, no political party has even come close to the two-thirds threshold for the governorship, thus rendering an entire provision of the 1952 Constitution completely moot and inoperative.[14]

It should also be noted that the 1952 Constitution requires redistricting every ten years, after each census, through a so-called Constitutional Board led by the Chief Justice and by two additional members, each of whom must be from a different political party. Note, once again, that the constitutional structure is designed for a two-party system.

As noted above, Section 2, Article I of the 1952 Constitution explicitly adopted the classic, three-branch republican structure. This implicitly includes the doctrine of the separation of powers. As per that model, '[t]he Legislative Power will be exercised by a Legislative Assembly'.[15]

This is a very broad concept and includes the general police power. As discussed further in Chapter 5, this general delegation of the legislative power is reinforced by Section 19 of the Bill of Rights which grants the Legislative Assembly even broader police powers to provide for the general welfare of the Puerto Rican People. In that sense, and unlike Article I of the federal Constitution, the 1952 Constitution makes no specific reference to the powers of the Legislature. This was intentional and reinforces the notion that the legislative power is broad and general in nature, subject only to the limitations adopted in the constitutional text, mostly through its rights provisions.

Internally, the Legislative Assembly operates as does the US Congress and most state legislatures: it has the power to adopt rules for its internal operations, is the only forum that can pass judgement as to the qualifications of its members, can elect its officers, may meet in ordinary and extraordinary sessions, its deliberations must be public, and its members enjoy parliamentary immunity.

[14] The two-thirds scenario is regulated by s 7(a) of Art III. Since the 1960s, all of the times where the expansion mechanism was used were done under s 7(b).

[15] Puerto Rico Constitution, Art III, § 1.

The Legislature also has broad power to structure the Executive Branch, particularly with regard to the creation, organisation, and operation of its administrative agencies. The 1952 Constitution also creates the office of the Comptroller, with broad powers to audit and supervise public spending in Puerto Rico. Under the constitutional structure, the Comptroller is considered a legislative officer, but one that must be nominated by the Governor and confirmed by an absolute majority of both legislative houses. Along with the Secretary of State, it is the only officer that requires bicameral confirmation.

Tracking the federal practice, the House of Representatives has the sole power of impeachment. But, unlike its federal counterpart, it requires a two-thirds majority in the lower house. As we saw, the Constitution makes it impossible for a single party to control more than two-thirds of either house, meaning that impeachment presupposes some sort of, at least, bipartisan consensus. If this threshold is met, then the matter passes to the Senate, which will hold an impeachment trial presided by the Chief Justice. In order to successfully remove an official, the 1952 Constitution requires a three-quarters majority in the upper house. Again, the constitutional structure is meant to remove officials only when there is a wide consensus in favour. It is not meant to be used for purely partisan purposes and advantage.

With regard to possible bases for impeachment, the text limits the reasons to 'treason, bribery, other felonies (*delitos graves*), and those misdemeanors (*delitos menos graves*) that imply depravation'.[16] The use of the words *delitos* strongly implies typification in the Criminal Code. But, because it is an explicitly political process, it is up to each house to determine whether a particular conduct is impeachable.

Finally, the legislative process itself is similar to the federal Congress and other state legislatures: members of either house can present bills that can be referred to one or several committees for their consideration. All bills require bicameral approval. If the same text is approved in both houses, it goes to the Governor for his or her signature. The Governor has 10 days – Sundays excluded – to either sign it, veto it, or let the period lapse. If the period lapses, the bill will become law, unless the 10-day period ends after the legislative session has concluded. In these circumstances, the Governor's inaction constitutes a pocket veto.

If the Governor vetoes a bill, it can be overridden by a two-thirds majority vote in each house. Considering that, as a historical and structural matter, a Governor is basically guaranteed, at least, one-third of each legislative chamber, his or her veto can only be overcome with support from legislators from his or her own party. As a historical matter, overriding an executive's veto is a very rare

[16] Puerto Rico Constitution, Art III, § 21. The term 'depravation' can be defined as conduct that implies moral turpitude.

occurrence. This has considerably expanded the political power of the governors, who are almost always the presiding officer of their respective parties.

B. Executive Branch

In 1952, the PPD was the dominant electoral force. As mentioned above, it routinely gained more than 60 per cent of the vote. Within the PPD, Luis Muñoz Marín was the undisputed paramount figure. First elected to the Senate in 1932 under the Liberal Party ticket, Muñoz Marín – a former Socialist – quickly acquired national recognition. The son of Luis Muñoz Rivera, himself the former head of the Autonomous Government in 1897 and also Resident Commissioner from 1911 until 1916, Muñoz Marín was renowned for his oratory skills.

After breaking with the Liberal Party, Muñoz Marín established the PPD in 1938 and, in 1940, the party won a majority of the seats in the Senate. After being elected President of the Senate, Muñoz Marín forged a close alliance with Governor Rexford Tugwell, who had been one of Franklin Delano Roosevelt's allies during the New Deal. This alliance resulted in the adoption of progressive reforms that were aimed at improving the living standards of poor and working-class Puerto Ricans, both urban and rural.

A former advocate of Puerto Rican independence (*independentista*), Muñoz Marín would steer the PPD into a position of accepting US domination over the island. This eventually resulted in the creation of the Commonwealth (*Estado Libre Asociado*). After 1952, the PPD became nearly synonymous with the Commonwealth status.

After Congress allowed Puerto Ricans to elect their first Governor in 1948, Muñoz Marín won by a landslide, obtaining more than 60 per cent of the vote. When the Constitutional Convention was convened, Muñoz Marín was elected as a delegate, while also serving as Governor of Puerto Rico and President of the PPD.

It is not hard to see that the figure of Muñoz Marín would directly influence the Convention's approach to the Executive Branch. Simply put, what eventually became Article IV of the 1952 Constitution was made in the image of Luis Muñoz Marín, very much in the way that Article II of the US Constitution was designed for – or at the very least thinking of – George Washington.

Section 1, Article IV of the 1952 Constitution vests the executive power in an elected Governor, to be chosen through direct popular vote at every general election for a four-year term. As with the members of the Legislature, there are no term limits. In fact, it should be noted that Muñoz Marín would serve as the elected Governor of Puerto Rico for four consecutive terms, similar in fact to the position of FDR in the US, from 1949 until 1965.

Like the US President, no person under 35 can be elected to the post of Governor. Also like in the federal sphere, all members of the Cabinet are to be appointed by the Governor, generally subject to Senate confirmation. During the deliberations of the Constitutional Convention the Socialist Party made a proposal to allow for the direct election of Cabinet officers, as is the system in many US states. It was thoroughly rejected by the PPD. This strengthened the Governor's control over the Executive Branch.

In other words, the Convention adopted a unitary Executive where only the Governor would be subject to popular election and where all executive officers would be subject to gubernatorial appointment. This is Puerto Rico's version of strong presidentialism.

Puerto Rico has no Lieutenant Governor. Again, the presence of Muñoz Marín explains why. The rejection of the creation of the office of Lieutenant Governor, then, was based on a concern shared by PPD delegates that the person who held that office could rival Muñoz Marín's unquestioned leadership. A similar thing happened with regard to the bicameral nature of the Legislature. During the deliberations of the Constitutional Convention, there were proposals to adopt a unicameral Legislature. These were rejected, mostly because the person who presided over that single body could equal Muñoz Marín's stature and authority as Governor.[17]

In the end, the Convention agreed to name the appointed Secretary of State as first in the line on the constitutional order of succession. In order to give that office – in the event of succession – some semblance of democratic legitimacy, it would be subject to confirmation by *both* the Senate and the House of Representatives, unlike other Cabinet officers, who only require the approval of the upper house.

Still, the Executive Branch is not all-powerful in the Puerto Rican constitutional order. In fact, the Constitutional Convention purposely limited some of the powers conferred on that office by the organic Jones Act. For example, under the Jones Act, the Governor had the power to suspend the writ of *habeas corpus*, subject to legislative confirmation. In the 1952 Constitution, that power was given to the Legislative Assembly exclusively.[18] It was an intentional transfer of power from one branch to another.

Unlike the powers of the Legislative Assembly, the 1952 Constitution does enumerate the powers of the Governor. Section 4, Article IV delegates to the chief executive the following duties, powers, and responsibilities, inter alia: to execute the laws; call for an extraordinary session of the Legislature; to appoint executive officers; to be commander-in-chief of the militia; to call up the militia and the *posse comitatus* to address any grave disturbance to the public order, rebellion, or invasion; to proclaim martial law when there is a rebellion or invasion – or imminent danger of one – and it is required by the public safety, subject to immediate legislative approval; to grant pardons and commutations.

[17] The Speaker of the House of Representatives at the time, Ernesto Ramos Antonini, was also a towering figure in his own right, who could rival Muñoz Marín. If he had presided over a unicameral Legislature, his stature would have grown even further.

[18] This issue is discussed in greater detail in Ch 5.

The Governor's *legislative* powers are mostly statutory and political in nature. As a historical practice, governors double as presidents of their respective political parties. As such, they chair their party's legislative conference, made up of the Governor and all representatives and senators elected under the party banner. This practice is found in most of the by-laws of the main political parties in Puerto Rico and considerably enhances the Governor's influence over the legislative process.

Another source of executive participation with regard to legislative norms is the historical practice of statutory delegation of quasi-legislative power to executive agencies, as well as to the Office of the Governor. The doctrine and practice of delegation in Puerto Rico is not as strict as in the federal sphere, allowing for considerable delegation of quasi-legislative power to administrative entities, including independent agencies and state-owned corporations.

The broad scope of delegated quasi-legislative power, combined with: (1) the Governor's historical role as president of his or her party – and thus their control over their party's legislative conference; (2) the Constitution's grant of the veto power; and (3) the almost inevitable situation where a Governor's party will control, at least, a third of each legislative chamber, creates a perfect storm for presidentialism. Specifically, any Governor has the ability to effectively block any legislative attempt to overrule the Executive Branch's legislative choices. Think of the following scenario. The Legislative Assembly passes a bill delegating broad quasi-legislative power to a particular administrative agency that is accountable to the Governor. Exercising that delegated power, the agency adopts a legislative rule establishing a particular norm. The Legislature disagrees with the substance of that rule. The Legislature's only option is to pass another bill overruling the rule. But, in order to do so, the Legislature needs the Governor's signature. This means that a sitting Governor would have to publicly disagree with his or her agency's legislative rule when, in all likelihood, the agency acted in accordance with the Governor's wishes in the first place. This all but guarantees a veto. In that scenario, the Legislature would need to mobilise two-thirds of its members to override the veto. But, as we saw, the Governor's party, almost inevitably, will control at least a third of the Legislative Assembly, thus almost guaranteeing that the veto will stand. The end result is a strengthened Executive Branch at the expense of the Legislature.

Much of the power that governors in Puerto Rico wield comes not from Article IV of the 1952 Constitution but from their status as party leaders and the broad scope of delegated quasi-delegated power which is exercised by the agencies under his or her control, or that is given directly to the Governor. The constant use of executive orders during the COVID-19 pandemic, authorised by statute in cases of emergency, is a testament to this phenomenon, where the Legislative Assembly could not muster sufficient votes to reclaim the delegated power. As a result, most of the normative rules that Puerto Ricans had to follow – from vaccine and mask mandates to curfews – came not in the form of legislated statutes but as executive decrees issued solely by the Governor, subject only to highly deferential judicial review.

C. Judicial Branch

As to the Judiciary, the Constitutional Convention again looked to the federal model, settling on a system of gubernatorial appointment, subject to Senate confirmation. While this system was eventually adopted through consensus, it is worth noting that other proposals – one of them decidedly more democratic and the other less so – were also considered.

The proposal put forth by the Republican Statehood Party (PER) was probably the least democratic. It called for the formation of a 'Judicial Council', composed of distinguished jurists, former judges, and law professors, to recommend candidates to the Governor. According to the PER, this would ensure that merit would be the overriding factor in the selection of judges.

The Socialist Party (PS) vehemently opposed this idea, claiming that it would turn the Judiciary into a self-perpetuating, elitist institution, mostly made up of conservative men of property of European descent who had access to the prevailing power structure and elite education. The specter of *Lochner* was still fresh in their minds.

As a result, the PS proposed the opposite of the PER's approach: the election of judges, as was the practice in many US states. This was part of an overarching agenda on the part of the PS to democratise Puerto Rican society, including its governmental structure and the private sphere. According to one of the PS's leaders in the Convention, they would push for democracy and election at every level, from the dog catcher to the bishop. The PS's model was also designed to avoid single party control, limiting the number of candidates that political forces could nominate.

The PS's proposal was based upon many factors, all of which shared a democratic characteristic. First is the basic desirability of popular selection as opposed to the exercise of power by unelected bodies. Second is the view that certain sectors of society, particularly those of humble origin, would only be able to access entities like the Judiciary through the ballot box. In other words, the only way to diversify elite institutions was through democratic intervention. A working class lawyer lacked the connections needed to successfully navigate an appointment process normally dominated by the privileged. And third is the fierce conviction that the judiciary needed to be a majoritarian instrument that would not thwart progressive legislation. Again, the spectre of *Lochner* loomed large.[19] The PER strongly opposed the Socialists' plan, fearing it could lead to demagoguery.

[19] This issue is related to the PS's attempt to limit the power of the courts to strike down progressive legislation.

For its part, the governing PPD opted for the federal model: gubernatorial appointment with senatorial confirmation. This fit perfectly with the dominant role of Muñoz Marín, as it would give him the absolute advantage of initiating the process through nomination. A friendly Senate would most likely support the Governor's choice.

During the deliberations of the Convention, the PER made its position quite clear: they preferred the Judicial Council route, but under no circumstance would they support popular election. The possibility of appointment and confirmation constituted an acceptable alternative. The PS took the opposite approach: they preferred popular election, but under no circumstance would they support the Judicial Council. The possibility of appointment and confirmation would also be an acceptable alternative.

As a result, the PPD's first preference happened to be the PS's and PER's second choice. Since the PS and the PER would veto each other's primary proposal, appointment and confirmation became the consensus choice.

It should also be noted that the PS, while unable to obtain popular election for judges, was successful in its attempt to include a mandatory retirement age – 70 years – for the Judiciary, including the Justices of the Supreme Court. This was meant to avoid the development of a judicial elite that could hold on to power during important moments of social change and transformation.

As with the US federal system, the composition of the Supreme Court is mostly dependent on biological factors, namely, the death or forced retirement of judges. For decades after the 1952 Constitution was adopted, the PPD was able to appoint a majority of the Justices. In 2009, the PNP – the conservative successor to the pro-statehood PER founded in 1967 – was finally able to muster its own majority. That signified a rightward turn by the Court in terms of legal philosophy, as well the reality that a majority of the Court would now be generally hostile to the 1952 constitutional project, mostly associated with the PPD.

D. Political Parties

Political parties in Puerto Rico enjoy explicit constitutional status. They are mentioned more than 20 times in the constitutional text in six different provisions in four separate Articles. This is the result of the fact that the political parties existing at that time led the drafting process. Every single delegate to the Constitutional Convention belonged to a political party and was elected under their lists.

Parties are first mentioned in Section 4 of Article III (Legislative Branch), which requires that the two additional members of the constitutional board that convenes every ten years to review legislative districts must belong to different political parties.[20] Section 7 of Article III is completely devoted to the participation of minoritarian political parties in the Legislature. As we saw, the 1952 Constitution requires that at least one third of each legislative chamber must belong to a party or parties different from the majority. Such is the dominant role of parties in the political process that Section 8 requires that any vacancy that is created in an at-large seat must be filled exclusively by the party to which the incumbent belonged.

Section 12 of Article V (Judicial Branch) categorically prohibits judges from making economic contributions to political parties and from belonging to their governing boards. This is indicative of several things: first, that membership in political parties was expected to remain widespread, which required an explicit constitutional provision prohibiting judges from engaging in explicit partisan activity; second, that judges would be selected among active members of a political party, and the constitution needed to contain the most potentially egregious conflicts of interest; and finally, that the appointment model for judges established in Article V needed to be shielded from external partisan influences.

Because of their constitutional status and quasi-governmental nature, political parties are also subject to direct regulation by the Legislative Assembly,[21] as long as it does not interfere with the general right to association recognised in Section 6 of the Bill of Rights. Finally, Section 6 of Article IX protect parties from changes in their electoral status by explicitly requiring that all changes which weaken or eliminate their rights in any quadrennial period to be enforceable only after the following election cycle.

IV. AMENDMENT: SUBSTANTIVE AND PROCEDURAL LIMITATIONS

Probably one of the most undemocratic aspects of the 1952 Constitution is Article VII, which deals with the amendment procedures and mechanisms. We have already analysed the colonial nature of Article VII, particularly with regard to the substantive limitations imposed on the People's ability to alter their own founding document. We now focus our attention on the remaining substantive limits on constitutional amendments and, most importantly, the considerable procedural obstacles that thwart the available avenues for popular modification of the constitutional order.

[20] The third member of the board is the sitting Chief Justice. Note that the constitutional system limits the participation on the board to two members, anticipating the two-party system that would dominate Puerto Rico until 2020.

[21] Puerto Rico Constitution, Art VI, § 4.

A. Substantive Limitations

There are two main types of substantive limitations on the Puerto Rican People's amendment power under Article VII of the 1952 Constitution. As noted above, the first type relates to compatibility with specific federal instruments that, not coincidentally, establish and formalise Puerto Rico's colonial relationship with the US. This requires a more detailed look at these sources to identify the specific limitations they impose. The second type of substantive limitation are mostly conceptual: (1) a ban on the abolition of the Bill of Rights; and (2) a ban on altering the republican form of government. We start our analysis with the first type of substantive limitations to Article VII amendments or modifications.

As discussed earlier, Article VII of the 1952 Constitution names several specific federal instruments with which any and all amendments to the Puerto Rican text must be compatible. One of them is obvious: the US Constitution. As we saw, there is nothing normatively surprising in this fact. No state constitution can contradict the US Constitution. That is a direct consequence of the Supremacy Clause. What did stand out about this was the US Congress's insistence on incorporating it explicitly into the text of Article VII of the 1952 Constitution.

Also, as a result of the Supremacy Clause, federal statutes supersede state law, even those that have constitutional rank. But it is a different thing altogether to expressly state that hierarchy as an explicit substantive limitation on state constitutional amendment possibilities. It seems that Puerto Rico's territorial status allows, or even emboldens, Congress to act much more aggressively than it would with a state constitution.

The federal statutory enactments listed in Article VII are: (1) the Puerto Rico Federal Relations Act; (2) Public Law 600; and (3) Public Law 447 (Joint Resolution) (3 July 1952).

The Puerto Rico Federal Relations Act is made up by the remnants of the organic 1917 Jones Act, which was substantially modified and curtailed after the adoption of Public Law 600 and the 1952 Constitution. Once Congress approved the Constitution, the 1917 Act was restyled as the Puerto Rico Federal Relations Act. Article's VII ban on constitutional amendments or modifications that contradict this Act reflects Congress's desire to maintain ultimate control over Puerto Rico's territorial status. It becomes, for example, a formal legal impediment to unilateral independence, or even attempts at annexation, without congressional acquiescence. In that sense, the 1952 Constitution is still subordinate to the Jones Act of 1917, as modified.

The other two statutory enactments are two sides of the same coin: Public Law 600 authorised – and thus imposed conditions on – the drafting of the 1952 Constitution, while Public Law 447 (Joint Resolution) gave final congressional approval to the Puerto Rican constitutional text.

One apparent consequence of Article VII's reference to these two particular congressional enactments is that the Puerto Rican People could not remove what Congress explicitly required or imposed, nor incorporate what Congress explicitly prohibited or rejected. This could include, for example, the ill-fated Section 20 of the Bill of Rights, which included an expansive list of socio-economic rights that Congress found too radical in 1952. Would Article VII allow a federal court to block an attempt to reintroduce Section 20 to the Bill of Rights? Or would it require an affirmative congressional statement of disapproval?

While Section 20 was the most known instance of congressional rejection, the same thing could apply to instances of Congressional textual imposition. For example, Congress in 1952 required that the Puerto Rican constitutional text explicitly allow parents to send their children to private school as a way to comply with the 1952 Constitution's requirement that all school-age children enrol in the public education system. Can an Article VII amendment abolish private education in Puerto Rico and establish a public monopoly in, for example, elementary education?

While the first type of Article VII substantive limitations refer to actual compatibility with specific federal instruments, the second type is more conceptual and, possibly, more difficult to enforce. There are two manifestations of this type: (1) a ban on the abolition of the Bill of Rights; and (2) a ban on altering the Constitution's 'republican form of government'.[22]

A simple analysis of these textual limitations demonstrates their many potential enforcement challenges. What stops short of becoming an abolition of the Bill of Rights? Is it enough to leave just one constitutional right in a text that currently has over 50? How far can a substantial revision proceed before it is characterised as the functional equivalent of an abolition? Does it have to be the current version of the Bill of Rights or can it be any Bill of Rights, even one that is wholly different from the one adopted in 1952?

B. Procedural Limitations

Because of its central role in Article VII and its explicit democratic deficits, we focus most of our attention on an analysis of the amendment procedures themselves. The first thing that stands out is that any and all formal constitutional change must begin with the Legislative Assembly. It is important to note, however, that the Legislature does not possess the power to unilaterally alter the constitutional text. But it does have the exclusive power to initiate constitutional amendments. In other words, only the Legislature can get the amendment ball rolling.

[22] For a brief analysis on the content of this requirement, see n 12 above.

This structure is the result of an over-confidence in representative democracy manifested during the deliberations of the Constitutional Convention which were entrenched throughout the constitutional text. The main absent actor is the People, who cannot directly initiate an amendment process. When it comes to the amendment process, the People constitute a substantially passive entity that is called upon only at the end.

There are only two mechanisms for formal constitutional change under Article VII. One is very broad and the other considerably more narrow. This limits the options available to the Legislature somewhat, as there is no clear middle-ground alternative that can be pursued. The available mechanisms sit at the extremes.

The first option is the adoption of individual amendments. It starts with both houses of the Legislature adopting concurrent resolutions which require, at least, a two-thirds majority in favour.[23] The two-thirds majority is calculated on the basis of the entire membership of each chamber, regardless of vacancies or abstentions. Note that the Executive Branch plays no part in this process, since concurrent resolutions are not subject to the Governor's signature or veto.

If the requisite majority is achieved in both houses, then the amendment goes to the People, who must ratify it through referendum. A simple majority of those who participate will be enough to approve the amendment. There is no minimum threshold in terms of voter participation. This means that the only supermajoritarian requirement applies in the initial legislative stage; the People are not so bound.[24]

Article VII limits the number of individual amendments that can be put to the People in a single referendum at three. Each proposal must be voted on individually, allowing the public to pick and choose between the amendments that are presented to them. The textual requirement of no more than three individual amendments at each referendum has been subject to judicial interpretation, which has, in turn, made it considerably more flexible, creating something of a de facto middle point.

The Supreme Court of Puerto Rico has interpreted the three-amendment rule to not mean that each individual textual change constitutes a separate amendment. It will consider a series of textual modifications as a single amendment if there is a 'single purpose' that is common to all of them.[25] The objective of the three-amendment rule is to avoid logrolling.

[23] A three-quarters majority is required if the Legislature wishes to celebrate the referendum on the same day as the general election.

[24] The Constitutional Convention rejected a proposal to require a two-thirds majority in the referendum.

[25] See *Berríos Martínez v Gobernador II* 137 DPR 195 (1994). In *PIP v ELA* 186 DPR 1 (2012), the Supreme Court went even further, as it held that a substantial overhaul of Art III regarding the composition of the Legislative Assembly was to be considered one single amendment.

This allows the Legislature to propose an amendment that would impact several constitutional provisions, but only as incidental to achieve single end. Suppose that there is a proposal to establish the office of Lieutenant Governor. Because of the structure of Article IV, this would require modifying more than one of its sections. For instance, the proposal would need to include the office in the section that deals with age requirements for executive office. It would also need to change the section that deals with gubernatorial succession. But because all of these multiple changes are *incidental* to a single proposal, the amendment would be counted as one and the same.

It should be noted that the 'single purpose' doctrine would not allow, for example, the Legislature to propose a whole new 'Article III' and completely transform the Legislative Branch under the guise of being one single idea. The 'single purpose' doctrine merely avoids the incidental impact on more than one provision from couting as multiple amendments. The bottom line is whether it is an indivisible proposal that can elicit a simple yes or no from the voters on each single idea.

The second option is to call a new constitutional convention for a 'revision of this Constitution'.[26] As with the first option, the Legislative Assembly would need to approve a concurrent resolution with the requisite two-thirds majority in each chamber. This would trigger a referendum asking the People of Puerto Rico if they agree to the organisation of a new constitutional convention. The Constitution requires that this referendum take place at the next general election, in order to assure maximum voter participation.

If the voters vote in favour of the proposal, then elections would be held for the members of the new constitutional convention in a manner established by statute. Any and all the revisions to the Constitution made by the new convention, including a whole new document, would then be submitted to the People for a final up or down vote.

The main conceptual challenge in this scenario is the scope of the 'revision' that the new constitutional convention could carry out. In other words, whether Article VII always allows for a *general* revision or would it also allow for a more limited, *partial* revision; for example, limiting the convention to reviewing some parts of the Constitution, but forbidding it from considering others.

Some argue that the use of the general word 'revision', the lack of textual reference to a more limited alternative, and the impossibility of controlling a 'runaway convention' once it has been elected by the People, means that any constitutional convention can always carry out a general revision of the Constitution.[27] I disagree.[28]

[26] Puerto Rico Constitution, Art 7, § 1.

[27] See JJ Álvarez González and AI García Saúl, 'Derecho Constitucional' (1991) 65 *Revista Jurídica Universidad de Puerto Rico* 799, 875.

[28] See JM Farinacci-Fernós, 'Cómo cambiar nuestra Ley Suprema: Un análisis del Artículo VII de la Constitución de Puerto Rico' (2019) 2 *Amicus Revista de Política Pública y Legislación Universidad Interamericana de Puerto Rico* 153.

At least formally, the type of convention mentioned in Article VII seems to be an example of constituted power, not an exercise of constituent power. In any event, it poses a limit on its constituent authority. As such, it is nominally beholden to the conditions and limits that the Legislature, as the initiating party, decides to impose.

The text of Article VII seems to back up this idea. It states that once the People approve the proposal to call a convention in a referendum, the elections to the new convention will be held *in the manner established by statute*. Moreover, there is the fact that the *authority* of the new constitutional convention derives from a popular referendum. If the proposal submitted to the People by the Legislature stated explicitly that the convention would be called for some specific or limited task, one could argue that, at least from a purely legal perspective, a convention that exceeds the stated task would have acted outside its legal authority and contrary to popular will.

Of course, there is always the possibility that a convention can go rogue. But that is a permanent political possibility that lies outside the control of the current legal order.[29] But supposing that the current legal order survives, it should be able to rein in a rogue convention that attempts to violate its charge, which would have been adopted by legislative action and popular ratification.

Since 1952, the Legislative Assembly has never used the second option, in any of its manifestations. All attempts at constitutional modification have been made using the single amendment procedure. It can be deduced that the stakes in any revision process, whether general or partial, are too high for the current political class.

The 1952 Constitution has not been amended frequently. The last successful change was in 1970, when an amendment was passed to lower the voting age to 18. Since then, there have been few formal proposals made by the Legislature. All have been defeated in popular referenda.

For example, in 1994, the Legislative Assembly passed a concurrent resolution including three amendments: (1) to permanently fix the number of Justices in the Supreme Court to 9 and eliminate the Court's ability to initiate a process to increase or decrease its size; (2) to abolish the absolute right to bail in criminal cases, thus giving discretion to the Legislature on when to deny it; and (3) to set term limits for several elected officials. The Supreme Court of Puerto Rico struck down the last proposal, holding that it amounted to a series of amendments lacking a single purpose.[30] The Court concluded that the voters should have the right to vote in favour of term limits for senators, but not necessarily

[29] See JM Farinacci-Fernós, 'The Constitution is Dead, Long Live the Constitution! The Creation, Endurance and Modification of Modern Revolutionary Constitutions' (2020) 25 *Barry Law Review* 35.

[30] *Berríos Martínez v Gobernador II* (n 25).

for representatives, and vice versa. As such, it decided that the third proposal exceeded Article VII's allowed maximum of three amendments per referendum. In any case, the People of Puerto Rico soundly rejected both remaining proposals.

In 2012, another attempt was made to amend the Constitution. Two proposals were made: (1) a substantial reduction in the size of both houses of the Legislative Assembly; and (2) another effort to eliminate bail in criminal cases as an absolute right and allow the Legislature to withhold bail in the most egregious cases. Even though the Supreme Court allowed the referendum to continue – holding that the first amendment had, in fact, a 'single purpose', even though it substantially overhauled Article III[31] – the amendments were again soundly rejected in the corresponding referendum.

In summary, during the last 30 years, all attempts to modify the Constitution have failed. It is worth noting the nature of the proposed amendments. Notice that *twice* the Legislative Assembly attempted to eliminate the absolute right to bail in criminal cases and that *twice* it was soundly rejected by voters. It can be argued that proposals made to *eliminate* constitutional rights have not been well received by the public, while amendments *granting* rights, like lowering the voting age, have prevailed.

Notice also that the 1994 and 2012 proposals would have limited democratic avenues. First, by expanding the Court – thus giving the governing party two additional appointments – and removing the modification mechanism which allowed for inter-branch coordination on the matter. Second, by substantially reducing the size of the legislature, thus giving more power to fewer people, and further decreasing the possibility of third-party representation. It should therefore not be surprising that, although these measures gained super-majorities in both legislative houses, including bi-partisan support from the main political parties, they were firmly rejected by the voters. It would seem that while elected representatives may favour reducing democratic institutions, the population at large does not.

This brings us to the fatal democratic flaw of Article VII. As analysed previously in this chapter, some of the most undemocratic characteristics of the 1952 Constitution have to do with the electoral system, legislative representation, and the composition of the Executive. Some of the examples mentioned referred to the first-past-the-post model, plurality elections, unavailability of citizen-driven legislative initiatives, and so on.

The problem is that, in order to change those undemocratic elements, many of which directly impact the composition of the Legislative Assembly, these *must first be approved by a supermajority of the Legislature*. In other words, the Legislature itself would have to consent to a constitutional change that would considerably alter the way it is selected.

[31] *PIP v ELA* (n 25).

There is absolutely no incentive for legislators to do so. First, because any structural change in a democratic and participatory direction would make it harder for them to be elected. Second, because the main parties, who are not able to garner majoritarian electoral support but can muster pluralities that translate into super-majoritarian numbers in terms of legislative seats, would be consenting to their own demise.

This creates a vicious cycle: the People may want to get rid of their current representative system because it is not sufficiently democratic. The only way to do so is through formal constitutional alteration. And the two mechanisms for constitutional change must necessarily be initiated by the Legislature. This would require the election of pro-constitutional reform candidates. But the current system is stacked against these candidacies. That is precisely why the public wishes to change it in the first place.

There would either need to be a sudden change of heart within the main parties – perhaps if they realised they could benefit from a more democratic approach, if only to thwart the electoral possibilities of their partisan rivals – or a massive popular electoral response outside of the current two-party culture that would ensure the election of a supermajority to then put the issue to the People. As with many instances of constitutional amendment, this would mean that the People need first to overcome the systemic problem in order to then be in a position to fix it.

One possible solution is to generate a critical mass situation where a super-majority of the Legislature is persuaded to adopt a constitutional amendment *to change the procedural requirements of Article VII instead*. In other words, the best route to fixing the Constitution is to first fix Article VII. Although the same super-majoritarian problem may arise, there could be a better chance of generating sufficient political pressure on the Legislature to, instead of directly embracing structural changes to the specific issues discussed earlier, agree to an overhaul of the amendment mechanisms themselves.

This possibility has been discussed in the aftermath of the events of the so-called 'Summer of '19'. The political upheaval experienced during several months in the summer of 2019 revealed many of the democratic deficits of the 1952 Constitution, particularly in terms of the role of the public with regard to the structure of government. This revelation has had two immediate effects: a national conversation as to (1) those structural problems; and (2) the difficulty of fixing those problems because of the procedural limits of Article VII. As such, Article VII has also been identified as one – in fact probably the main – structural problem.

5

The 1952 Constitution (Substance)

I. A SUBSTANTIVE, PROGRESSIVE, AND SOCIAL CONSTITUTION

THE 1952 CONSTITUTION includes a variety of judicially enforceable, mostly progressive, substantive provisions that make it stand out among the constitutions of other states and territories of the US. These provisions were the result of the Constitutional Convention's conviction that a constitution should not just be a basic structural framework for the effective operation of democratic self-government, but that it should become the foundation for a fairer and more just society. In that sense, they concluded that the constitutional text should reflect the deeply held views of the Puerto Rican People, particularly with regard to social rights and economic justice, so it could be used to further social reform and, to some extent, transformation.[1] Of course, this transformation was limited to the possibilities allowed under colonialism and the dominant capitalist model, which remained mostly unchallenged.

As we saw in Chapter 3, this meant that the content of the Constitution was the object of social deliberation and analysis even before the Convention first met in 1951. The process that led up to the Convention generated important social agreements among the population on several important substantive issues, particularly socioeconomic ones. Among these were matters regarding labour rights, the education system, ending exploitative economic conditions, the eradication of discrimination, and the general notion of a fairer and more equitable society.

But the colonial character of Puerto Rico's constitutional process meant that the deliberations of 'We the People' were subject to final approval by the federal Congress, a body where Puerto Ricans were not directly represented. One of the greatest challenges for the Constitutional Convention was convincing a Cold War-era Congress to accept a territorial constitution full of progressive provisions, particularly with regard to individual rights and

[1] M Tushnet, 'Constitution-Making: An Introduction' (2013) 91 *Texas Law Review* 1983 ('The precise issues constitution makers confront vary widely and depend on the specific historical circumstances in which they operate'). In the Puerto Rican context, the prevailing historical circumstances pointed in the direction of social reform, particularly with regard to labour issues, education, and discrimination.

substantive public policy. Curiously, most – though not all – of these provisions managed to survive the congressional axe.

The combination of substantive provisions and the availability of judicial enforcement made Puerto Rico's Constitution something of a trailblazer, especially in 1952. Specifically, the Constitution's Bill of Rights adopted important enforceable socioeconomic rights, including horizontal individual and collective labour rights, among others. While Chapter 6 deals with the actual enforcement of these provisions after adoption, from a purely conceptual point of view, the progressive nature of the Bill of Rights adopted in 1952 should not be discounted. On the contrary, it serves as one of the main pillars of the entire constitutional project.

It should be noted that, while the Puerto Rican Bill of Rights is found in Article II of the 1952 Constitution, there are other important substantive provisions in other parts of the constitutional text, particularly Article VI, that should be treated as part of the Bill of Rights proper.[2] Our analysis includes provisions found in both articles, though most of our attention will focus on Article II.

Before diving into individual provisions, several conceptual clarifications are warranted. Many of these explain the important differences between the Puerto Rican and federal constitutional experiences.

First, the 1952 Constitution includes both civil and political rights, as well as socio-economic rights. The inclusion of judicially enforceable socioeconomic rights distinguishes the Puerto Rican text from its federal counterpart. But even as they pertain to civil and political rights, the Puerto Rican articulations tend to be considerably more expansive and numerous than those found in the US Constitution. In other words, there are two separate qualitative differences between both texts: categorical with regard to socioeconomic rights; and relative as to the reach, effect, and strength of political rights.

Second, the 1952 Constitution also includes both vertical and horizontal rights. In other words, many of the constitutional rights found in the text are enforceable both against state actors as well as private parties. In fact, some of the rights discussed below actually apply only to private actors, not the government. And even those rights that are primarily vertical – that is, those that require state action for their operation – also have indirect or secondary horizontal effect. This can take the form of statutory interpretation of legislation that has substantive links with the constitutional text, as well as through private causes of action under Puerto Rican civil law.

[2] According to José Trías-Monge, a delegate at the Constitutional Convention and future Chief Justice of the Puerto Rican Supreme Court, the substantive provisions found in Art VI of the 1952 Constitution should be treated as though they are part of the Bill of Rights established in Art II. See J Trías-Monge, *Historia Constitucional de Puerto Rico*, vol 3 (Editorial de la Universidad de Puerto Rico, 1982) ('*parte de la Carta de Derechos*').

Third, the 1952 Constitution also includes positive and negative rights. This means that some constitutional rights actually empower citizens to require government action and to recruit the Judiciary in this respect. It should be noted that there is no exact correlation between civil-political and socioeconomic rights on one side and positive and negative rights on the other. They are not inherently linked. In fact, there are instances of civil and political rights that are positive in their effect, as well as socioeconomic rights that operate negatively as a shield to protect against action initiated by others.

Finally, the 1952 Constitution includes more than simply individual rights. Some of the rights included in the text are collective, meaning that they must be exercised by two or more persons, not to mention those substantive provisions that identify the community as the main interested party, although each individual member of the community can require their enforcement.[3]

As we can appreciate, there are numerous variables that allow for many different conceptual combinations and outcomes with respect to constitutional rights in Puerto Rico. This basic fact distinguishes the 1952 constitutional text from its federal counterpart. But the differences are not merely conceptual, they are also substantive and practical.

II. HUMAN DIGNITY, EQUALITY, AND DISCRIMINATION

We start our analysis of the substantive content of the 1952 Constitution with Section 1 of the Bill of Rights. This is not just the result of obedience adhering to some numerical sequence or order. The Puerto Rican framers made the deliberate choice to include the most important substantive provision of the Constitution in the very first sentence of Section 1 of Article II: 'Human dignity is inviolable'.[4]

This simple sentence constitutes the backbone of the entire Puerto Rican constitutional structure. This is not hyperbole or literary rhetoric; it is the expressed will of the 1952 Constitutional Convention.[5] As a result, the dignity clause has three separate normative roles.

[3] For a more in-depth discussion of these concepts, see JM Farinacci-Fernós, 'Looking beyond the Negative-Positive Rights Distinction: Analyzing Constitutional Rights According to their Nature, Effect and Reach' (2018) 41 *Hastings International and Comparative Law Review* 31.

[4] The mere existence of this clause distinguishes the Puerto Rican text from its federal counterpart. While Justice Thomas may insist that the US Constitution 'contains no "dignity" Clause' (see *Obergefell v Hodges* 576 US 644 (2015) at 735 (Thomas, dissenting)) no Puerto Rican judge could claim the same. The normative implications of this, even textual, difference cannot be overstated and should not be minimised.

[5] It should be noted that, since 1952, the Puerto Rico Supreme Court has identified the intent of the framers as determinative in terms of constitutional interpretation. See JM Farinacci-Fernós, 'Originalism in Puerto Rico: Original Explication and its Relation with Clear Text, Broad Purpose and Progressive Policy' (2016) 85 *Revista Jurídica Universidad de Puerto Rico* 203.

First, it stands as an independent standard sufficient to resolve any legal dispute. In other words, there can be instances of violations of human dignity that empower a person to pursue a judicial claim, based exclusively on the dignity clause of Section 1 as their cause of action. This would mean that the dignity clause can be used, by itself, as a normative command and as its own judicially enforceable cause of action.

Second, it acts as a permanent complement to every other provision found in the 1952 Constitution. This means that all other individual clauses and sections in Articles II and VI can and should be combined with the dignity clause. This combination creates a normative force greater than the sum of its individual parts. As a result, the dignity clause becomes a permanent addition to all the other provisions in the Bill of Rights – one could say, the entire 1952 Constitution – that strengthens its normative content.

And third – and probably most importantly – the dignity clause directly supplies the actual substantive and normative content of all the other constitutional provisions found in the 1952 text. In other words, in addition to their combined effect – specific provision plus the dignity clause – the latter becomes the source of meaning for the former. All constitutional provisions must be interpreted through the prism of the dignity clause. It is unsurprising, then, that the dignity clause has been one of the most cited provisions in the decisions of the Puerto Rico Supreme Court,[6] as well as being copied by the framers of other state constitutions, most notably Montana.[7] In that sense, the dignity clause serves as a *primus inter pares* among constitutional provisions in general and constitutional rights in particular. It also functions as a normative Rosetta Stone.

The dignity clause, however, is not entirely original. Following the devastation of World War II, the concept of human dignity and its inviolable nature came to the fore and was central on the international stage. As a result, direct references to human dignity can be found in the United Nations Charter, the Universal Declaration of Human Rights, the Interamerican Declaration on the Duties and Rights of Man, as well as in the West German Basic Law of 1949. These legal texts were adopted at the end of the 1940s and their importance was not lost on the Puerto Rican framers who met in San Juan from 1951 until 1952.

What has been original is the judicial enforcement of the human dignity clause by Puerto Rican courts. Although it has not lived up to its full potential

[6] See CE Ramos González, 'La Inviolabilidad de la Dignidad Humana: Lo Indigno de la Búsqueda de Expectativas Razonables de Intimidad en el Derecho Constitucional Puertorriqueño' (2011) 45 *Revista Jurídica Universidad Interamericana de Puerto Rico* 185.

[7] See JM Farinacci-Fernós, 'Curious In-Laws: The Legal Connections between Montana and Puerto Rico' (2018) 79 *Montana Law Review* 187.

by any stretch,[8] it has nonetheless had a direct impact on the development of Puerto Rican constitutional law. If used to its fullest potential, the dignity clause would become the most powerful weapon in Puerto Rico's constitutional arsenal, an outcome that would be completely aligned with the stated goals and intentions of the constitutional framers.

As discussed in Chapter 6, one of the main obstacles to this enterprise is the influence of federal judicial practices over Puerto Rican courts.[9] Because there is no human dignity clause in the US Constitution, many Puerto Rican courts are tempted to underenforce this pivotal provision since they lack a federal counterpart to lean on. But that misses the point of the Constitutional Convention's approach to substantive rights. While there is definitely federal influence on the constitutional text, particularly with respect to the island's governmental structure and basic civil and political rights, the Convention purposely deviated from the federal model to turn the Constitution into a key ingredient in Puerto Rico's social transformation. The dignity clause was meant to lead the way.

The rest of Section 1 deals with equality and discrimination. This is evidence of the framers' views that equality and anti-discrimination are inherently linked with human dignity. As a result, these provisions benefit from the superior normative force generated by the dignity clause.

It should also be noted that the Puerto Rican Bill of Rights includes a *separate* provision concerning the equal protection of the law, similar to the 14th Amendment to the US Constitution. This has two important implications. First, this means that the 1952 Constitution does not limit itself to a vague reference to equal protection as its main normative weapon against discrimination and in favour of equality. As we are about to see, the remaining sentences of Section 1 are much more assertive than the more generalised equal protection clause found in Section 7. And second, that there is a combined effect between the specific text of Section 1 and the general clause included in Section 7. If we add to this equation the intentional choice of the Puerto Rican framers to include the equality and anti-discrimination provisions in Section 1, right next to the dignity clause, then we come up with a powerful normative cocktail. Anti-discrimination and equality were at the forefront of the Puerto Rican Constitutional Convention's agenda and constitute a key component of the entire constitutional project.

[8] See CI Gorrín Peralta, 'La Declaración Universal de los Derechos Humanos en la Jurisprudencia del Tribunal Supremo de Puerto Rico' (2010) 44 *Revista Jurídica Universidad Interamericana de Puerto Rico* 1. Professor Gorrín Peralta notes how, in general, several rights included in the 1952 Constitution that were imported from international treaties and text have been underused by the Puerto Rican Supreme Court. However, compared to other jurisdictions, it is fair to conclude that the dignity clause has not been actually mothballed or ignored as symbolic text. It is still an enforceable and central part of the Puerto Rican constitutional project.

[9] There are also ideological considerations at play. For decades, a majority of the Justices on the Supreme Court of Puerto Rico have been considerably more conservative and cautious than the founding generation in general and the framers in particular.

This was not the result of accident or chance. Puerto Rico in 1951–52 was an unequal society that yearned for greater social justice. Among the most pressing problems were discrimination on account of class, sex, race, and circumstances of birth.

The issue of class cannot be separated from the debate concerning labour rights. But because labour rights were given considerable attention by the 1952 framers, they will be discussed separately. But more generally, as discussed in previous chapters, Puerto Rican society during the first decades of the twentieth century was very unequal with regard to wealth distribution. Exploitation gave rise to class distinctions, stigmatisation, and systemic discrimination. The Convention explicitly addressed that situation.

As noted above, the Puerto Rican Constitutional Convention resorted to international instruments such as the Universal Declaration of Human Rights and the Interamerican Declaration of the Rights and Duties of Man as part of their drafting process. With regard to the anti-discrimination language in Section 1 of the Bill of Rights, the Convention mostly relied on the Universal Declaration of Human Rights, copying most of its classifications.[10]

But the Convention deliberately modified some of those classifications. The Universal Declaration-referenced 'economic position' was one of them. The Puerto Rican drafters thought it was both under and over-inclusive. As to the former, the term 'economic position' would leave out other social characteristics associated with class, like one's appearance, neighbourhood, and socially imposed stigmas. As to the latter, the framers were worried that the term could be used to strike down progressive economic legislation meant to address class inequalities. Thus, the framers opted to use the term 'social origin'. With this term, the Convention made clear that progressive economic legislation was in, while discrimination based on social stigmas was out.

During the deliberations of the Convention with regard to this issue, delegates from the Socialist Party offered an amendment to add the word 'condition' to the prohibition, in order to outlaw discrimination based both on social origin as well as social condition. Unfortunately, since there was no opposition to the amendment, the legislative history regarding the meaning, reach, and effect of this new prohibited classification is extremely scarce. But all roads point to a broad conception of social and class discrimination that included both the circumstances of a person's birth and early years (origin), as well as any social stigmas or class-based circumstances that could be acquired later in life (condition).

[10] The list that appears in the Universal Declaration of Human Rights is: race, colour, sex, language, religion, political or other opinion, national or social origin, economic position, birth and any other condition. Section 1 of the 1952 Constitution's Bill of Rights includes race, colour, sex, birth, social origin or condition, and political or religious ideas. Note the textual similarities between these two sources, including the choice of sequence. See JM Farinacci-Fernós and G Rivera-Vega, 'Los Usos de Fuentes Transnacionales en el Derecho Puertorriqueño (Parte I)' (2015) 51 *Revista Jurídica Universidad Interamericana de Puerto Rico* 189.

The shift from 'economic position' to 'social origin or condition' allowed the framers to fill the legislative record with explicit references to the progressive nature of the constitutional project, particularly with regard to issues of social class. On the one hand, progressive economic legislation and wealth distribution measures could not be challenged on the ground that they unduly discriminated against upper-income groups. On the other hand, discrimination and stigmatisation based on one's social and economic situation – almost inherently directed against the poor and working class – would be constitutionally prohibited.

The issue of sex was also a central concern of the 1952 process. The historical marginalisation of women from society was extensively debated during the deliberations of the Constitutional Convention. It is worth mentioning that there was only *one* woman elected as a delegate: María de Libertad Gómez, who also served as Vice-President of the Convention. This was evidence of the institutionalised marginalisation of women that the Constitution was meant to address.

The result of this approach was the establishment of a categorical ban on discrimination on the basis of sex, then understood to encompass both biological and sociocultural distinctions and characteristics. As with the classification regarding social origin or condition, the 1952 Constitution's prohibition as to discrimination on account of sex did not stop at the text. On the contrary, the official legislative record is full of references to the explicit goal of eradicating sex discrimination in Puerto Rican society, and to encourage greater participation by women in the social, political, and economic spheres.

Racism in Puerto Rico is a complex issue that lies beyond the scope of this book. But the problem of racism was of concern to the Puerto Rican framers, who chose to include an express prohibition on account of both race *and* colour, as per the Universal Declaration of Human Rights. This was done a *decade* before the passage of the federal Civil Rights Act in 1964. At least with regard to positive law, the Puerto Rican struggle against legalised racism predates the federal response to this problem and, instead of merely adopting statutory legislation, it was entrenched in the constitutional text.

Finally, there is the issue of birth. The prohibition against discrimination on account of birth was imported from international sources. Yet the Constitutional Convention explicitly rejected the meaning of birth as used in those sources and supplied its own autochthonous content. While the concept of 'birth' was seen as signifying the *place* where a person was born, the Puerto Rican framers gave it an alternative meaning: the marital status of a person's parents.

The issue of so-called illegitimate children was a daunting social and legal challenge. The civil law at the time adamantly distinguished between children born in and out of wedlock. As a result, thousands of children were denied their parentage and rights to participate in the inheritance of their parents.

By 1952, there was an emerging consensus that this sort of discrimination should have no place in Puerto Rican society. The time had come to recognise the inherent dignity of all children, regardless of their parents' marital status. Eventually, the Puerto Rico Supreme Court would use the Bill of Rights' express prohibition against discrimination on account of birth to strike down the legal structure that perpetuated the unequal treatment of children in terms of their right to inherit.[11]

The remaining text of Section 1 of the Bill of Rights after the dignity clause reads:

> All men are equal before the law. There shall be no sort of discrimination because of race, colour, sex, birth, social origin or condition, nor because of political or religious ideas. Both the laws and the public education system will embody these principles of essential human equality.

The list regarding prohibited discrimination closely mirrors Section 2 of the Universal Declaration of Human Rights. It should be noted that the Puerto Rico Supreme Court has held that the list established in Section 1 triggers strict scrutiny and is open-ended, meaning that other classifications can be found to fall within the constitutional prohibition.[12]

As explained above, the 1952 Constitution's commitment against discrimination does not end with Section 1. It also has an equal protection clause – as per the US Constitution – in Section 7 of the Bill of Rights. This is consistent with the fact that discrimination, marginalisation, and unequal treatment were central to the framers' progressive and reformist constitutional agenda. This has two key implications. First, it reinforces the explicit intent of the framers that the list of outlawed discrimination adopted in Section 1 of the Bill of Rights is not *numerus clausus*. That means that there could be other classifications that also activate strict scrutiny.

Second, it turns Section 7 into a residual clause of sorts that builds upon the express list established in Section 1 and the other classifications that can be inferred from that clause. This means that the general right to the equal protection of the laws found in Section 7 starts at a higher level than its federal counterpart, since Section 1 – which has no equivalent in the US Constitution – established a firm, broad, and potentially expanding floor of basic quality, on top of which Section 7 is able to build further.

III. OTHER POLITICAL RIGHTS

As discussed above, the 1952 Constitution has two main substantive differences from its federal counterpart when it comes to rights. First, the Puerto Rican text includes judicially enforceable socioeconomic rights. These are discussed

[11] See *Ocasio v Díaz* 88 DPR 676 (1963).
[12] See *De Paz Risk v Aponte Roque* 124 DPR 472 (1989).

further below. Second, while the 1952 Constitution also includes several civil and political rights that mirror the federal text, there are important differences between the approaches with regard to these types of rights.

To begin with, the 1952 Constitution includes additional civil and political rights that are not explicitly found in the US Constitution. Second, even for those rights that are found in both documents, the Puerto Rican text tends to be more expansive, assertive, and normatively forceful. This can be appreciated both in terms of classic political rights – such as privacy – and in the rights of criminal defendants, such as the adoption of an explicit and categorical exclusionary rule.

Even though, as we examined in Chapter 4, the structure of the 1952 Constitution has deep democratic flaws and deficits, the substantive content of the constitutional text has explicit democratic aspirations, particularly with regard to the individual right to vote. Section 3 of the Bill of Rights states that the 'laws shall guarantee the expression of the popular will through universal, direct, equal and secret suffrage and shall protect the citizenry from any coercion against the exercise of the vote'. This text was mostly imported from Article 21 of the Universal Declaration of Human Rights.

The four pillars of the right to vote established in Section 3 have important historical roots as well. As to its universal character, it should be stressed that the right to vote in Puerto Rico was originally recognised only for men of property. That gradually changed, through consistent expansion of the franchise, eliminating gender disparities and economic considerations. The 1952 Constitution represents the culmination of a decades-long process of democratisation in terms of the individual right to vote, but within a passive system of representative democracy.

The other aspect of the right to vote which merits special attention relates to its secret nature. For decades, there were countless instances of people 'voluntarily' waiving their right to a secret ballot, purportedly as a unilateral show of support for a particular party or candidate, that was, in fact, the direct result of pressure from powerful interests, such as employers, religious institutions or family members. In Puerto Rico, the right to a secret ballot represents one of those instances where an individual right cannot be waived, regardless of personal will.

Section 3 of the Bill of Rights deals with religion. While the US Constitution focuses on the dichotomy between free exercise and the prohibition regarding an establishment of religion, the Puerto Rican text has a two-stage structure. This structure was explicitly stated by the framers during the Constitutional Convention and informs the normative content of the text. The text of Section 3 reads: 'There shall be no law regarding the establishment of any religion nor to prohibit the free exercise of religious worship. There shall be complete separation between church and state'.

Note that the first sentence is very similar to the so-called religious clauses of the First Amendment of the US Constitution, although the Puerto Rican provision tends to specify that the free exercise is limited to worship, and not to any and all religious practices in general. The second sentence has two important roles. First, it clearly establishes a wall of separation between church and state. This categorical language has historical roots in the substantial influence of the Catholic Church in Puerto Rico, including over public policy. The second sentence was meant to firmly establish the secular nature of the government.

The second role is even more important than the first. The Puerto Rican constitutional framers made explicitly clear that both the establishment clause and the free exercise clause must be interpreted *in light of the second sentence*. In other words, independently of textual sequencing, the second sentence is actually normatively dominant. The starting point is the separation between church and state, to which we can then add the dual clauses adopted in the first sentence of Section 3.

The Puerto Rican secular project has been under constant strain; first from the Catholic Church, but more recently from Protestant sects, particularly those that adopt a very militant attitude towards morality.[13] But the text is still there and serves as, at least, an important reminder of the secular nature of the Puerto Rican constitutional project.

The freedoms of speech, press, and association have constitutional status in Puerto Rico, and for the most part mirror their federal counterparts. Still, because of a historical practice that pre-dates the 1952 Constitution, the Puerto Rico Supreme Court tends to interpret and apply these freedoms far more broadly than the US Supreme Court. This practice began with an expansive interpretation of federal constitutional rights and, later on, of the local rights recognised in the Jones Act of 1917. In other words, even those political rights that were imported from the federal constitutional text have enjoyed an independent life from their federal counterparts. As a result, rights such as freedom of speech – even though they were directly imported from the US Constitution – have greater strength in the Puerto Rican case than in the federal sphere.

Specifically, Section 4 of the Bill of Rights addresses freedom of speech and press, as well as the right to assemble peacefully and petition the government for the redress of grievances. The combined effect of these four rights is the

[13] The irony is that, 70 years later, many Protestant sects – currently in the ascendancy – are now leading the charge *against* the separation of church and state. One explanation for this inconsistency is changed circumstances, where these sects are now much more influential and powerful than they were in 1951–52 as comparted to the Catholic Church, so they are now willing to disregard the separation they once counted on when they were in a clear minority. Another explanation might be that the Protestant sects of the middle of the twentieth century were not as politically assertive as they are now. In any event, it is quite ironic that the same currents that fought substantially for a strict separation between church and state are now the ones eager to dissolve it.

existence of a greater one: freedom of expression in general.[14] It also includes a general right of freedom of thought.

For its part, Section 6 deals with a separate right of association and organisation. But because of the turbulent character of Puerto Rican politics during the 1940s and early 1950s, the framers included an explicit limitation on the exercise of these rights: the lawful nature of the association and an explicit ban on military or quasi-military organisations. This was an overt response to the militancy of the nationalist movement in Puerto Rico at that time.

This historical experience also explains why the Constitutional Convention intentionally opted to omit any reference to a right to bear arms. It is one of the very rare instances in which the 1952 Constitution does not, at least, mirror the minimum federal rights floor. Again, this was not an oversight: it was a deliberate act on the part of the governing party at the time, the PPD, to avoid giving the nationalist movement any legal standing to pursue their revolutionary goals.[15] As to these issues, the framers were reacting to a particular problem of the time, and not as architects of a future society. As with the Third Amendment to the US Constitution, the Puerto Rican text is not immune from the perils of contemporary ordinary politics and self-interest on the part of the governing party.

Barring these historical characteristics, the right of association recognised in Section 6 closely mirrors the same right in the federal sphere. Yet, there has been evident value in its separate textual existence, as opposed to being lumped in with the freedoms that are directly related to the individual expression of ideas. In that sense, Section 6 actually adds normative content: the collective exercise of the right of association and a separate right to lawful organisations as to their own existence.

Another example of a Puerto Rican enhancement of a federal constitutional right is due process. Section 7 of the Bill of Rights has two different components. The first one is explicitly substantive as opposed to procedural. The first sentence of Section 7 states: 'It is recognized as a fundamental right of every human being the right to life, liberty, and the enjoyment of property'.

In terms of the objects of the right, this provision of Section 7 mirrors the federal due process clauses. Yet, some important differences should be appreciated.

First, the Puerto Rican clause's explicit substantive content. Unlike the perennial debate in the US regarding the legitimacy of substantive due process, the

[14] Although the word 'expression' does not appear in the text of Section 4, its given title is, precisely, 'freedom of expression', which confirms the view that the four freedoms contained in this section make up a broader right to expression.

[15] Curiously enough, the right to bear arms has a separate and autochthonous history in Puerto Rico. At the height of the Spanish repression during the nineteenth century, Puerto Rican revolutionaries defended the right to bear arms as an essential component of individual and collective liberty, in opposition to tyrannical government. It was, as such, seen as a vital political right.

Puerto Rican framers made the intentional choice to adopt two separate clauses, one substantive and one procedural. In other words, the notion of substantive due process has clear textual roots in Puerto Rico, albeit with a distinct normative content.

Second, note that with regard to property, the right refers to its *enjoyment*, not to the acquisition of property as such. This is explained by the Puerto Rican framers' rejection of the *Lochner* era and by their social approach to the concept of property. In that sense, it also becomes quite clear that the substantive content of liberty in this clause refers mostly to personal autonomy and not economic *laissez-faire*. We will return to the issue of substantive due process when addressing Section 8's explicit protection of privacy rights.

The third sentence of Section 7 refers to the procedural version of due process: 'No person shall be deprived of their liberty or property without due process of law'. On the one hand, the textual similarities to the federal clauses are undeniable. But note also that the Puerto Rican clause omits the concept of life, which is mentioned in the substantive clause. This was an intentional omission to make clear that life could never be taken away, no matter how much due process was given.

This explains why the second sentence of Section 7 makes an explicit reference to the death penalty,[16] instead of it being located in the cruel and unusual punishment clause in Section 12 of the Bill of Rights. In that sense, while the death penalty ban clause in Section 7 should be read jointly with the cruel and unusual punishment clause in Section 12, the framers' intentional decision to locate the former in Section 7 was meant to confirm the already explicit statement that life is a fundamental right that can never be taken away.

The existence of the death penalty ban clause in Section 7 directly impacts the normative content of the cruel and unusual punishment clause in Section 12. The former establishes an irreducible normative minimum on top of which the latter can build upon. This is a reminder of the formula we saw with regard to the equal protection clause found in Section 7 and the specific list of prohibited classifications in Section 1.

Something similar happens with the interaction between the substantive right to liberty in Section 7 and the explicit privacy (*intimidad*) provision found in Section 8.[17] Precisely because of the explicit nature of Section 8's privacy clause, the substantive component of liberty can build upon this foundation

[16] 'The death penalty shall not exist'. Note the categorical language used in this provision.

[17] The textual formulation of the privacy clause is normatively irrelevant. It states: 'Every person has the right to protection of law against unwarranted attacks against their honor, their reputation, and their family or private life'. This text was directly imported from Art V of the American Declaration of the Duties and Rights of Man. See Farinacci-Fernós and Rivera-Vega (n 10). More than textual importation, it was a normative one. More than a privacy clause, s 8 establishes a normatively broader concept: intimacy and personal autonomy.

and thus offer a broader space of constitutional protection. This is important because Section 8's normative content is, by itself, quite significant. This means that anything that is built on top of it will have even greater normative reach and effect.

Because of historical experiences, the Puerto Rican framers decided to complement the general privacy clause of Section 8 with a precise protection of private telephone conversations. The text, found in Section 10, reads: 'Telephone communications shall not be intercepted'. The categorical nature of this provision produces a dual protection: against uninvited state intervention and between private parties proper.

The general privacy clause of Section 8 has become a hallmark of Puerto Rican jurisprudence, accounting for many of the most watershed decisions of the island's Supreme Court. This includes historic holdings regarding issues such as divorce,[18] breastfeeding in the workplace,[19] and living wills.[20]

Like its federal counterpart, the Puerto Rican Bill of Rights explicitly bans slavery and indentured servitude. Section 12 does carve a limited exception: work that can be imposed by court judgment as punishment for a felony. However, the rest of the clause has a broader reach than the federal text, transcending the historical origin of the federal provision. This includes, for example, exploitative labour conditions that are unacceptably similar to servitude. In that sense, Section 12's nature is hybrid: it is both civil and political, as well as socioeconomic. In addition, this provision has the strongest normative connection with the dignity clause discussed earlier.

In addition to the due process clause, Section 7 also prohibits the impairment of contracts. Like its federal counterpart, this clause has been considerably weakened. In fact, *it was nearly omitted from the constitutional text altogether*. In that sense, even if there were to be a contracts clause comeback at the federal level, the Puerto Rican clause would remain normatively harmless. The main operation of this clause in Puerto Rican jurisprudence is mostly limited to possible government attempts to destroy its own legitimate obligations. Yet, as outlined above, the framers made it abundantly clear that the police power would trump most considerations, except the most egregious violations of basic fairness.

In a similar vein, Section 7 also gives basic legal protection against liens that affect an individual's essential livelihood. However, the language used in this clause is very direct and has very little independent normative value. It simply orders the Legislature to establish the minimum legal protection against liens. The precise content of that legal protection is thus delegated entirely to legislative judgment. The only scenario rejected by constitutional imperative is a total

[18] *Figueroa Ferrer v ELA* 107 DPR 250 (1978).
[19] *Siaca v Bahia Beach Resort* 194 DPR 559 (2016).
[20] *Lozada Tirado v Testigos de Jehová* 177 DPR 893 (2010).

absence of such protection. This, for example, would impede a Legislature from only giving nominal protection.

Section 9 the Bill of Rights refers to the government's eminent domain power. Like the US Constitution's Fifth Amendment, the Puerto Rican text states that private property shall not be taken for public use, unless it is accompanied by just compensation, in the manner prescribed by law.

Two things make the Puerto Rican provision stand out. First, even though it is basically the same text, the normative content is different. This is due to both historical and ideological reasons. As to the former, it is simply the product of the fact that the Puerto Rican clause was adopted by the framers at a time when the federal doctrine was not particularly protective of property rights. As to the latter, it is a sequel to the same logic that we saw with regard to the substantive property clause found in Section 7; in particular, the existing consensus at the time regarding the social role of property and that collective interests trump individual ones.

Second, Section 9 includes additional text providing a very specific and detailed process regarding the taking of printing presses or similar equipment. It establishes a *categorical ban* against the taking of any printing press, for any purpose. Such is the extent of the protection, that the text also addresses the possibility of a taking of a building that houses a printing press or similar equipment. In such circumstances, the Constitution allows for the taking of a building only after a judicial declaration of public utility and necessity through a statutorily prescribed process. If the taking must take place before such judicial declaration can be obtained, Section 9 states that it can only be done after a suitable alternative locale has been identified where the equipment can be transferred within a reasonable period.

This particularly detailed provision has historical roots, although they were not entirely Puerto Rican. It was proposed by the Socialist delegation to the Constitutional Convention, apparently as a response to the experiences of left-wing and labour organisations in Europe who had been victims of this type of government repression. As a result, although this particular rule is included in the takings provision, it should also be seen as an extension of the freedom of the press established in Section 4 of the Bill of Rights.

Finally, the Puerto Rican Bill of Rights includes other standard provisions found in many classic constitutions. For example, it entrenches the principle of civilian rule over the armed forces,[21] bans the bestowing of titles of nobility,[22] and requires prior legislative approval in order for a public official or employee to receive foreign gifts or recognitions.[23]

[21] Puerto Rico Constitution, Art II, § 13.
[22] Puerto Rico Constitution, Art II, § 14.
[23] ibid.

The provisions we have analysed so far are, at least at their core, easily recognisable by liberal legal systems. But, as we have also seen, this core is not minimalist. On the contrary, the text and normative reach are considerable. This is consistent with the progressive-liberal view that dominated the Constitutional Convention.

IV. CRIMINAL PROCEDURE GUARANTEES

The 1952 Constitution includes a substantial set of rights that protect persons who are subject to the criminal justice system, including many that apply before they have been formally arrested. This was done *before* the Warren Court's aggressive expansion of the rights of criminal defendants during the 1960s.

Section 10 mostly deals with searches and seizures. Some of the language resembles the federal text, while some of its clauses are wholly original. As a general matter, Section 10 protects persons against unreasonable searches and seizures, as per the Fourth Amendment of the US Constitution.

Section 10 also includes a categorical ban against the tapping of telephone lines, regardless of the possibility of judicial authorisation. An interesting note is that, when this provision was debated during the Constitutional Convention, there was a federal statute that also prohibited wiretapping. In that sense, the Puerto Rican framers were simply entrenching in their local constitution text that was already applicable law at the federal level. But the twist is that the federal statute that served as the basis for this part of Section 10 was eventually repealed. Yet, with regard to Puerto Rico, the ban is still in force because of its constitutional status. Such is the power of constitutional entrenchment, which was not lost on the framers.

Section 10 also includes a warrant requirement clause as a general matter. In particular, it requires that all warrants be issued by a court, and only then when there is probable cause based on a sworn statement, describing with specificity the place to be searched and the people or persons to be seized.

More importantly, Section 10 includes a categorical exclusionary rule which, in addition, makes no textual distinction between civil or criminal cases: 'Evidence obtained in violation of this section shall be inadmissible in the courts'. In that sense, the Puerto Rican framers decided to give constitutional status to a judicial doctrine imported from the federal jurisdiction. But the difference between the Puerto Rican and federal exclusionary rules is not merely a matter of form; it is also of kind. The Puerto Rican clause gives considerably more normative protection than the federal rule.

Section 11 has two main parts. First, a list of rights that apply 'in all criminal processes'. While this list also tracks the language of the Sixth Amendment, note that the Puerto Rican text applies to 'all criminal *processes*' and not 'all criminal *prosecutions*' as in the federal Constitution. This is yet another example of the Puerto Rican Constitution expanding on the federal text.

Among the rights that are established in this first part of Section 11 are the right to: (1) a speedy and public trial; (2) be notified of the nature and cause of the charges against them, including receipt of a written notice of the charges; (3) confront the witnesses against them; (4) obtain the compulsory calling of witnesses for their defence; (5) the assistance of counsel; and (6) enjoy the presumption of innocence.

The second part of Section 11 addresses additional individual guarantees. The first clause requires detailed analysis, and it pertains to jury trials. Before diving into the specifics of the jury trial system, it should be noted that there are no jury trials in civil cases in Puerto Rico. Therefore, the entire normative content of the jury system in the island is limited to the criminal sphere.

Section 11 states that there shall be a right to a jury trial for all felonies. Specifically, the text refers to the right to an impartial jury made up of 12 neighbours who may reach a verdict with no less than nine votes. In other words, the 1952 Constitution does not require unanimity for felony convictions. While the Legislature can require unanimity, it is constitutionally authorised to permit majority verdicts, as long as there are, at least, nine jury members in favour of a particular outcome. It should be noted that the jury clause's requirement of a minimum of nine affirmative votes for a verdict applies to both convictions and acquittals.

The historical reasons for this deviation from the federal rule are not flattering. The distinction is rooted on the practice of political persecution, particularly against the militant pro-independence movement. By eliminating unanimity, the possible not-guilty votes of pro-independence jurors could be neutralised. It is the political equivalent of the racial and religious prejudice basis for the similar Oregon and Louisiana state constitutional provisions regarding non-unanimous juries. It is one of those rare instances where the Puerto Rican equivalent of a federal constitutional right offers less protection to its titleholder.[24]

Section 11 also adopts from the federal text a general right against self-incrimination. Yet, in the Puerto Rican tradition of adding more content instead of just copying mechanically, Section 11 makes a direct reference to the prohibition on using an accused person's silence against him or her. This goes beyond simple self-incrimination. With regard to double jeopardy, Section 11 does limit itself to simply copying from its federal counterpart.

[24] It should be noted that the non-unanimous jury verdict rule is no longer in effect in Puerto Rico. With regard to guilty verdicts, the US Supreme Court decision in *Ramos v Louisiana* 140 S Ct 1390 (2020) applies with full force in the island. In that case, the Court ruled that the Sixth Amendment, as applied to the state and territories, requires unanimity for guilty verdicts. With regard to acquittals, the Puerto Rico Supreme Court held that, since the guilty verdict rule has now changed because of the *Ramos* decision and because – in their estimation – one of the goals of the Puerto Rican framers was to establish symmetry between both types of verdicts, then the same unanimity rule applicable to guilty verdicts would also apply to acquittals. See *Pueblo v Centeno* 2021 TSPR 133. This is an ever-rarer instance of an entire clause of the Puerto Rico Constitution that has been put beyond use without formal amendment.

The right to bail constitutes a sharp departure from the federal rule. While the text recognising the right is somewhat modest ('Every accused person shall have the right to be freed on bail before a guilty judgment'), its main normative strength comes from the official Report by the Bill Rights Commission of the Constitutional Convention, which explicitly states that this is an *absolute* right that cannot be denied to anyone for any crime. It is a categorical rule that takes away judicial discretion to deny bail, as is the practice in the federal sphere.

The bail clause has to be read concurrently with two other constitutional provisions, which directly follow it in the text of Section 11. First, the categorical constitutional requirement that any accused person who, for some reason, was unable to post bail – even though, as just noted, it should have been available – and was thus taken into physical custody *must* be set free if more than six months elapse between their incarceration for failing to post bail and the start of their criminal trial.

This means that, although the criminal trial could still be held after the six-month period, the accused would be freed in the meantime. This serves as the counterpoint to the absolute right to post bail, creating a two-fold system that is meant to prevent people who are presumed to be innocent from needlessly being in jail: First, there is a categorical requirement that a judge must establish bail. If the person is able to post it, they go free pending their trial. Second, if a particular accused person was unable to pay the amount imposed, then the mere passage of time would grant them a charge-free bail; the cost, unfortunately, would be to spend six months in jail. But, if that period elapses without the trial having started, the accused is to be freed unconditionally, exactly as if he or she had posted bail from the start. The latter mechanism has been dubbed as the poor-person's bail.[25]

The historical purpose behind this system was the previous experience of people charged with crimes, denied bail or, because of their economic limitations, being unable to post bail, then spending extended amounts of time in jail without even being put on trial, much less being found guilty beyond a reasonable doubt. In that sense, it combines the constitution's express adoption of the presumption of innocence and the prohibition on discrimination on account of social origin or condition. Its class nature is evident.

The second related provision is the Constitution's requirement that bail and fines shall not be excessive. Although admittedly vague and subjective, it does create a workable legal standard that allows for judicial enforcement. When taken together, these three clauses generate a formidable normative scheme meant to limit the government's ability to deprive a person of their liberty before they are found guilty in a trial or admit their guilt in a judicial proceeding.

[25] *Vázquez Alejandro v Supte. Bayamón* 183 DPR 711, 720 (2011) (Hernández Denton, dissenting) ('*la fianza de los pobres*').

Finally, Section 11 also includes a textually categorical ban regarding imprisonment because of debt. The historical practice this was meant to prohibit were instances where a poor person was sued to collect on a debt, a judgment was issued ordering payment, the defendant was unable to pay, and then the issuing court would find them guilty of civil contempt for failing to obey the judgment, thus resulting in the defendant's incarceration. The ban is also related to a more general historical practice in other parts of the world were there would even be formal criminal liability for failing to pay a debt.

Interestingly enough, this clause of Section 11 represents a rare instance where a broader text trumped the stated, more limited, purpose of the framers. While the original purpose of the ban was to prevent people who could not pay from being imprisoned for failing to pay a debt, the Supreme Court held that the textual reach of the clause was broader, also covering instances in which a person who could pay, but chose not to, would face jail time as a result.[26] The Court rejected that possibility, meaning that, regardless of whether the failure to pay a debt was the result of lack of means or lack of will, the ban was applicable. The only known exception to this rule is for situations of child support payments, where failure to make those payments can result in incarceration. It is an exception rooted in compelling considerations of public policy.

The 1952 Constitution's also includes other classic liberal rights and provisions such as prohibitions regarding *ex post facto laws*, as well as *bills of attainder*. These are addressed in Section 12.

The issue regarding *habeas corpus* warrants closer analysis, due to its normative, historical, and structural implications. The normative structure regarding *habeas corpus* is part of a larger scheme that addresses emergency situations. Some of these are mentioned in different parts of the constitutional text, including instances outside the Bill of Rights proper. In that sense, the normative scheme regarding emergency powers adopted in the 1952 Constitution is the result of the combination of different provisions found in separate articles.

We begin with the writ of *habeas corpus* established in Section 13 of the Bill of Rights, which states:

> The writ of *habeas corpus* shall be granted with speed and free of costs. The privilege of the writ of *habeas corpus* shall not be suspended, unless where, in cases of rebellion, insurrection or invasion, the public safety so requires it. Only the Legislative Assembly shall have the power to suspend the privilege of the writ of *habeas corpus* and the laws the regulate their issuance.

Several features stand out. First, note the declaration as to the existence of a general, albeit implied, right of *habeas corpus*. Second, also note that the text establishes a single exception to this general rule which, in turn, requires the

[26] *Díaz Aponte v Comunidad San José* 130 DPR 782 (1992).

presence of two factual situations: (1) that there is an actual rebellion, insurrection or invasion (no other circumstances would trigger the exception); and (2) that, they, in addition, constitute a threat to public safety. Absent any of these factual circumstances, the writ of *habeas corpus* cannot be suspended.

The only institution authorised to suspend the writ of *habeas corpus* in these extraordinary situations is the Legislature. This was an intentional design choice meant to address a historical problem: that, prior to the enactment of the Constitution, the Jones Act gave the power to suspend the writ to the Governor. The transfer of the power from the Executive to the Legislative is part of the general ideological tendency of the Constitutional Convention, which had great faith in the legislative process as the focal point for addressing social problems.

Section 4 of Article IV (Executive Branch) authorises the Governor to declare martial law in similar circumstances that would allow for the suspension of *habeas corpus*. Specifically, it allows the Governor to declare martial law when public safety requires it in situations of rebellion or invasion, or imminent danger of either of these. Note that this is largely similar to the *habeas corpus* language established in Section 13 of the Bill of Rights.

This is so because the original draft of Section 13 gave the Governor the power to both declare martial law and suspend the writ of *habeas corpus* in extraordinary circumstances. The Constitutional Convention made important changes to this scheme. First, it gave exclusive power to the Legislature with regard to the suspension of *habeas corpus*. The Governor was completely excluded from that decision. This would mean, for example, that a Governor can declare martial law but he or she cannot, in addition, suspend the writ of *habeus corpus*.

The second decision made by the Convention was to give the Legislature a deciding role as to the issue of martial law. Section 4 of Article IV also states that, while the Governor has the *initial* power to declare martial law, the Legislative Assembly must 'meet immediately by its own initiative to ratify or reject the proclamation' of martial law. This means that, with regard to the possible suspension of the writ of *habeas corpus*, the Legislature is the sole relevant institutional actor. With regard to martial law, the Legislature cannot invoke it, but it has the ultimate say as to whether it should remain or cease.[27]

V. SOCIOECONOMIC RIGHTS

The Constitutional Convention that met between 1951 and 1952 was not just interested in establishing the structures of the Puerto Rican government and

[27] Another relevant provision is s 17 of Art VI, which allows the Governor, in the event of invasion, rebellion, pandemic or any other similar circumstance which creates a state of emergency, to summon the Legislative Assembly to a place that is different from its usual meeting place, but subject to the Legislature's agreement with regard to that decision. Once again, the Legislative Assembly is given a central role.

the political rights that allow them to function effectively within a basic democratic framework. The constitutional drafting process was generally seen as an opportunity to address the most pressing social and economic challenges facing the country at that time. This included the eradication of extreme poverty and economic exploitation.

At the top of the list was the development of a comprehensive and robust public education system with constitutional status. As a result, education is mentioned twice in the Bill of Rights, most prominently in Section 5, both as a right and as a general governmental responsibility. The relevant text states:

> Every person has the right to an education that propends to the full development of their personality and that strengthens respect for the rights of man [*sic*] and of fundamental liberties. There shall be a public education system, which will be free and entirely non-sectarian. Education shall be free of charge in elementary and secondary school and, to the extent that the State facilities allow it, shall be mandatory for elementary school [...] Neither public property nor funds shall be used towards sustaining schools or educational facilities that are not the State's. Nothing included in this provision shall impede the State from granting any child non-educational services that are established by law for the protection and welfare of children.[28]

Section 5 generated considerable debate within the Constitutional Convention. While part of the leadership wanted to limit the text to merely aspirational language, a majority of the drafting body decided to adopt an operational text that could be judicially enforced, if necessary. This was one of many instances in which the 'backbenchers' of the Convention managed to assemble together a majority to adopt more progressive measures against the wishes of the official leadership of the PPD.

Several things stand out in Section 5: first, the combination of an individual right to an education with an affirmative command on the state to establish a public education system, which shall be free of charge all through high school; second, the constitutional requirement that said education be of a particular nature (one that emphasises respect for 'the rights of man and of fundamental liberties');[29] third, the explicit requirement that it be secular in nature. This was adopted at a time when the Catholic Church had a considerable presence with regard to educational facilities.

Similar to many state constitutions in the US, the Puerto Rican framers adopted language that prohibits public financing of private religious education. But unlike many of its brethren,[30] the 1952 Constitution does not single out

[28] The omitted text refers to the possibility of complying with s 5's requirement of mandatory public education attendance through a private school.

[29] Note that the constitutionally established public education system is designed as humanistic, pluralistic, and progressive.

[30] See *Espinoza v Montana Department of Revenue* 140 S Ct 2246 (2020).

religious entities. On the contrary, it establishes a categorical ban on any direct financing of any *private* educational facility, be it secular or religious. Public funds shall only benefit public schools. The only exception to this constitutional mandate is services that are offered directly to children, such as transportation or food.

Why was public education so important to the Puerto Rican framers in 1952? The answer can be found in Section 15 of the Bill of Rights, which bans child labour. In particular, this provision prohibits any minor under the age of 14 from engaging in any work or occupation that imperils their health or morals, or that in any way threatens their life or physical integrity.[31]

The goal was to move children from working in the factories and the sugar fields to learning in the classroom. The right to an education would be useless if most children were working in hazardous jobs. And just banning child labour was not enough, as this could lead to thousands of children being on the streets and engaging in antisocial behaviour. Both policies were needed. This responded both to a moral imperative and an economic reality. As to the latter, the Puerto Rican framers knew that a population whose young are systematically deprived of an education is condemned to permanent deprivation and poverty.

Section 5 has not remained merely aspirational. It has generated continued litigation and has been the legal basis for important judicial decisions. For example, in *Asociación de Maestros v Srio de Educación*,[32] the Puerto Rico Supreme Court invalidated a statutory programme that allowed parents of students in public schools to use public funds to enrol them in a private institution. The Supreme Court reaffirmed the clear mandate of Section 5 that no public funds could be used to finance or directly benefit any private educational institution.

While Section 15 deals with the economic exploitation of children in particular, Section 16 deals with the general problem of the exploitation of workers. This provision establishes the minimum individual labour conditions allowed in Puerto Rico, regardless of the employer's or the employee's will. It is an irreducible constitutional floor that applies universally ('[E]very worker …') without the possibility of individual waiver, regardless of personal will.

The main conditions are: first, the right for individuals to freely choose their occupation and, most importantly, to resign from it at any time. This was meant to abolish the historical practice of lengthy labour contracts that denied workers the possibility of accepting other positions. Also note that the unilateral right to resign was not accompanied by an authority for the employer to unilaterally fire or dismiss an employee. This was no accident; it was the result of the Convention's judgment that workers and employers are not equally placed with regard to their bargaining power.

[31] The other provision found in s 15 prohibits children under 16 years from being sent to prison or jail. This adds to the view that the Puerto Rican framers wanted to protect children from exploitation and other situations that jeopardise their potential development as productive members of society.

[32] *Asociación de Maestros v Srio de Educación* 137 DPR 528 (1994).

Second, there is a right to receive 'equal pay for equal work'. This clause was primarily meant to address the gender gap in wages. But the text was not limited to gender issues or just wages. It establishes a broader legal standard applicable to compensation, with the goal of erasing all forms of unjustified differential treatment when it comes to wages and other material benefits. While this language seems to be symbolic or aspirational, it is anything but. It can serve as the sole basis for a judicial cause of action in case of violations by an employer.

Third is the right to a 'reasonable minimum wage'. At first glance, this seems like a toothless clause made up of abstract wording. But actually, the 1952 Convention intentionally used this language to make sure it would be effective in the future, rather than fixing a specific number that would very quickly become anachronistic due to inflation. It should be noted that the phrase 'reasonable minimum wage' served as a sort of term-of-art in 1952, which stemmed from the legislation that was in place at the time. This term referred to compensation that was sufficient to guarantee to every worker, and their family, the ability to cover their daily expenses and provide them with decent living conditions.

Fourth, there is a right to be protected against employment conditions that may risk their health or personal integrity. This has been interpreted by the Puerto Rico Supreme Court to encompass both the physical ('health') and mental or internal ('personal integrity') realms.[33] This provision acts as a sort of minimum OSHA requirement. Also note that, in addition to being a right that employees enjoy, it also serves as an affirmative obligation towards employers. This reminds us of the education provision, which also combines an individual right with an affirmative obligation, indicative of a *positive* right. While Section 5 refers to government, Section 16 refers to both public and private actors.

Fifth is the right to an eight-hour working day, with, at least, a time-and-a-half overtime pay if that period is exceeded.[34] The Legislative Assembly is empowered to increase this minimum overtime pay through statutory enactment. As can be appreciated, this provision is particularly detailed and rule-like. While some members of the Convention objected to this type of constitutional text, they were firmly overruled by a majority that wanted to entrench important labour rights, uncertain whether a future legislature would succumb to employer pressure and eliminate the labour movement's legislative victories.

Note that Section 16 applies to both public and private employers. It expressly omits the requirement of state action. In fact, it could be argued that public employers are an incidental or secondary object of the text, which focuses primarily on private entities.

[33] *García v Aljoma* 162 DPR 572 (2004).

[34] The original intent of the framers, which is clearly identified in the records of the Convention, is that overtime pay would be required if anyone worked over the eight-hour limit during any 24-hour period, as opposed to just in any given calendar day.

This has evident historical connotations. Economic exploitation by way of substandard employment conditions was mostly a direct byproduct of a capitalist system. It would make little sense to protect only public employees in the Constitution. This goes to the heart of the *social* Constitution, which attempted to address the main ills of Puerto Rican society, particularly in the economic sphere, through progressive policy enactments.

The public-private distinction is even more substantial with regard to Sections 17 and 18, which deal with the collective rights of workers, particularly with unionisation. These provisions are actually inapplicable against the central or municipal governments. The subject of the rights recognised in these two sections are workers employed in the private sector and state-owned corporations that function as if they were private entities.[35] In other words, these provisions turn the state action doctrine upside down: these constitutional rights operate mainly against private employers. The only state actors towards which these rights are cognisable are those that are economically identical to private entities, but just happen to be state owned. This is the strongest manifestation of the horizontal nature of the 1952 Constitution.

With regard to these workers, Section 17 recognises their right to engage in collective bargaining through representatives of their choosing. In other words, it gives constitutional protection to the right to unionise. As a result, employers are constitutionally bound to engage in good-faith collective bargaining with their employees.

In order to facilitate the effective exercise of the rights recognised in Section 17, Section 18 further recognises the right of these workers to strike, establish pickets, and engage in any other lawful concerted activities. Because the Convention concluded that these rights were fundamental to ensure social justice in the labour realm, Section 18 states the only allowed instances for the possible impairment of the right to strike: situations in which a particular strike creates a 'grave emergency' that threatens public health, public safety, or essential public services.

It should be noted that, during the deliberations concerning the text of Section 18, a majority of the Convention amended the original proposal regarding the possible limitation of the rights included therein. The original proposal allowed for limitations in a broad array of scenarios, for example, if a strike posed an imminent danger to the general welfare. This proposal was amended in favour of a much stricter set of instances which could justify a limitation on collective labour actions. In other words, Section 18 rights can only be curtailed in the most extraordinary of circumstances.

[35] During the 1930s and 1940s, Puerto Rico had several economically active entities that generated profits, which were owned by the government. These included, for example, a glass factory. These entities operated as if they were private companies, but instead of individual shareholders, the owner was the Puerto Rican government. Legally, these are identified as 'public corporations'.

These provisions demonstrate the strength, both ideologically and culturally outside the Convention, as well as politically inside the constitutional framing body, of the labour movement and its main tenets. In fact, it should be noted that two of the most discussed rights during the deliberations of the Constitutional Convention were overtime pay and the right to strike. In that sense, the 1952 Constitution has a distinct and undeniable labour DNA.

It should also be noted that much of the normative content of Sections 17 and 18 is, with regard to most private employers, currently displaced by the National Labour Relations Act (NLRA). Of course, should that statute be repealed or modified at any time so as to allow for state norms to operate, these constitutional provisions would spring into action. This is not specific to the colonial condition of Puerto Rico. The NLRA's preemption provision applies to all the states. The important point here is that, regardless of the currently displaced status of Sections 17 and 18 in terms of the employees of private enterprises that impact interstate commerce, those sections still form part of the social and progressive Constitution, and contribute to its overall ideological identity.

As we saw earlier, all three participating parties at the Convention had labour leaders among their delegates. This meant that the labour question would be central during its deliberations. More importantly, this demographic composition reflected the social reality of the time. The labour movement in Puerto Rico had been relatively strong during the preceding decades, and the constitutional entrenchment of labour rights was one of its top social priorities. Without labour rights, economic growth was merely another term for exploitation and substantial inequality. The social Constitution was seen as an important tool in the struggle for a more just distribution of wealth and more decent living conditions for the working people.

VI. SECTION 19

Section 19 of the Bill of Rights has three important clauses that warrant further analysis with regard to substance. The first two are closely related and refer to interpretive issues.

The first one requires a *broad* interpretation of constitutional rights, both enumerated and unenumerated. In that sense, it is a hermeneutic command to courts on the part of the constitutional framers. This first clause reads: 'The foregoing enumeration of rights shall not be construed restrictively …'. While at first glance this clause seems to simply refer to the existence of unenumerated rights, both the stated intent of the framers – as documented in the Constitutional Convention's official records – and basic interpretive rules require a different conclusion: that both enumerated and unenumerated rights should be read expansively.

In that sense, it is the second clause which directly addresses the issue of unenumerated rights. It partially mirrors the Ninth and Tenth Amendments of the US Constitution. Once these rights are identified in a particular situation, the clause requires judicial recognition as if it were part of the constitutional text. This clause concludes the first sentence of Section 19: '… nor does it contemplate the exclusion of other rights not specifically mentioned which belong to the people in a democracy'. The use of 'nor' confirms the view that there are two separate rules in this first sentence.

As seen, the first clause refers to interpretation of rights in general, and the second one establishes the existence of unenumerated rights. Finally, note the substantive characteristic of these unenumerated rights: 'belonging to the People in a democracy'. This gives courts the required normative standard used to identify unenumerated rights. In other words, unenumerated rights should not be invented wholesale, but must be consistent with the rest of the Bill of Rights. These rights should further a progressive, democratic society. Section 19 is, thus, a residual clause that allows for the identification of such rights.

A third clause completes Section 19 and is found in its second sentence. It states that the enumeration of rights in Article II and elsewhere 'shall not restrict the power of the Legislative Assembly to adopt statutes in order to protect the life, health and welfare of the People'. This single sentence has great normative effects.

First, it gives textual form to the inherent police powers possessed by state legislatures within the federal constitutional system. Precisely because these police powers are inherent, the effect of textualising them serves to *strengthen* them. In other words, there is a combined effect that results from the sum of the inherent police powers with the text of Section 19.

This was purposeful and brings us to the second point. The Puerto Rican framers were convinced that, in order to adequately address the substantial social and economic challenges facing Puerto Rican society at that time – or at any time for that matter – an interventionist state was required. This has several ideological and structural consequences.

On the one hand, it rejects a *laissez-faire* approach to the role of government in society and the economy. While the more classical view sees the government as an impediment to freedom –and, as such, its powers must be constantly limited and monitored – the more modern approach adopted by the Constitutional Convention was that a progressive-minded, democratic government was actually essential to the pursuit of social justice.[36]

On the other hand, it also rejects the orthodox view that individual rights and government power are, inherently, at odds with each other. The Puerto

[36] See generally, JM Farinacci-Fernós, 'Post-Liberal Constitutionalism' (2018) 54 *Tulsa Law Review* 1.

Rican framers had a different model in mind; one in which individual rights actually interacted productively with government power in order to build a fairer and freer society. The lessons of the *Lochner* era still loomed large during the deliberations of the Constitutional Convention. The use of individual rights – mostly on the part of privileged and economically powerful groups – as an obstacle to government-led social justice measures was a historic experience the framers wanted desperately to avoid.

Third, note that the main subject of this second sentence of Section 19 is the Legislature. As discussed both in Chapter 4 and above in this one, the Legislative Assembly is the main protagonist of the Puerto Rican constitutional project.

More than a pure issue of structural design, the privileged status given to the Legislature also has ideological and practical connotations: it is the ideal body for the enactment of socially transformative legislation. While the 1952 Constitution entrenched much of the social legislation that existed at that time, the framers intended that legislative work to continue and to build upon the new constitutional floor that was being laid. Section 19 was meant to give explicit articulation to that idea and to remind the Legislative Assembly of its constitutional role and its historical responsibility.

VII. OTHER SUBSTANTIVE POLICY PROVISIONS

Article II of the 1952 Constitution is not the only source of substantive policy. There are important provisions found elsewhere – particularly Article VI – that deal with general matters. A few stand out and all of them share a clear progressive bent.

First, there is the natural resources clause found in Section 19 of Article VI, which adopts as public policy 'the most effective conservation of the [Commonwealth's] natural resources, as well as their greatest development and harnessing for the general benefit of the community …'. According to the Puerto Rico Supreme Court, this clause has two operations: first, as a stand-alone provision that can be called upon to resolve any legal question regarding environmental issues; and second, as a standard by which to analyse the sufficiency of any statutory or regulatory enactment that deals with natural resources.

The natural resources clause was intentionally added to the constitutional text with the explicit understanding that it would not constitute aspirational language. On the contrary, its proponents emphasised its operative character.[37] Although judicial underenforcement continues to be a problem in Puerto Rico,[38] the island's Supreme Court has recognised that the natural resources clause has a real normative bite.

[37] This is another instance of a majority of backbenchers defying their party leadership in order to adopt a progressive provision.

[38] Farinacci-Fernós (n 5).

Second, there is the historical buildings clause – also found in Section 19 – which adopts as public policy 'the conservation and maintenance of buildings and places that have been declared to have historic or artistic value by the Legislative Assembly'. Like the natural resources clause, this provision is not meant to be merely symbolic or aspirational. It constitutes binding public policy. Of course, it delegates to the Legislature the power to designate a particular building or place as having historic or artistic value. But the Legislature is not free to wholly disregard this policy. And more importantly, once there has been a legislative designation, that action acquires constitutional force.

The third clause of Section 19 relates to the rehabilitation of convicted persons. Specifically, it establishes as public policy the 'regulation of penal institutions so that they fulfil their purposes effectively, and tend to, within available resources, the adequate treatment of delinquents to further their moral and social rehabilitation'. This clause has generated considerable case law throughout the years,[39] cementing its status as an operative part of the 1952 Constitution.

One of the greatest economic challenges facing Puerto Rico during the first decades of the twentieth century was the concentration of wealth and power in the hands of agricultural corporations, particularly in the sugar industry. A distinct articulation of this centralisation of corporate power was the acquisition by these entities of substantial pieces of land.

In order to curtail the economic and – consequentially – political power of these mostly foreign corporations, the Puerto Rican Legislature adopted statutory limitations on the number of acres a particular company could own. As with labour rights, many of the framers wanted to further entrench this historically significant substantive policy enactment, upgrading it from a statutory provision to a constitutional clause.

Section 14 of Article VI directly addresses the issue of corporate ownership of land as a matter of constitutional law. It states:

> No corporation is authorized to engage in the business of the buying and selling of real estate property; nor shall they be allowed to possess or hold this type of property except those that are rationally necessary to carry out the purposes that led to their creation; and the domain and management of lands belonging to any corporation authorized to engage in agricultural endeavors shall be limited, through their founding charter, to an amount that shall not exceed five hundred acres; and this provision shall be understood as impeding any member of an agricultural corporation from having any interest in any type of corporation of a similar kind.

Section 14 crystallises the framers' concerns regarding excessive corporate power, particularly as to considerable real estate holdings. While modest in its specific normative reach as a distinct constitutional provision, its ideological

[39] See, eg, *Rivera Sierra v Supte Anexo 500 Guayama* 179 DPR 98 (2010).

component is evident and speaks to the overall nature of the entire constitutional project. As far as the 1952 Constitution is concerned, excessive corporate power is a social problem that must be addressed through the constitutional entrenchment of limitations to that power. In the particular context of a relatively small island, one of the fundamental limitations must be restrictions regarding land holdings.

The last provision that merits further attention is Section 9 of Article VI, which establishes an across-the-board ban regarding the use of public funds for purely private ends: 'Public funds or property will only be disbursed for public ends, and for the sustainment and operation of state institutions, and in all cases authorized by law'. This provision has also generated a considerable amount of case law, in an attempt to fine-tune the boundaries between the private and public spheres. The main goal of this text was to avoid the diversion of public funds to benefit private economic interests that have little or no social value.

The Article VI provisions discussed above point to a unifying theme: an emphasis on the common good over individual interests. This is accomplished through the protection of public funds, property, and goods, and the establishment of limitations over excessive private power, particularly of an economic nature.

VIII. CONGRESSIONAL ANTI-SOCIALIST VETO AND PUERTO RICAN COLONIAL ACCEPTANCE

The Constitutional Convention's crowning substantive and social achievement was going to be Section 20. Section 20 of the Puerto Rican Constitution's Bill of Rights included an important catalogue of socioeconomic and human rights that, while not necessarily designed to be directly justiciable by themselves, were meant to be the main driving force behind Puerto Rico's public policy, constitutional development, and social construction. This catalogue committed the island's government to fundamental human rights, such as, inter alia, the right to work, social security, healthcare, housing, and nutritional sustenance. Many of the specific items included in Section 20 are found in the Universal Declaration of Human Rights and the American Declaration of the Duties and Rights of Man.[40] But the provision itself was a Puerto Rican product.[41] Because of its significance, it is worthwhile reproducing the text in its entirety:

> The Commonwealth also recognizes the existence of the following human rights:
>
> The right of every person to receive free primary and secondary education.

[40] In particular, s 20 incorporates text found in Arts 22, 23(1), 25 and 26(1) of the Universal Declaration, as well as Arts VII, XI, XII and XIV of the American Declaration.

[41] In a vain attempt to minimise congressional resistance to the content of s 20, Convention President and Resident Commissioner Antonio Fernós-Isern tried to emphasise that several state

> The right of every person to obtain work.
>
> The right of every person to enjoy a standard of living adequate for himself and for their family's health, welfare and, especially, food, clothing, housing, medical care and necessary social services.
>
> The right of every person to social protection during unemployment, sickness, old age or physical disability.
>
> The right of every woman while pregnant or during her nursing period and the right of every child, to receive special care and assistance.
>
> The rights set forth in this section are intimately linked to the progressive development of the Commonwealth's economy and require for their full effectiveness sufficient resources and agricultural and industrial development that the Puerto Rican community has yet to achieve.
>
> In their duty to encourage the integral liberty of the citizen, the People and government of Puerto Rico will endeavor to promote the greatest possible expansion of its productive system, assure the fairest distribution of its economic results, and achieve the best understanding between individual initiative and collective cooperation. The Executive Branch and the Judicial Branch will keep present this duty and consider the laws that tend to fulfill it in the most favorable way.

As can be appreciated, Section 20 was meant to guide legislation and executive action, as well as judicial enforcement, in quite a progressive, and even radical or transformative, direction. This requires two separate discussions: first, the substantive content and operation of this text; and second, the colonial nature of Section 20's eventual demise. We begin with its operative effect.

At first glance, it would seem that Section 20 was nothing more than an aspirational statement of a purely symbolic nature. But the closer one looks the better one can appreciate the operational side of this provision. There is more than meets the eye when it comes to Section 20.

As discussed above, the Puerto Rican framers had great confidence in the role of the Legislative Branch as the conduit for the collective aspirations of the Puerto Rican People –particularly its working-class majority – and as the main instrument for the enactment of even more profound socioeconomic policies and legislation that furthered the main substantive blueprint established in the social Constitution.

As a result, Section 20 was not meant to completely dislodge legislative creativity. While the social Constitution establishes the goal, it is up to the Legislature to chart the way. In that sense, Section 20 does not command specific legislative action. However, once that legislative action has been taken, then Section 20 transcends the aspirational realm and becomes normatively operational.

constitutions at the time also had similar provisions, such as California, Colorado, Florida, Kansas, Louisiana, Mississippi, Montana, New York, Oklahoma and Texas. See A Fernós-Isern, *Original Intent in the Constitution of Puerto Rico: Notes and Comments Submitted to the Congress of the United States* (LexisNexis, 2002) 48.

This is done through a direct command to the Executive and Judicial branches: 'The Executive Branch and the Judicial Branch will keep present this duty and consider the laws that tend to fulfill it in the most favorable way'. In other words, once the Legislature has enacted a particular statute that relates to any of the issues identified in Section 20, the Constitution *requires* direct and specific executive and judicial action with regard to implementation and interpretation.

This constitutes a very deliberate division of normative labour. With regard to the Legislature, Section 20 assumes a passive stance: it simply establishes a mostly unenforceable general public policy, trusting the Legislature to – in its own judgment concerning the availability of resources and the adequacy of a particular policy – determine the specific manner in which these general public policies are to be pursued. But with regard to the Executive and the Judiciary, Section 20 changes tack and assumes a much more aggressive posture: it orders these branches to enforce and interpret these statutory enactments through the prism of the normative content adopted in Section 20 itself.

This means that the main operative feature of Section 20 is to serve as a comprehensive and robust interpretive tool that gives additional normative weight to those statutory or regulatory enactments that address the substantive issues identified in the text. This, in turn, requires a closer look at the actual substantive issues that were incorporated in Section 20.

The first thing that stands out is the characterisation made by the text: that the Commonwealth 'recognizes the existence of the following human rights'. The use of the phrase 'recognizes the existence' takes us back to the operative issue. On the one hand, the Constitution acknowledges that these rights are real and should be addressed. On the other hand, it gives the Commonwealth government sufficient leeway concerning its implementation.

As to the second phrase, 'the following human rights', the text consciously incorporates an ideological concept that had recently gained strength in the aftermath of World War II: human rights. The use of this term clearly indicates the intent of the framers to connect the 1952 Constitution with the international human rights regime that was being developed at the time.

But which human rights? The selection made by the Constitutional Convention speaks volumes with regard to the ideological leanings of its members and the founding generation in general.

First is 'the right of every person to receive free primary and secondary education'.[42] Sound familiar? This is directly related to the general right to education established in Section 5 of the Bill of Rights. As discussed above, there was some disagreement among the drafters as to whether education would be an operative right or whether it would be merely declaratory. This clause in Section 20 was meant to adopt the latter alternative.

[42] This corresponds to Art 26(1) of the Universal Declaration of Human Rights (1948).

But, as we saw, the Convention decided to incorporate the education clauses as an independent operative provision of the Constitution. However, the text of Section 20 was not amended. The result is a combination between Section 5 and this clause that strengthens the general normative power of the right to an education. Finally, notice the reaffirmation of the tuition-free nature of the public education system that the 1952 Constitution establishes.

Second is 'the right of every person to obtain work'.[43] This relates to the labour rights recognised in several clauses in the Bill of Rights, particularly Section 16. This right is essential to make sense of the other ones. If a person does not possess a right to earn a living in the first place, and keep that job under reasonable circumstances, then the other rights become illusory.

Note also that the right to obtain work is listed second in the list of recognised human rights, right after the right to an education. This is evidence of the consensus that existed in Puerto Rican society in general and the Constitutional Convention in particular with regard to the dignity of labour and its central role in the creation of wealth. This, in turn, required the adoption strong legal protections, including through the constitutional text.

Third is 'the right of every person to enjoy a standard of living adequate for himself and for their family's health, welfare and, especially, food, clothing, housing, medical care and necessary social services'.[44] This clause also has strong connections with the labour issue. As discussed above, the operative right to a reasonable minimum wage established in Section 16 of the Bill of Rights requires that workers be paid a wage that is sufficient to address their needs and those of their families, and to enjoy a decent standard of living. This clause in Section 20 elaborates on that goal. The objective was that every person, particularly those that worked for a living, be able to receive wages that allowed them to enjoy the standard of living described in this provision.

Notice also that the items that make up this basic standard of living are deeply rooted in social justice considerations. When one takes into account that the main vehicle for obtaining this material state is through employment that pays a living wage, one can really appreciate the social worldview of the framers and their commitment to the interests of working people and the necessary correlation that should exist between honest work and a decent life.

Fourth is 'the right of every person to social protection during unemployment, sickness, old age or physical disability'.[45] This general right to social security is meant to address circumstances in which a person is incapable of fully providing for themselves. In these situations, there is a social and governmental responsibility to take care of the most vulnerable. Notice, then, the common denominator between the rights mentioned so far, ie making sure that working

[43] This corresponds to Art 23(1) of the Universal Declaration of Human Rights (1948).
[44] This corresponds to Art 25(1) of the Universal Declaration of Human Rights (1948).
[45] ibid.

people have the tools to live a decent life: tuition-free public education for the children of the working classes, a general right to obtain and maintain one's employment, the right to earn a living wage that supplies the basic necessities of a dignified existence, such as clothing, food and housing; and, finally, the right to obtain social assistance when, due to circumstances such as unemployment, sickness, old age or disability, a person is not able to work and thus provide for themselves.

Fifth is 'the right of every woman while pregnant or during her nursing period and the right of every child, to receive special care and assistance'.[46] This provision is meant two protect two particularly vulnerable groups in society, specifically under a capitalist system: (1) pregnant women who, as a historical matter, were susceptible to employment discrimination and lack of economic support during a period in which they were unable to work; and (2) young children, who, precisely because of the ban on child labour, require social assistance to ensure they enjoy and make the most of their childhood.

One final point regarding Section 20's substantive content refers to its last paragraph:

> In their duty to encourage the integral liberty of the citizen, the People and government of Puerto Rico will endeavor to promote the greatest possible expansion of its productive system, assure the fairest distribution of its economic results, and achieve the best understanding between individual initiative and collective cooperation.

The ideas incorporated in this text constitute a perfect example of the ideological worldview of the Constitutional Convention, which attempted to combine progressive liberalism with moderate socialist – or maybe social-democratic – proposals.

This statement reflects the Convention's attempt to combine progressive liberalism with moderate socialist aims. Note the harmonisation between individual liberty and the collective good. The paragraph's reference to 'the fairest distribution of its economic results' constitutes the most explicit statement regarding a just distribution of wealth.

This brings us to the second issue: how Section 20 became the main target of congressional intervention and the principal victim of colonialism. When the Constitutional Convention approved its final version of the text, it sent it to Congress for its consideration and approval, as required by Public Law 600. This was not merely a pro forma gesture. On the contrary, as discussed above, Congress did, in fact, use its veto power over the finished text.

The reasons for Congress's direct and explicit intervention in the actual content of the constitutional text are mostly geo-political, historical, and ideological. Specifically, it was the result of Cold War politics. Section 20 was

[46] This corresponds to Art 25(2) of the Universal Declaration of Human Rights (1948).

considered too 'socialistic' at a time when the US, particularly the national political leadership, was embracing anti-communism as a defining characteristic. References to 'the fairest distribution of its economic results' and 'achieve the best understanding between individual initiative and collective cooperation', as well as the incorporation of so many 'human rights' of a socioeconomic nature were a step too far for Congress at the height of the Cold War.

It did not seem to matter that many of these rights could also be found in many state constitutions or that they were taken directly from international documents that the US had been instrumental in drafting and adopting just four years earlier, like the UN Declaration of Human Rights. It was evident that FDR's 'Second Bill of Rights', which Section 20 mirrors in many respects, was no longer viewed as sufficiently American or patriotic in the 1950s.

The result was clear: Congress required the elimination of Section 20 of the Bill of Rights as a condition for the approval of the entire constitutional text. The Constitutional Convention, which had celebrated Section 20 as its crowning achievement, submitted to Congress's will and accepted what a then-delegate, and future Chief Justice of the Puerto Rico Supreme Court, characterised as nothing short of a humiliation.[47]

Although Section 20 of the Bill of Rights was formally deleted, it has not been entirely exiled. For example, most printed versions of the Constitution still include Section 20. Sometimes it is accompanied by an asterisk. Section 20 has also found itself into the pages of the Puerto Rican Supreme Court's Reports.[48] The humiliation of its deletion has been partially compensated by an insistence in keeping it alive as part of the Puerto Rican Constitution's incomplete promise of a fairer society.

[47] Trías-Monge (n 2) 212 ('*esta humillación*').
[48] See Ch 6.

6

Puerto Rico under the 1952 Constitution

I. INTRODUCTION

WHAT HAS HAPPENED since 1952 in terms of Puerto Rico's constitutional project? This question raises two important issues: first, how has the 1952 Constitution actually been implemented in practice? Addressing this issue will facilitate a contrast between the promise of its text and the concrete experiences of reality, thus allowing a greater and more complete understanding of the entirety of the constitutional project; and second, what role has the 1952 Constitution played after its ratification in terms of the colonial relationship, the country's democratic deficits and aspirations, and the material challenges facing Puerto Rican society?

Several decades have elapsed since the current constitution was adopted. For 70 years, the 1952 Constitution has ruled over a society of more than three million people. This has allowed the accumulation of substantial experiences that complement the text and structure of the formal constitution. This experience is as important as the actual text of the constitution.[1]

After centuries of only having purely external constitutional norms, and after a historic process that culminated in the adoption of an autochthonous constitutional text for the first time, Puerto Rico now has its own institutions, jurisprudence, and legal gloss, albeit of a colonial nature, with all the ideological and normative limitations this implies. The 1952 Constitution sits at the centre of this new intricate system, though not alone. It still reports to a higher, federal, power. But when it comes to everyday life in Puerto Rico, the constitutional project has played, and still plays, an important and visible part.

Like many other constitutions around the world, Puerto Rico's lives in two different time periods. First, as a historical product of 1952. Second, as a legal

[1] The claim is not that the 'practical' or 'material' constitution is the 'real' constitution, as opposed to the 'formal' version. On the contrary, one of the normative claims of this book is that most of the gap between the 'practical' and the 'formal' constitution should be resolved in favour of the latter. Here the point is simpler: that, in any case, we must account for the practical constitutional events that have transpired in Puerto Rico during the last 70 years, in order to measure, among other things, the effectiveness of the Constitution, as well as its actual role in Puerto Rican everyday life and recent history.

norm that has influenced and been influenced by the historical events that followed ratification. This merely works to increase the intensity of the 1952 Constitution's contradictions.

Some things have changed since 1952, others have not; some for the better, others for the worse. There is no inherent correlation between these two sets of value judgements. It is a dynamic process that moves in many directions, accompanied by its own internal and external contradictions – the point being that there are no categorical truths or answers. Seventy years do not pass in uniform fashion. But after these tensions and contradictions are accounted for, there is no denying the importance of post-ratification events as part of the complete picture of the Puerto Rican constitutional project.

With this in mind, we can begin to address the multiple constitutional and historical experiences that Puerto Rico has accumulated since 1952. Specifically, this chapter will focus on the following issues: (1) the evolution of the colonial problem and debate; (2) the stagnation of Puerto Rican democracy and its subordination to the status question; (3) the intensification of social tensions, including an emerging political leadership that strayed from the more progressive roots of the 1952 Constitution; and (4) the approach taken by Puerto Rico's institutional actors, particularly the Supreme Court, to the constitutional text and its role in social life.

Our preliminary conclusions are as follows. First, that the 1952 Constitution was turned into a weapon – or, at the very least, into an unwitting tool – against Puerto Rico's effective decolonisation. In some respects, it even worsened the colonial problem by masking it without generating any real change in the Puerto Rico-US relationship. Meanwhile, it gave dangerous cover for the US in the international and domestic spheres with respect to its imperialist practices in Puerto Rico. Malavet's characterisation is harshest: 'Although locals are governed by locals, the power is still wielded by the United States … through careful legal and social constructions of citizenship'.[2] But, as discussed below, this does not paint a complete picture of the contradictory nature of the 1952 regime.

Second, that the Constitution was partially successful in creating a relatively stable internal political system but remained constantly marred by its external and internal democratic insufficiencies and colonial underpinnings. That 'success' also created a hollow and problematic two-party system. The persistence of the status question as a central question in terms of identity and direction overshadowed policy matters as the main driving force in Puerto Rican electoral politics, contrary to the substantive nature of the 1952 Constitution.

This became a recipe for a democratic short circuit: the public was voting according to status preferences, but the parties were governing according to their socioeconomic policy views. If we add to this equation the passive role given

[2] PA Malavet, *America's Colony: The Political and Cultural Conflict Between the United States and Puerto Rico* (New York University Press, 2007) 29.

by the 1952 Constitution to the People with regard to constitutional or statutory enactments, as well as the intentionally designed strictures of the electoral system, it is not hard to see how, simultaneously, Puerto Rico became a 'stable', yet evidently dysfunctional, representative democracy.

Several additional factors worked against the 1952 Constitution's attempt at creating a universally acceptable and fully functional political structure.

First is the 1952 Constitution's perceived complicity in the perpetuation of the colonial condition. Since the political parties were becoming mostly organised around the status question, the colonial characteristics of the constitution made it impossible for important political and social groups to accept it wholeheartedly. The colonial problem merged with the democratic issue to create scepticism about the political structures of the Constitution. This impacted on both the statehood movement – which saw the Constitution as a distraction from the ultimate goal of annexation – and the independence movement, which considered the Constitution as an apologist tool for colonialism.

In the end, only the Popular Democratic Party (PPD) was left to defend the structural and political components of the 1952 Constitution or to adopt them as their own historical project. The lack of universal acceptance pressured the PPD into becoming the only apparent unconditional supporter of the entire constitutional project, including its colonial and undemocratic characteristics. This was accomplished by the PPD's transformation from a big-tent social reformist party into the main stalwart of the Commonwealth formula associated with the 1952 Constitution, sacrificing its social components along the way. Ironically, the PPD's enthusiastic adoption of a Commonwealth-status-centred political programme allowed it to focus almost exclusively on the status-political aspects of the Constitution, substantially relegating what was supposed to be the main component of the constitutional project: its social and progressive substantive content. This, in turn, made the other parties – also organised along status lines – reject the Constitution, regardless of its social content.

Second is the PPD's continued electoral erosion. Thus, a political and electoral system that was designed for a dominant political party soon saw itself deprived of its material underpinnings, adding to the democratic short-circuit. As discussed further below, the PPD's electoral dominance ended quite decisively in 1968 and has not returned since. In other words, the existing political system was designed for an electoral reality that ceased to exist decades ago.[3]

Third is the stagnation of the colonial system and the hollowing out of a collective project that could be channelled through the 1952 Constitution's

[3] When the 1952 Constitution and the Commonwealth status were adopted, the PPD became the natural party of government: first, because of its uncontested electoral might; second, because its social reformism mostly coincided with the liberal-progressive substantive content of the constitutional text; and third, because it was the only established political party to fully embrace the Commonwealth arrangement, which made it the obvious channel for its development through the governmental structure created by the 1952 Constitution. As is explained in Ch 7, the PPD has ceased to be the natural party of government under the 1952 Constitution.

political structures. Institutional politics seemed to fail systematically as a vehicle for social transformation and the effective implementation of the popular will. This, in turn, further eroded confidence in the constitutional system's ability to deliver social progress.

And the final preliminary conclusion regarding the social and material situation in Puerto Rico is that Puerto Rico's institutional actors have not been able – or have been unwilling – to maximise the Constitution's potential with regard to substantive policy, thus frustrating one of the main objectives of the Constitutional Convention: that the constitutional text would play a central, decisive, and driving role in shaping Puerto Rican society in a direction of greater social justice, economic prosperity, and wealth distribution.

One possible explanation for this phenomenon is rooted in history, geopolitics, legal culture, and colonialism. Puerto Rico's 1952 Constitution was adopted at the *end* of an important political and ideological cycle that was quickly swallowed up by Cold War politics and an ideological turn to the Right, particularly by the statehood movement as a whole (after the dissolution of the Socialist Party in 1954) and by the PPD in particular. For decades, the Puerto Rican Left would exist, almost exclusively, within the ranks of the independence movement, which lacked a significant working-class base. This meant that the social Constitution in particular was left without defenders that would ensure, or at least attempt, to implement it to the maximum.

This is somewhat similar to the events surrounding the Portuguese Constitution of 1976. Adopted at the height of a highly charged progressive atmosphere – in the Portuguese case, a successful and radicalised popular uprising with explicit socialist characteristics – the 1976 Constitution soon found itself an orphan when the right-wing parties quickly separated themselves from its radical content and objectives, and the Socialist Party abandoned its Marxist roots and embraced neoliberalism. This left the Communist Party as the sole defender of the Constitution's socialist goals. As a result, the Constitution's substantive content became isolated and underenforced, thus ineffective, culminating in a series of constitutional reforms that eliminated most of its operative revolutionary language.

There were, to be sure, important success stories in Puerto Rico with regard to social justice, consistent with the original constitutional promise made in 1952. But those experiences were limited and sporadic. Several waves of economic recession added to the challenges, while the substantive constitutional text took a backseat to ordinary party politics, the advent of neoliberalism, the weakening of the labour movement, and the primary focus on the issue of the island's political status.

The end result of this historical experience has been that the institutional actors charged with implementing the 1952 Constitution have not been willing or able to enforce it to its maximum potential. Quite the contrary, the constitutional text has generally been applied in its minimum form, respecting its basic textual core while mostly ignoring its transformative potential.

II. A HISTORY OF JUDICIAL UNDERENFORCEMENT AND NOMINAL LIP SERVICE

After the adoption of the constitutional text in summer of 1952, elections were held in November of that year. Once again, the PPD won in a landslide, netting some 65 per cent of the vote. The PIP, which had been absent during the deliberations of the Constitutional Convention, came in a relatively strong – yet objectively distant – second with 19 per cent. The PER obtained 13 per cent, while the Socialist Party received 3 per cent. The Socialist Party would dissolve itself in 1954, with most of its members joining the reformist PPD. A minority joined the PER. Even fewer still joined the PIP.

This left the PPD as the sole remaining true defender of the constitutional *project* itself. While the PPD managed to obtain these astronomical electoral results, the project seemed safe for now. But, even under these circumstances, it strengthened the view that the 1952 Constitution was mostly a creature of the PPD, instead of We the People as a whole.

The PPD's absolute control of the island's governmental structure meant that it would very quickly appoint all members of the Supreme Court of Puerto Rico. One might assume, then, that having political allies in the branches charged with the implementation of the Constitution would usher in a new era of aggressive constitutional enforcement. But, as noted above, the political winds were changing, mostly to the Right – primarily because of Cold War-era geopolitical considerations, exacerbated by colonialism and economic dependence. Also, Puerto Rican courts were still mostly American creatures, shaped by the previous organic acts, as well as by procedural rules and structures imported from the federal and state jurisdictions. These judicial structures would severely limit the ability of courts to become effective enforcers of the Constitution's substantive text. This was a recipe for constitutional underenforcement. Most of the more transformative aspects of the 1952 Constitution were left to the political branches.

Still, the Constitution did not become a mere background player in Puerto Rican jurisprudence. And with regard to constitutional meaning and interpretation, the Puerto Rican Supreme Court soon announced a central role for the legislative record of the Constitutional Convention. In that sense, Puerto Rico became an 'originalist' jurisdiction as early as 1954.[4] I have labelled this originalist approach as *original explication*.[5] The result is a mixed bag of partial underenforcement, particularly as it relates to its maximalist potential.

[4] For a more in-depth discussion on the methodological history of the Supreme Court of Puerto Rico with regard to the 1952 Constitution, see JM Farinacci-Fernós, 'Originalism in Puerto Rico: Original Explication and its Relation with Clear Text, Broad Purpose and Progressive Policy' (2016) 85 *Revista Jurídica Universidad de Puerto Rico* 203: 'Since the adoption of the Constitution in 1952, *originalism has been at the forefront of constitutional adjudication in Puerto Rico*, years before it would become an object of debate in US legal scholarship. Originalism has been used constantly and repeatedly by the Supreme Court' (ibid 211).

[5] ibid.

For decades, the Supreme Court's approach to constitutional interpretation has given determinative weight to the stated expressions of the delegates to the Constitutional Convention during its official deliberations. This includes issues relating to communicative and normative meaning, possible applications through examples, purpose and intent, among many others. The main tools for this approach have been the reports of the Convention's commissions when presenting their respective drafts of the text for each Article of the Constitution, as well as the debates and statements of the framers when considering each constitutional provision.

In addition, Puerto Rico's transcript-like record allows for greater empirical certainty. Also, as discussed in Chapter 3, the Puerto Rican framers were well aware that their statements during the deliberations of the Convention would be used as an authoritative source in future judicial interpretations. As such, they took great care in designing their interventions so as to facilitate this objective.

Finally, the, at least perceived, democratic legitimacy of the 1952 process has allowed the Supreme Court to justify its originalist tendencies. In other words, by directly quoting from the Convention's internal reports or the statements of the delegates during its deliberations, the Court has attempted to tap into the legitimacy of the framers, thus strengthening the legitimacy of its own rulings. In other words, it would not be the Supreme Court deciding on its own what the constitutional text meant, but the delegates themselves through empirically accurate and normatively authoritative legislative history.

However, although the Court would strongly rely on the democratic credentials of the 1952 process, the impact of colonialism meant that a considerable amount of the potentially transformative substantive content of the Constitution has been sacrificed. In other words, the democratic nature of the process supplied the basis for the selection of a particular interpretive *method*, but colonialism beat radicalism with regard to jurisprudential *substance*. It seems that, in terms of Puerto Rico's post-1952 constitutional experience, colonialism has been in the substantive driving seat, with democratic legitimacy playing an auxiliary role, and progressive substance left mostly marginalised as a constitutional player.

But marginalisation does not mean total disappearance. Depending on the particular historical and political context, different substantive parts of the 1952 Constitution have been used by the Supreme Court to address important policy matters. A decade-by-decade analysis offers a glimpse of this phenomenon.

The 1960s were characterised by rearguard actions regarding labour rights and discrimination on the basis of the circumstances of birth. In *Mun de Guaynabo v Tribunal Superior*,[6] the Puerto Rico Supreme Court held that the minimum wage provision found in Section 16 of the Bill of Rights applies to

[6] *Mun de Guaynabo v Tribunal Superior* 97 DPR 545 (1969).

municipal employees. This was the result of the broad language used in that provision, which addresses the right of 'every worker'. In *AD Miranda, Inc v Falcón*,[7] the Court made general statements praising the 1952 Constitution's pro-labour rights policy. The lip-service approach had begun.

But the most important decision of that decade addressed the rights of children born out of wedlock. *Ocasio v Díaz* is probably considered one of the most important Supreme Court cases during the 1952 constitutional era.[8]

Section 1 of the Bill of Rights prohibits discrimination, inter alia, on account of 'birth'. While the original semantic meaning of this term could be subject to debate – for example, that it addresses the place or social circumstances of birth – the delegates to the Constitutional Convention made explicit their intent that 'birth' only addressed the civil status of parents with regard to their children, specifically, to proscribe differentiations between so-called legitimate and natural children.

But the legislative history seemed to include a catch: the Bill of Rights Committee Report suggested that the prohibition with regard to birth would only protect children – with regard to their inheritance rights – born after 1952. But the continued legal distinction between children born within and outside wedlock for the purposes of inheritance was becoming untenable, particularly when faced with the seemingly absolute – and thus not time-restrained – language of Section 1. As a result, the Court held in *Ocasio* that Section 1's command was categorical and limited its possible retroactive application to *deaths* that occurred prior to 1952 where, presumably, a deceased person's estate was already divided up.

Puerto Rican legal history regards *Ocasio v Díaz* as the island's own *Brown v Board of Education*.[9] Even though *Ocasio* was a discrimination case, while the others mentioned above deal with labour issues, they share a common thread: the 1952 Constitution's promise of social equality.

The 1970s was the decade of the rise of the right of privacy, the strengthening of anti-discrimination provisions – particularly with regard to sex – and the continued erosion of labour protections, particularly in the collective realm. This trend seemed to signify a shift from the more socialistic characteristics of the 1952 Constitution to a more individual-centred form of progressive liberalism. This had the effect of retroactively characterising the ideological basis of the Constitution itself. In other words, the struggle to define the 1952 Constitution did not stop at the moment of its adoption. On the contrary, it has been a constant process that, during the 1970s, produced a significant shift.

[7] *AD Miranda, Inc v Falcón* 83 DPR 735 (1961).

[8] *Ocasio v Díaz* 88 DPR 676 (1963).

[9] See A Rodríguez Rodríguez, 'Palabras de la Hon. Anabelle Rodríguez Rodríguez en ocasión del acto de cierre editorial de la Revista de Estudios Críticos del Derecho de la Universidad Interamericana de Puerto Rico' (2015) 11 *Clave Revista de Estudios Críticos Del Derecho* 1, 3; *Domínguez Castro v ELA* 178 DPR 1, 157 (2010) (Fiol Matta, dissenting).

Just like other parts of the world, including the US, Puerto Rico during the 1970s was characterised by the struggle to obtain real equality between men and women. Puerto Rican law was no exception to this important trend.

While the Supreme Court had announced as early as 1972 in *Wackenhut v Rodríguez Aponte* that *all* the classifications mentioned in Section 1 of the Bill Rights – race, colour, sex, birth, social origin, social condition, political beliefs, and religious beliefs – were subject to strict scrutiny,[10] in its 1975 decision in *Zachary International v Tribunal Superior*,[11] the Court adopted a strong approach to legal distinctions between men and women that were based on the archaic view that women were somehow inferior to or weaker than men. It should come as no surprise that this landmark constitutional anti-discrimination case involved labour rights.

Privacy was also a hallmark of Puerto Rican jurisprudence during the 1970s. In *Figueroa Ferrer v ELA*,[12] the Supreme Court held that the state could not limit the right to obtain a divorce to only a few discrete instances – mostly of an at-fault nature – that required couples to share intimate details during court proceedings. Instead, the Court concluded that the constitutional right to privacy explicitly adopted in Section 8 of the Bill of Rights allowed couples who mutually wished to divorce to do so, without any ulterior explanation. *Figueroa Ferrer* not only revolutionised family law, but it also established privacy as one of the most powerful weapons in the constitutional arsenal.

But while privacy and anti-discrimination issues were making headlines, collective labour rights were being weakened, mostly accompanied by 'living constitutionalist' rhetoric. For example, in *ELA v Hermandad*,[13] the Court upheld an injunction issued against a labour union that was picketing an employer's house during a labour dispute. Here, the right to privacy trumped the combined effect of free speech and concerted labour activities. It was a liberal triumph over the more class-oriented possibilities of the Constitution.

But the most devastating blow to constitutional collective labour rights came in *AAA v UIAAA*.[14] As in many other parts of the world, in Puerto Rico the 1970s was a period of labour militancy and struggle. In this case, a particularly strong strike was carried out by the workers at Puerto Rico's state-owned water and sewage company. Section 18 of the Bill of Rights guarantees workers of private and state-owned companies that operate as private businesses the right to strike, picket and carry out concerted activities. Section 18 also contains a single exception to the exercise of these constitutional rights: if there is a grave emergency where the public health and security, as well as essential public services, are clearly in danger.

[10] *Wackenhut v Rodríguez Aponte* 100 DPR 518 (1972).
[11] *Zachary International v Tribunal Superior* 104 DPR 267 (1975).
[12] *Figueroa Ferrer v ELA* 107 DPR 250 (1978).
[13] *ELA v Hermandad* 104 DPR 436 (1975).
[14] *AAA v UIAAA* 105 DPR 437 (1976).

An injunction was sought by the management of the water and sewage company against the union strike. The union claimed that its strike was protected by Section 18 of the Bill of Rights, and that the extraordinary exception established in that provision was inapplicable to its case. If it did apply, the union reasoned, then management could stop any successful strike which, by definition, supposes a stoppage of production.

One could be forgiven for thinking that a possible strike at a state-owned water and sewage company constitutes, by itself, a grave emergency that puts essential public services in clear danger. But the Supreme Court recognised that the constitutional history of Section 18 did not support such a conclusion. In its Opinion, the Court acknowledged that the delegates to the Constitutional Convention actually amended the original draft of Section 18 to make it *harder* to stop a successful strike. In other words, they amended the text of Section 18 to strengthen the effectiveness of the right to strike.

Originally, the text of Section 18 allowed for limitations to the right to strike if there was an *emergency*. The delegates added the adjective *grave* and explicitly stated that a successful strike, by itself, could never constitute a grave emergency. Also, the original text allowed the Legislature to limit the right to strike if there was an *imminent threat* to public health and security, as well as the general welfare. The first change as to this issue was the replacement of *imminent threat* with *clear danger*. In the delegates' estimation, imminent meant future, while clear danger required present circumstances. In other words, one would need to wait for the strike to actually impact these public interests before being able to stop a strike action. The second change was the substitution of *general welfare* with *essential public services*. This was meant to narrow the circumstances in which Section 18 could be invoked to derail a successful strike.

In *AAA v UIAAA*, the Supreme Court recognised all of these normative qualities found in Section 18. It also recognised that Section 18 was drafted by known labour leaders who wanted to entrench a powerful collective right to strike by workers. But the Court in the 1970s was not as radical as the delegates who met in 1951–52. Again using living constitutionalist language, the Court basically said: that was then, this is now. In the end, it upheld the injunction because, in their estimation, society had had enough of the strike.

In summary, the 1970s saw a Supreme Court willing to be radical with regard to liberal issues such as privacy, free speech, and anti-discrimination, but unwilling to be so with regard to issues related to class struggle, like collective labour militancy. Its sympathies with labour issues were mostly limited to the individual realm.

The 1980s saw a similar trend: a strengthening of the Constitution's progressive individual rights in the labour context, but continued erosion in the collective sphere. In *Academia San Jorge v JRT*,[15] a divided Court held that the

[15] *Academia San Jorge v JRT* 110 DPR 193 (1980).

right to unionise, recognised in Section 17 of the Bill of Rights, did not extend to religious schools. Again, a liberal right (free exercise of religion) trumped a class-based one (unionisation and collective bargaining).

But in *Amy v Adm Deporte Hípico*,[16] and *Arroyo v Rattan Specialties*,[17] the Court issued two of the most daring decisions in its entire history. Both deal with individual labour rights, and both constitute a sharp break with US jurisprudential paradigms. In *Amy*, the Court revived the ill-fated Section 20. As discussed in Chapter 5, Congress deleted this provision, finding it too radical and socialistic. The Constitutional Convention obliged and excluded it from the final version.

But Section 20 remained in a limbo state, formally erased but symbolically alive, almost always printed in the official publications of the constitutional text. In *Amy*, the Court finalised its resurrection. It stated that the right to obtain employment – and by extension many of the other rights identified in Section 20 – was of such a nature that it existed even if not formally codified in the constitutional text. But, instead of channelling the right through Section 19's residual clause, the Court instead opted for an expansive interpretation of the right to life guaranteed in Section 7. While mostly symbolic in nature, with very little in the way of specific normative content, *Amy* was a powerful decision for many reasons.

First, it finally recognised the central role of work in society and Puerto Rico's constitutional project. It seemed unnatural that, given the strong labour presence in the Constitutional Convention and, in turn, in the constitutional text itself, the right to obtain and maintain one's employment should stay hidden forever. However symbolic or short-lived, it was a necessary reconnection between the original constitutional project and its working class foundations, and Puerto Rican jurisprudence.

Second, it was a sort of vindication for the humiliation suffered in 1952 when Congress demanded Section 20's elimination from the official constitutional text. By resurrecting Section 20 through case law, with an explicit reference to that ill-fated provision, the Supreme Court stood up for what the delegates in 1952 were politically incapable of doing. *Amy* restored Puerto Rico's collective constitutional pride and gave legitimacy to the informal practice of including Section 20 in the published versions of the 1952 Constitution. People could now argue that, although Congress had eliminated it in 1952, the Supreme Court reinserted it in 1985.

Third, *Amy* signalled the possibility of embarking once again on the progressive track originally laid out by the Bill of Rights in general and Section 20 in particular. Why stop at the right to obtain work? If Section 20's heart still beats, could it usher in a new era of progressive jurisprudence? Although the Supreme Court has not yet pulled the trigger, the promise is still there.

[16] *Amy v Adm Deporte Hípico* 116 DPR 414 (1985).
[17] *Arroyo v Rattan Specialties* 117 DPR 35 (1986).

The other case of this period that can be characterised as a watershed in Puerto Rican case law is *Arroyo v Rattan Specialties*. This case combined two fundamental elements of Puerto Rico's constitutional project: the right to privacy and Section 16's recognition of individual labour rights. In *Arroyo*, a private employer was concerned with theft in his establishment. Suspecting possible employee participation, he decided to have each employee tested with a polygraph. An employee challenged the move, citing his constitutional right to privacy and to protection of his personal integrity at the workplace.

The Supreme Court sided with the employee. It held that the general right to privacy entrenched in Section 8 of the Bill of Rights was strong and broad enough to protect an employee from an employer's attempt to, almost literally, get inside their heads. In *Arroyo*, the Court reaffirmed that the right recognised in Section 8 did not require state action and nor did it require further legislative enactment. In other words, the constitutional right to privacy had horizontal (*erga omnes*) effect and operated on its own (*ex proprio vigore*). While this could seem odd or even foreign to the legal culture in the US, it has become the bread and butter of Puerto Rican constitutional law.

Around the world, the 1990s was a decade of environmental awareness. As we saw in Chapter 5, Puerto Rico's 1952 Constitution included operative language regarding the preservation of natural resources for the general benefit of the community. After decades of obscurity, this language – found in Section 19 of Article VI – was given new energy in a pair of decisions handed down by the Supreme Court. In both cases,[18] the Court cited from the records of the Constitutional Convention, which clearly stated that the language of Section 19, Article VI was not aspirational or symbolic in nature, but operative and binding. As a result, the Supreme Court ruled that:

> this provision is not merely an inconsequential statement nor a declaration of general principles of an exhortative nature. Actually, *it is a command that must be obeyed rigorously and that trumps any statute, rule or municipal ordinance that is contrary to it*. (emphasis added)[19]

Quite a statement, indeed. In particular, the Court has stated that Section 19 has a dual role: (1) as an independent rule of law that is sufficient to resolve any relevant controversy; and (2) as a legal standard through which relevant statutes, rules or ordinances should be interpreted and analysed.[20]

While more recent Supreme Court decisions have heralded a disastrous environmental policy – in defiance of Section 19[21] – the groundwork laid down during the 1990s is still solid and awaits a much-needed course correction.[22]

[18] See *Paoli Méndez v Rodríguez* 138 DPR 449 (1995) and *Misión Ind PR v JCA* 145 DPR 908 (1998).
[19] *Misión Ind PR v JCA* (n 18) 919 (author's translation).
[20] ibid 919–20.
[21] See, eg, *Lozada Sánchez v JCA* 184 DPR 898 (2012).
[22] See *Empresas Loyola v Com Ciudadanos* 186 DPR 1033 (2012).

Hopefully, the current Supreme Court will rediscover Section 19 and its own jurisprudence before it is too late.

The 1990s also saw a moderate, yet consistent, vindication of individual labour rights, mostly found in Section 16 of the Bill of Rights. In *Dolphin Int' of Puerto Rico v Ryder Truck Lines*,[23] a company sued, among others, some of its former employees who had resigned from their posts in order to accept employment offers from one of its main competitors. The plaintiff argued that such action constituted an illegal interference with a legitimate contract. With regard to the rank-and-file employees who simply changed employers, the Supreme Court reminded readers that Section 16 of the Bill of Rights protects the right of every worker to *resign* at any time, and that this right was not subject to contractual limitations, given its nature as a generally unwaivable right.

Once again, a trend seems to emerge. With regard to collective labour rights, the Court is, at the very least, hesitant to effectively enforce them. Quite the opposite, it has consistently weakened their normative force, leaving them as marginal provisions in the constitutional text. However, when it comes to individual labour rights, the Court feels more comfortable with their enforcement, although it does not do this as aggressively as it could, considering the strength of the legislative record and the clear intentions of the framers.

If we add to this situation the Court's consistent protection of other rights that centre around the individual as a political unit, such as privacy, prohibition on discrimination, and free speech, a clear picture is revealed: a classic liberal-progressive view with regard to constitutional law that sacrifices more collectivist, class-oriented and pro-labour militancy constitutional provisions. While this liberalism is undoubtedly progressive, it is hardly radical or revolutionary.

The twenty-first century has been, so far, a conservative frustration of the 1952 Constitution's most progressive or radical provisions and general policies. It seems to prove that, regardless of the constitutional text or its accompanying authoritative legislative history, it is still up to concrete institutional actors to determine the actual development of constitutional law. In other words, it requires constant political victories both at the time of adoption and all through its future enforcement. As such, the constitutional project is subject to changes in the political winds which, in turn, translate into a dominant judicial philosophy that, in Puerto Rico's most recent experience, is quite conservative and mostly at odds with the original constitutional project.

This is so, even though the current conservative majority in the Puerto Rico Supreme Court labels itself – ironically – as originalist. As can be appreciated from statements made in this book, originalism in Puerto Rico must be, because of historical requirements, inherently progressive or transformative.

[23] *Dolphin Int' of Puerto Rico v Ryder Truck Lines* 127 DPR 869 (1991).

While lip-service is given to the general ideological infrastructure of the 1952 Constitution, the actual doctrine that has emerged recently is anything but. The 1952 Constitution's promise of radical social transformation is still pending.

But the evident conservative turn in the dominant judicial philosophy regarding constitutional enforcement in the 1990s coexisted with numerous social movements that still aspire to greater measures of social justice and material redistribution. Several examples stand out, mostly related with student and union activism.

Probably the main social and class struggle of the 1990s was the popular resistance to privatisation of the government-owned telephone company. Since the 1930s, the Puerto Rican government has had considerable instances of direct involvement in the island's economy and productive sectors. Puerto Rico has a rich history of government-owned entities that generate substantial income. In its heyday, this included, for example, profitable bottle factories.

In the 1970s, the Commonwealth government nationalised the private telephone company, at a time where direct government intervention in productive economic activity was seen as a positive alternative. But by the late 1980s, neoliberalism had taken a hold of the main political parties in Puerto Rico. While the PPD's attempt to privatise the telephone company during the 1980s failed, the PNP picked up the privatisation project in 1997. This generated militant resistance from the unionised telephone workers, the broader labour movement, and the general public. What followed were some of the greatest class-based mobilisations since the upheavals of the 1970s. In the end, however, the privatisation went through, which exemplified the privatisation wave of the 1990s in Puerto Rico and around the world.

Other labour sectors were also active during this period, including the then-strongest unions in Puerto Rico, such as the government-owned electricity company workers' union (UTIER) and the main teachers' union (FMPR). These two unions and their struggles implicate many of the substantive policy provisions found in the 1952 Constitution. For example, the FMPR aggressively defended the requirement in the Bill of Rights Section 5 that public funds could only be used for public schools. UTIER defended the notion of government ownership over strategic sectors, such as energy production, as well as worker participation in its earnings.

Another source of social mobilisation from a progressive perspective was based on the numerous student movements at the state-owned university (UPR), particularly its main campus in Río Piedras. During the 1990s, most of the demands from the student movement related to resisting rises in tuition fees, privatisation, and the presence of the US military, particularly the Reserve Officers' Training Corps. This militancy also coincided with more general anti-militarist sentiment, which culminated in substantial protests against the US-led wars in Afghanistan and Iraq.

The UPR example combines many of the substantive elements found in the constitutional project: first, a defence of higher education as a right instead of a commodity or a privilege; second, the struggle for state-owned entities that resist the profit motive and, instead, focus on providing quality public services and goods. The student protests also implicated important political rights, such as free speech.

This period of social mobilisations must be analysed in the context of the shifting economic realities in Puerto Rico. As we have seen, Puerto Rico's economic structure has been a dysfunctional creature of colonial capitalism. This structure is based on several key aspects.

First is the near absolute displacement by US capital of the local bourgeoisie. This began at the dawn of the twentieth century. While there was significant direct economic activity on the part of governmental entities during the 1930s and 1940s – which explains the economic worldview that permeates the 1952 Constitution, including its direct references to productive, state-owned enterprises – the complete takeover of the Puerto Rican economy by US capital was accelerated during the 1950s and 1960s. As a result, displaced local Puerto Rican capital opted to become an auxiliary entity in partnership with American capital. This had two direct effects: (1) the absence of a local economic elite that would adopt independence as their historic project; and (2) the absolute dependence of the Puerto Rican economy on US markets, both in terms of exports and imports.

The second key aspect is that the near total takeover by US capital of the Puerto Rican economy was accompanied by federal and local tax exemptions, which incentivised US capital investments, but deprived Puerto Rico of most of the benefits, whether through taxation or reinvestment. This meant that, no matter how productive economic output was or how hardworking the Puerto Rican People were, the island's economy would not reap most of its benefits. Quite the opposite: this model generated considerable capital flight, which resulted in a growing public debt, wage stagnation, and lack of capital reinvestment. All of this hampered the Puerto Rican economy from becoming self-sustainable.

The third key aspect of Puerto Rico's dysfunctional colonial economy after the adoption of the 1952 Constitution has been the failure of this economic model to address the basic material needs of the Puerto Rican People. This, in turn, has generated considerable social and economic tensions that, during the economic recession of the 1970s, threatened to explode. The systemic response was a substantial inflow of federal economic assistance, particularly through welfare programs, such as food stamps. This had several effects: (1) it avoided a humanitarian crisis; (2)it strengthened the relationship of dependence between Puerto Rico and the US; and (3) it failed to solve the structural problems of the economy, which would still be marred by chronic unemployment, an eroding tax base, austerity measures, and wealth inequality.

This material reality made the 1952 Constitution's social and economic project difficult to implement. The fact that institutional actors were mostly unwilling to do so further weakened the 1952 Constitution's relevance with regard to economic development, particularly its most progressive and potentially transformative content.

Another obstacle to the achievement of the substantive goals of the 1952 Constitution has been the Puerto Rico Supreme Court's recent adoption of a relatively strict version of justiciability as a condition for judicial intervention. The increased difficulty of gaining access to the court system in order to assert the implementation of important constitutional provisions has become an indirect mechanism in the service of underenforcement.

Unlike the US Constitution, Puerto Rico's constitutional text makes no reference whatsoever to 'justiciability' or the 'case or controversy' requirement. It should be noted that attempts to entrench these requirements in the 1952 Constitution were unsuccessful.

But regardless of this notable textual omission, in 1958 the Supreme Court of Puerto Rico held that the concept of justiciability was inherent to the judicial power and the nature of courts in general.[24] The opinion issued in that case reads as a sort of bizarre *Marbury v Madison*, where the Court lays out the fundamental tenets of justiciability and the case or controversy requirement, which had the effect of substantially curtailing the jurisdiction of Puerto Rican courts, including the Supreme Court. In other words, the Puerto Rico Supreme Court, under the guise of judicial self-restraint, considerably overreached itself when it imposed a requirement that is not to be found in the text of the 1952 Constitution. In one move, the Court incorporated into Puerto Rican constitutional law doctrines such as political questions, advisory opinions, standing, mootness, and other related concepts.

The 1958 decision was followed by a relatively moderate approach to justiciability questions. This avoided the most drastic consequences of that watershed opinion. For many decades, for example, the Supreme Court adopted very flexible, liberal, and expansive conceptions of the standing doctrine, going as far as to recognise the Legislature's plenary authority to grant standing to any person, regardless of their injuries.[25]

But the emergence of a considerably more conservative majority within the Supreme Court in recent years has noticeably put the brakes on with regard to access to courts for the adjudication of important policy matters. The main tool in that arsenal has been a weaponised version of justiciability, particularly in terms of the standing and mootness doctrines. The issue of standing has been especially worrisome, since it has been used to thwart efforts by important social sectors to ask for judicial relief in instances of constitutional violations by powerful economic forces. Environmental cases have been the primary victims of this trend.[26] Only time will tell whether this trend will continue or whether,

[24] See *ELA v Aguayo* 80 DPR 552 (1958).
[25] See *CUD v CSP* 174 DPR 174 (2008).
[26] See *Fund Surfrider v ARPE* 178 DPR 563 (2010).

through judicial u-turns or constitutional amendment, the doctrine of justiciability will be relegated to its previous, more benign, articulation.

III. THE ILLUSION OF DECOLONISATION, AUTONOMY, AND SORT-OF EQUAL TREATMENT

After the 1952 Constitution was adopted, US diplomats – aided by the PPD leadership – rushed to the United Nations to petition that Puerto Rico be removed from the list of territories that were still subject to colonialism. They argued that, by adopting the 1952 Constitution, Puerto Rico had achieved a sufficient level of self-government that merited its deletion from the list. As Malavet points out, however, 'most observers concluded that the [PPD] presented the constitution and [Act 600] as creating an improved but transitional form of self-government'.[27]

Nonetheless, in 1953, the UN General Assembly passed Resolution 748(VII), which stated, inter alia: (1) 'that the people of the Commonwealth of Puerto Rico, by expressing their will in a free and democratic way, have achieved a *new constitutional status*' (emphasis added); (2) 'that it *stems* from the documentation provided that the association of the Commonwealth of Puerto Rico with the United States of America has been established as a *mutually agreed association*' (emphasis added); (3) that the People of Puerto Rico had '*effectively exercised their self-determination*'; and (4) that 'in the framework of their Constitution and of the compact agreed upon with the United States of America, the people of the Commonwealth of Puerto Rico have been invested with *attributes of political sovereignty* which clearly identify the status of self-government attained by the Puerto Rican people as that of an *autonomous political entity*' (emphasis added).[28]

As a result, the UN General Assembly resolved that 'the Declaration regarding Non-Self-Governing Territories and the provisions established under it in Chapter XI of the Charter *can no longer be applied to the Commonwealth of Puerto Rico*' (emphasis added).[29] This meant that the US was no longer required to send periodical reports on the situation in Puerto Rico and that there was no further need to decolonise the island. Although in 1960 the UN adopted Resolutions 1514(XV) and 1541(XV), which meant that the 'Puerto Rican case' could be addressed by the Special Committee on Decolonization, the truth is that Resolution 748(VII) created the impression that Puerto Rican colonialism had been surpassed and that Puerto Rico had achieved an acceptable level of self-government. In 1972, the United Nations explicitly linked the Puerto Rican

[27] Malavet (n 2) 71.

[28] Cessation of the transmission of information under Art 73e of the Charter in respect of Puerto Rico, UNGA Resolution 748 (VII) (27 Nov 1953) UN Document A/RES/748(VIII).

[29] ibid.

situation and Resolution 1514(XV).[30] Moreover, '[d]espite the Compact and the degree of integration in certain economic sectors, the United Nations continue to view Puerto Rico as a separate national entity'.[31]

As is discussed in Chapter 7, the impression given in 1953 was, at best, a naïve illusion and, at worst, an intentional fraud on the international community and the Puerto Rican People. But Resolution 748(VII) heralded an extended period of radio silence regarding Puerto Rico's constitutional development in the context of its relationship with the US. This radio-silence allowed colonialism to fester for decades, with catastrophic consequences, both material and moral.

The myth of Puerto Rican decolonisation had two seemingly contradictory effects. On the one hand, it appeared that Puerto Rico had achieved a political status reminiscent of an associated republic: self-government, fiscal autonomy, differential tax treatment, and limited international participation, such as the Olympics.[32] On the other hand, US constitutional law seemed to indicate that Puerto Rico was to be treated on equal footing with other states, eliminating most instances of inferior treatment. Puerto Rico was to be *mostly* treated *as if it were a State*, except for structural constitutional considerations, such as full representation in the US Congress and the ability to select electors to the Electoral College.

Yet, it should be noted that there is US Supreme Court authority for the proposition that Congress can, under the Territorial Clause, in fact treat Puerto Rico differently from other states, as long as it has a rational basis for doing so.[33] Although some of these statements were made in passing, generating unclear normative value, they are considered good law and stand for the proposition that Congress has considerable leeway to legislate for Puerto Rico in a manner that would differ from what was applicable in the 50 states. In the end, whether Puerto Rico will receive the same treatment as the states or whether it will be treated differently is a matter left entirely to Congress, subject only to the most elemental requirements of the US Constitution and to the most deferential judicial scrutiny.

Congress has been inconsistent with regard to this power. In many instances, it has passed legislation that requires equal treatment for Puerto Rico. But other

[30] CI Keitner and M Reisman, 'Free Asociation: The United States Experience' (2003) 39 *Texas International Law Journal* 1, 32.

[31] ibid.

[32] In that sense, I have to disagree with Malavet's more absolutist position that the US still 'controls the political, past, present, and future of the island and its residents': Malavet (n 2) 49. While it is true that 'Congress giveth and Congress taketh away', meaning that Congress can take away Puerto Rico's local government powers (and in Chapter 7 we see that it has done so), the current reality is that Puerto Rico does have some measure of self-government, particularly as to local issues. Also, and probably because of important political factors in the US and internationally, it is very difficult to imagine that the US would take radical actions regarding Puerto Rico on the scale of unilateral annexation or, as some have suggested, selling Puerto Rico to a third party.

[33] *Califano v Torres* 435 US 1 (1978); *Harris v Rosario* 446 US 651 (1980).

instances remain, where living in Puerto Rico can mean receiving fewer social benefits than a person would be entitled to if they lived in any of the 50 states.

In any event, the issue of colonialism was not so simply swept away by a UN Resolution or even timid or ambivalent US Supreme Court pronouncements. Both the pro-annexation and pro-independence currents constantly denounced the Commonwealth as a mere continuation of the territorial condition, while even voices within the PPD recognised that Puerto Rico had not fully overcome the colonial problem. Issues such as the draft during the Vietnam War kept the colonialism question central in Puerto Rican politics.

During the 1970s, there were several struggles to further demilitarise Puerto Rico, particularly with regard to the military bases and live-ammunition drills carried out in the island-cities of Vieques and Culebra. While the protests managed to close the Culebra base and operations, the US Navy presence remained in Vieques until a new, massive protest movement emerged in 1999 after an errant bomb accidentally killed a Puerto Rican security guard.

What followed were the most massive popular mobilisations during the 1990s – in a similar vein to the protests against the privatisation of the state-owned telephone company a year earlier. While the anti-privatisation campaigns implicated socioeconomic policy and issues of public ownership over strategic economic sectors, the Vieques mobilisations directly implicated the colonial issue.

Unlike the mobilisations against the privatisation of the telephone company which failed to stop the sale – although they made 'privatisation' a dirty word for several years – the Vieques campaign managed to attain the ouster of the Navy from the island-municipality in 2003. It should be noted that, in addition to massive popular mobilisations, the Vieques campaign included a referendum in the island-municipality asking its residents whether they wanted the immediate exit of the Navy. Nearly 70 per cent of voters answered yes.

IV. DEMOCRATIC CRISIS: THE NEW TWO-PARTY SYSTEM, POLITICAL REPRESSION, AND ARMED STRUGGLE

As explained in Chapter 4, the political structure adopted by the 1952 Constitution was designed for a dominant party, namely, the PPD. But by late 1960s, the PPD's electoral dominance was being challenged, mostly fuelled by internal divisions and an ascendant statehood movement.

After serving four terms, for a total of 16 years in office, Governor Luis Muñoz Marín decided to stand down in 1964. In the elections held after the adoption of the 1952 Constitution, Muñoz Marín and the PPD continued to win outright: 65 per cent in 1952, 62.5 per cent in 1956, and 58.2 per cent in 1960. For its part, the pro-statehood PER was steadily rising in its electoral fortunes: 13 per cent in 1952, 25 per cent in 1956, and 32 per cent in 1960. The pro-independence PIP was going in the opposite direction: 19 per cent in 1952, 12.5 per cent in 1956, and an abysmal 3.1 per cent in 1960. In fact, during the 1960 elections, the PIP was beaten into fourth place by a new, short-lived party made up by mostly conservative pro-independence supporters: the Christian Action Party (PAC). The PAC obtained 6.6 per cent in the 1960 elections.

In 1964, the PPD's candidate for Governor, Roberto Sánchez Vilella, won with almost 60 per cent of the vote. The PER finished second with nearly 35 per cent, while the struggling PIP – after a record setting 19 per cent in 1952 – came in dead last with barely 2.8 per cent. The PAC received 3.3 per cent and disbanded shortly thereafter.

It would appear that the PPD's electoral dominance was not affected in any way in 1964: it won in *all* of Puerto Rico's municipalities. But the cracks were showing. First, there were substantial internal divisions, mostly generational in nature. And second, the PER had consolidated itself as the main opposition party and would soon be in a position to challenge the PPD's decades-long electoral dominance.

While Muñoz Marín had officially relinquished his leadership over the PPD and did not occupy the Governor's mansion, his presence and influence were still substantial. When Governor Sánchez Vilella attempted to embark on his own route, in opposition to important parts of his party's leadership, a showdown became inevitable. Eventually, Muñoz Marín's faction of the PPD managed to nominate a new candidate for Governor, effectively banishing the sitting Governor from the party. As a result, Governor Sánchez Vilella founded his own party, the People's Party (PP), led mostly by younger generations of now former *populares*.

Prior to the split, and while the divisions within the PPD were still heating up, the PPD government decided to hold a status plebiscite. While nominally held to test whether Puerto Rican society still backed the Commonwealth status established in 1952, the true motivation for the plebiscite was to energise the depressed PPD base, demoralised by the internal party squabbles. The gamble did not pay off.

When the 1967 plebiscite was announced, both the PIP and the PER decided to boycott it. Both parties immediately saw that the PPD was using the plebiscite to address its internal party feud and that it was not a true exercise of self-determination. But an important part of the PER leadership disagreed with their official party stance on the plebiscite. They decided to risk their positions in the PER by publicly breaking with the official leadership and decided to defend the statehood option in the plebiscite. Their gambit paid off.

While the Commonwealth option won easily, the margins were not what the PPD hoped for: 60 per cent for the Commonwealth and a surprising 39 per cent for statehood. It was the highest electoral tally for any pro-statehood force in the island's history. This energised the statehood movement. The rebels who broke with the PER leadership established a new party – the conservative New Progressive Party (PNP) – and aimed to unseat the weakened PPD in the 1968 elections.

This combination of a split within the PPD and a galvanised statehood movement – now coalesced around the PNP – led to a narrow PNP electoral victory in 1968. With 43.6 per cent of the vote, Luis Ferré was sworn in as Governor. But this electoral victory did not automatically signify the collapse of the *populares*. The combined vote of the PPD (40.7 per cent) and Sánchez Vilella's PP (11.7 per cent), meant that the pro-Commonwealth, nominally reformist parties still commanded majority support. In fact, the PPD held on to a one-seat majority in the House of Representatives and a three-seat majority in the Senate. The PIP remained stuck at 3.5 per cent.

The PPD, under a new generation of leaders, regained the governorship in 1972. Rafael Hernández Colón received 50.7 per cent of the vote, while Governor Ferré obtained 43.4 per cent, very similar to his 1968 total. The PP was mostly absorbed by the PPD, and it seemed that the *populares* had reclaimed their majority party status. But the damage had been done and a new two-party system emerged from the ashes. There would be no return to the pre-1968 PPD dominance. This produced a partial dislocation with the 1952 Constitution's political structure, which was not entirely designed for a true two-party system, much less a multi-party system.

This, mostly stable, two-party system operated for more almost 50 years, from 1968 to 2016, with the PNP and the PPD alternating the top positions of government. During that period, the PPD and the PNP controlled the governorship for 24 years each. The PNP became the dominant party, being the only one to break through the 50 per cent mark (1996, 2008), while the PPD victories were much narrower. The combined vote tally for both parties never slipped under 90 per cent and mostly held over 95 per cent.

But this two-party system should not be confused with political stability or the consolidation of a true democratic culture. The two-party system coexisted with militant opposition from, mostly left-wing, forces, mainly articulated through re-energised labour and student movements. This opposition did not match electoral results, which could be explained by the contradiction and misalignment of mostly plebiscitary elections and social mobilisation in the streets.

To add to the democratic shortcomings of the 1952 model was the fact that elections were more and more contested on the status question,[34] instead of socioeconomic policy. As a result, important sectors were voting for a party because of their shared status preference, only to see themselves opposing the actual socioeconomic policies implemented by the resulting governments. For example, many *penepés* (PNP) and *populares* (PPD) would dutifully vote for their respective parties because of their stance on the status question but confront

[34] This is known as a plebiscitary election. See also Malavet (n 2) 49 ('Native-born … political thinking is determined by the relationship between Puerto Rico and the current colonial power advocated by each person or political group'). However, as is discussed in Ch 7, this dynamic seems to be changing.

them when it came to implementing government policy. This dysfunction was the result of Cold-War politics.

Another important factor to consider is the unleashing of political repression, particularly against the labour, student, and independence movements. This repression followed the upsurge in militancy within these sectors, particularly during the substantial economic crises of the 1970s and 1980s. These crises were the result of the combination of worldwide recession with the shortcomings and exhaustion of the colonial economic system described above.

One of the leading organisations at this time was the Pro-Independence Movement (MPI), a non-electoral alliance of diverse independentist currents, including nationalist and socialist tendencies. The MPI made an affirmative effort to take the streets as an avenue for social and political protest and resistance. Founded in 1959 – the same year as the Cuban Revolution – the MPI quickly dislodged the Nationalist Party as the main vehicle for militant pro-independence activism. But, unlike the *nacionalistas*, the MPI made a conscious effort to connect the independence movement with other social struggles, particularly the labour and student movements. Many labour and student leaders were MPI members who sought to combine an anti-imperialist worldview with working class issues.

In 1971, the MPI became the Puerto Rican Socialist Party (PSP), which formally embraced Marxism-Leninism, although it still held on to a mostly nationalist worldview that gave priority to the goal of independence over the struggle for socialism. The PSP was never able to take off electorally, although it constituted a formidable political force.

Because of its activism, the MPI-PSP became a constant target of police repression.[35] This repression included the surveillance of activists and even political violence by rogue sectors of the security forces and of extreme right-wing groups, mostly made up of anticommunist Cuban exiles. In turn, this repression – in combination with the revolutionary fervour that swept Latin America from the 1960s to the 1980s – resulted in the creation of significant underground revolutionary groups that took up arms in their opposition to imperialism and colonialism, and for the establishment of an independent, socialist republic.

The most significant group was known as *Los Macheteros*, in reference to the instrument of choice of Puerto Rican land workers, the machete. Founded in 1976 as the Puerto Rican Workers' Revolutionary Party (PRTP), this group symbolised the combination of Marxist theory with pro-independence goals, and the fusion of the social and national questions. In 1978, the PRTP founded

[35] Although the PSP was the main embodiment of above-ground, left-wing organisations in Puerto Rico during this period, it was by no means the only one. Other notable groups include the Popular Socialist Movement (MSP) and the Revolutionary Socialist Party (PSR) – both of which would merge into the Workers' Socialist Movement (MST) – and the Puerto Rican Socialist League (LSP), among others.

its military wing, the Popular Boricua Army (EPB). The structure and strategy of this new organisation, as well as many of the other existing armed groups of the time,[36] was mostly modelled on the experiences of similar groups in Latin America, particularly the Uruguayan *Tupamarus* and the Argentinian *PRT-ERP*.[37]

The *Macheteros* carried out spectacular operations, including the destruction of 11 US warplanes at the Muñiz Air Base in 1981. This was the biggest loss of airpower for the US since the end of the Vietnam War, and it happened on US soil. The *Macheteros* were dealt a substantial blow in 1985, when most of its political leadership was arrested in a massive FBI operation. Afterwards, the revolutionary movement in Puerto Rico never fully recovered. The PSP was disbanded in 1993, with most of its members joining nationalist organisations that sidelined references to socialism and the class struggle.

Meanwhile, the PIP also experienced a generational change and an ideological transformation. The new party leadership embraced a social-democratic platform with explicit transformative language. Yet, the PIP remained committed to a non-violent strategy. Notwithstanding this new blood, the PIP was never able to fully take off electorally, normally hovering in the 3–5 per cent range and electing a single member to each legislative chamber. However, the PIP became a visible institutional component of the political system. During this period, the party system was clearly based on the status question, with each party defending a different status formula.

During this time, the 1952 Constitution was somewhat pushed into the background. Moreover, the PPD made tremendous efforts to claim the constitutional project solely as their own – albeit with regard to the establishment of the *Estado Libre Asociado* as a status formula – denying any emphasis to its progressive content.

The success of these efforts meant that the other parties, who rejected the Commonwealth status, continued their distancing from the 1952 Constitution which, because of these efforts by the PPD, was more and more seen as synonymous with the *Estado Libre Asociado* instead of with the just society that was promised by its substantive text. An example of this phenomenon was the transformation of 25 July – officially Constitution Day – into a partisan event where the PPD would focus exclusively on the status question.

In the end, 25 July became a divisive date, with each status alternative claiming a different historical significance. For the pro-autonomy *populares*, 25 July

[36] Among these were the Armed Forces of Popular Resistance (FARP), the Organization of Volunteers of the Puerto Rican Revolution (OVRP), and the People's Revolutionary Commandoes (CRP). Other, smaller groups, also operated during the 1970s and 1980s. Most of these groups, including the *Macheteros*, grew from the first wave of revolutionary organisations that emerged during the 1960s, like the Armed Revolutionary Independentist Movement (MIRA) and the Armed Commandos for Liberation (CAL).

[37] *Partido Revolucionario de los Trabajadores-Ejército Revolucionario del Pueblo*. These organisations were active in Argentina during the 1960s and 1970s.

meant the establishment of the Commonwealth in 1952. For the pro-annexation *penepés*, 25 July referred to 1898, when the US flag first flew over Puerto Rican soil. For the *independentistas*, the significance of 25 July was threefold: the violation of Puerto Rican sovereignty during the 1898 invasion; the farce and fraud of the Commonwealth established in 1952; and the murder of two pro-independence supporters during a police ambush in 1978. As a result, the substantive constitutional project adopted in 1952 became a mere asterisk.

7

Recent Developments Regarding the Puerto Rican Constitutional Project

I. COLONIALISM IN THE TWENTY-FIRST CENTURY

A. Colonialism's Constitutional Comeback

FOR YEARS, THE debate about the state of Puerto Rico's current colonial relationship with the US was mostly social, local, and personal – even folkloric – in nature, from family dinner-table discussions to heated debates in neighbourhood bars. It became a national sport with no definitive answers or resolution. The point was to have the conversation and establish distinctions and identities. A conclusive solution seemed inherently elusive and almost irrelevant.

This was facilitated by a persistent institutional silence from the three branches of federal government regarding the political and legal future of the island; there were only weak whispers from low-level officials or inconsequential processes. Reading tea leaves became a political pastime and livelihood. It was a period of recycled arguments and no new developments.

But since 2015, there has been a sudden resurgence of federal interest in Puerto Rico. Two branches stand out: Congress and the US Supreme Court. At first, they spoke separately. Lately, their communications have been more coordinated. This has substantially altered the paradigm under which the status question is currently discussed in both countries.

A quartet of the cases decided by the Supreme Court between 2016 and 2020, which can only be described as the *New Insular Cases*, broke the federal silence. Congress was not far behind, not to mention the resurgence of the issue of Puerto Rican statehood as a political talking point and possible partisan move on behalf of the US Democratic Party.

As we are about to see, this massive earthquake actually revealed that not much had changed since 1898. It is a contradiction of historic proportions: what had changed was that now we had absolute assurance that, in fact, things had stayed the same all this time. The Supreme Court declared it. Not so long after, Congress would act upon it with terrible consequences with regard to the prospect of Puerto Rican self-rule and the social fabric of the country.

First came *Puerto Rico v Sanchez Valle* in 2016.[1] That case dealt with whether the US Constitution's Fifth Amendment double-jeopardy clause prohibited Puerto Rican prosecutors from charging an individual after they had already been tried and convicted in federal court for the same conduct – in particular, whether the dual sovereignty doctrine, which allows an individual state and the federal government to separately prosecute an individual for the same unlawful conduct, applied to the Puerto Rico, given its specific relationship with the US.

Current US Supreme Court doctrine establishes that, since the federal government and individual US states are separate sovereigns, when each of them charges the same individual because of the same conduct, they are trying them for separate offences against different sovereigns. Therefore, in order to determine whether the dual sovereign doctrine applies, the charging jurisdiction must possess a separate sovereignty from the federal government.

In the case of US states, this separate sovereignty traces back to the founding of the US. Since the individual states were already sovereign when they created and joined the federal Union, their claim to sovereignty is not dependent on the existence of the US. States that were admitted after the creation of the Union share the same legal characteristic, albeit by a form of retroactive legal fiction. The same logic applies to Indian tribes: these are political units that pre-exist the US. As such, the source of their sovereignty is separate and independent from that of the federal government.

What about Puerto Rico? Is Puerto Rico's power to prosecute grounded on the existence of a separate sovereignty, distinct from the US? The federal Supreme Court answered no, quite forcefully. While the Opinion appeared to go out of its way to praise Puerto Rico's broad powers of self-government – more on that below, since Congress would soon after reverse most of it – the Court reminded us that the dual sovereignty question rested on a single historical fact: where did Puerto Rico's sovereign power to prosecute actually come from? If the answer was the US, then the doctrine would not apply, and double jeopardy would impede any additional prosecution. If the answer was the Puerto Rican People, then the doctrine would apply, and the prosecution could proceed.

Those who think that the 1952 Constitution was an exercise of sovereign, popular self-government believe that Congress relinquished its plenary powers over Puerto Rico in 1951 through Public Act 600 and with its eventual acceptance of the Puerto Rican Constitution through Public Law 447 in 1952. They focus on the language 'in the nature of a compact' that is constantly used in these congressional acts. If the 1952 Constitution was really in the nature of a compact, the argument goes, then Puerto Rico and the US became equal partners. As such, Puerto Rico should no longer be characterised as a subordinate territory of the US subject to Congress's plenary powers under the Territorial Clause of the US Constitution. The result would be that the 1952 process generated a separate sovereign entity that was wholly distinct from the US proper.

[1] *Puerto Rico v Sanchez Valle* 136 S Ct 1863 (2016).

Since the US Supreme Court has held that the Treaty of Paris legally transferred sovereignty over Puerto Rico to the US, any possible source of Puerto Rican sovereignty must necessarily be found after 1898. In that sense, the Court has completely ignored or rejected any argument based on the possibility that, before the Treaty of Paris was adopted, Spain had relinquished its sovereignty over Puerto Rico as both a legal and practical matter by way of the Autonomy Charter of 1897. The fact that sovereignty was legally transferred in 1898 was taken as a given.

Thus, the crucial question was: did Congress relinquish its plenary powers at any time after 1898. Specifically, did it do so during the 1951–52 constitutional process, as it did with the Philippines through the Philippines Independence Act of 1934, thus bestowing Puerto Rico with a separate source of sovereignty?

The Supreme Court held in *Sanchez Valle* that Congress did not, as a matter of fact, relinquish its power over the island in 1952, or at any other later date. On the contrary, the Court concluded that Congress had merely *delegated* some of its power, so that Puerto Rico could have enhanced home rule through locally elected institutions by way of a local constitution.

The Court also seemed to accept the US Solicitor General's position that the language regarding 'in the nature of a compact' merely indicated that the Puerto Rican People had accepted Congress' offer to write a territorial constitution; nothing more. That language did not change the nature of the relationship, nor did it amount to a recognition that the 1952 Constitution constituted a formal agreement among equals. And since Puerto Rico's prosecutorial powers were the result of congressional delegation, meaning that both federal and local prosecutions shared the same ultimate source of sovereignty, the double-jeopardy clause prohibited parallel criminal proceedings.

In that sense, *Sanchez Valle* settled a mostly historical question: whether the 1952 process constituted a paradigm shift as to the nature of the territorial relationship between Puerto Rico and the US. Particularly, did it constitute a point of no return with regard to Puerto Rican sovereignty? The answer was that it did not.

As a result, Puerto Rico was still subject to Congress's plenary powers under the Territorial Clause. In essence, all of Puerto Rico's self-government powers were the product of congressional delegation and not the exercise of sovereignty or true constituent power. According to the Supreme Court, Congress has never relinquished its sovereign power over Puerto Rico. That was true in 1898, 1952 and 2016 when the case was decided. It is still true today.

One of the main casualties of the *Sanchez Valle* decision was the theory of the compact. Not surprisingly, those who favour the current Commonwealth status are the main proponents of this approach. Before *Sanchez Valle*, it was, at least, a conceptually feasible argument.[2] Former PPD Governor Rafael

[2] See, eg, JA Otaño, 'Puerto Rico Pandemonium: The Commonwealth Constitution and the Compact-Colony Conundrum' (2004) 27 *Fordham International Law Journal* 1806, 1840–41;

Hernández Colón, himself a respected jurist, tried to hold on to the compact theory as long as possible. He pointed to language in the Opinion that seemed to state that, regardless of its origin, Puerto Rico still possessed considerable power over its internal affairs: 'Given the assertions by the US Supreme Court, we must conclude that Puerto Rico, as to its internal affairs, ceased to be a territory subject to the plenary powers of Congress'.[3]

Sanchez Valle, however, did not answer *how much* power had been effectively delegated. In fact, the majority Opinion in that case – penned by Associate Justice Elena Kagan – made several references to Puerto Rico's unique relationship with the US and its ability to operate as a fully autonomous political unit. But the walls of that question would soon start to close in. *Sanchez Valle's* praise of Puerto Rico's broad autonomy would quickly become hollow; first by a follow-up Supreme Court case and then by an Act of Congress. This would finally put the compact theory to rest for good.

During the same Term in which *Sanchez Valle* was decided, the Supreme Court of the US announced a second decision regarding Puerto Rico and its autonomy: *Puerto Rico v Franklin-California Tax Free Trust*.[4] While receiving less publicity than *Sanchez Valle*, probably because the latter focused directly on a matter of historical significance and decades-old partisan debate on the island, this second decision would start a recent and ongoing judicial process of reaffirming Puerto Rico's subordinate territorial status, which would, in turn, clear the way for the most direct instance of congressional intervention in Puerto Rican self-government since 1952.

As we have seen, Puerto Rico's economy has also suffered from the ills of colonialism. As explained above, US capital has completely dominated the island's economy since the dawning of the twentieth century. For decades, US corporations benefited from triple tax-exemption, including federal, state, and local taxes. Successive Puerto Rican governments have banked on an economic model of tax exemption for American capital in exchange for job creation.

Given the sheer domination of tax-exempt US entities, a significant part of the wealth generated in the island has fallen victim to massive capital flight. The wages that accompany job creation have not covered the difference. As a result, Puerto Rico's public debt has exploded, particularly during the last 30 years. Interest payments continued to eat away at the island's budget in a type of perverted and tragic Ponzi scheme. Eventually, Puerto Rico stood on the edge of bankruptcy.

CI Keitner and M Reisman, 'Free Asociation: The United States Experience' (2003) 39 *Texas International Law Journal* 1, 22 (stating that the 1952 process constituted 'a significant change in the Puerto Rico-United States relationship … despite the curious fact that many members of Congress seemed to believe that their legislative exercise did not alter the basic relationship').

[3] R Hernández Colón, 'The Evolution of Democratic Governance under the Territorial Clause of the US Constitution' (2017) 50 *Suffolk University Law Review* 587, 598.

[4] *Puerto Rico v Franklin-California Tax Free Trust* 136 S Ct 1938 (2016).

The problem was that Puerto Rico had been excluded from the protections of the federal Bankruptcy Code. But an easy solution appeared to present itself: the adoption of a local statute that allowed for public corporations and other state entities to file for bankruptcy. Several creditors objected, arguing that, while Puerto Rico was indeed excluded from the protections of the Bankruptcy Code, it was still subject to its preemption provision. As such, it appeared that Puerto Rico was stuck in limbo: it could not benefit from the protections of federal bankruptcy but was prohibited from adopting a local bankruptcy scheme on its own.

The Supreme Court of the US confirmed this limbo state. Through a considerably straightforward textualist lens, the majority Opinion – penned by Associate Justice Clarence Thomas – held that Congress had, indeed, excluded Puerto Rico from the protections of the federal Bankruptcy Code, but had still included it for purposes of preemption. Therefore, Puerto Rico's local bankruptcy statute was void.

What is most striking about the Opinion in *Franklin-California* is what it did not say. As a matter of statutory interpretation, the Court's reasoning was on solid ground. All sources confirmed that Congress had, in fact, intended this twisted outcome. But could Congress do that? Could Congress treat Puerto Rico in such a way that it could deny it the protections of the Bankruptcy Code while, at the same time, prohibit the adoption of a local statute? As noted, the Court did not address this issue. It just went without saying. Apparently, constitutionalised colonialism need not explain itself: it is what it is.

Unable to benefit from the protections of federal bankruptcy proceedings or to establish a local legal regime for that purpose, Puerto Rico was in imminent danger of defaulting on its debts without any legal safety net. This could trigger a dangerous political situation with an accompanying humanitarian crisis because of a breakdown of essential government services. Several powerful vulture funds in the US, which had bought much of Puerto Rico's public debt for cents on the dollar, decided to aggressively defend their economic interests that could be threatened by a hard Puerto Rican default.

In *Franklin-California*, the Supreme Court of the US gave a clear message: if Puerto Rico was going to be able to file for bankruptcy, Congress needed to act. And act it did, partially thanks to the efforts made by the vulture funds. Shortly after the decision, Congress passed the now infamous PROMESA statute.[5]

As relevant here, the Act allowed Puerto Rico and its dependencies to avail themselves of a special bankruptcy regime, specifically designed for the island. But there was a catch: Congress created a new body, called the Fiscal Oversight and Management Board, which would exercise substantial powers over Puerto Rico's fiscal and budgetary matters. Such was the scope of its power, that this

[5] Puerto Rico Oversight, Management, and Economic Stability Act (PROMESA), Public Law No 114-187 (2016).

unelected Board could overrule the decisions of the elected Legislature, as well as the popularly elected Governor.

The authority and nature of the Board has reignited the debate regarding colonialism. For many, the colonial nature of the Puerto Rico-US relationship had been more academic than real; akin to asking how many angels could dance on the head of a pin. But the creation of the Board and its unflinching use of its broad powers has hit home: cuts to pensions and education spending, direct interference in the legislative process, and so on. Colonialism has become clearly palpable by the general population both in material and political terms.

Evidently, the appointment of a Board of this type to oversee the entire fiscal and budgetary landscape of a political unit could not be imposed on a federated state of the Union nor an independent nation. But Puerto Rico's territorial status allowed Congress to implement its design. An outstanding issue remained: what was the nature of the Fiscal Oversight and Management Board? In other words, did it exercise the power of the US or was it merely a territorial entity exercising local powers? Had Congress created a federal overseer or had it directly and unilaterally amended the 1952 Constitution to include a new body at the top of the governmental hierarchy?

The answers to these questions would be crucial in determining the constitutional validity of the Board's composition. According to PROMESA, the members of the Board would be selected through an intricate system that included the President, as well as the leadership of both houses of Congress. Put plainly: the Board was not selected through presidential appointment and senatorial confirmation.

This led to an Appointments Clause challenge in the federal courts. The plaintiffs claimed that the members of the Board should be considered federal officers that must be appointed by the President and confirmed by the Senate, as must happen with any other principal officer of the US. The Board answered that it was a territorial body limited to local affairs, thus it was outside the reach of the Appointments Clause.

The Supreme Court of the US once again agreed to resolve a dispute related to the territorial nature of Puerto Rico. In *FOMB v Aurelius Investment, LLC*,[6] the critical issue was whether the nature of the powers exercised by the Board was federal or local. If it was the former, the Appointments Clause would apply, and the statutory scheme would be unconstitutional. If it was the latter, then it would be characterised as a valid exercise of Congress's general powers over the territories and not subject to the requirements of the Appointments Clause.

The Court held, in a unanimous decision, that the Board exercised power over local matters, and thus its members could not be characterised as federal officers. Among the main factors used by the Court in its decision was the fact

[6] *FOMB v Aurelius Investment, LLC* 140 S Ct 1649 (2020).

that PROMESA had explicitly created the Board as a body within the Puerto Rican government. In other words, the Board was not a separate entity but instead a new addition to the territorial governmental structure.

That would mean that Congress had exercised its powers under the Territorial Clause to effectively *modify* the Puerto Rican constitutional system by including an entity that does not exist under the 1952 Constitution or the statutes adopted under its authority. This was the functional equivalent of Congress amending the 1952 Constitution to alter the structure of the government of Puerto Rico.

This was extraordinary, as it represented the first time since 1917 since Congress had directly intervened in the composition of the Puerto Rican government though an express structural alteration. While in 1952 Congress had insisted that the Puerto Rican Constitutional Convention had to adopt a republican system of government – among other generalities – Congress had not played the direct role of architect as to the actual composition and structure of the Puerto Rican government. The situation in the *Aurelius* case was more reminiscent of the organic acts of the early twentieth century.

This constituted a culmination of the delegation rationale adopted in *Sanchez Valle*: the 1952 Constitution was the result of a delegation of Congress's powers under the Territorial Clause. It seemed that Congress had given in 1952, but Congress had taken away in 2016. The apparent gradual movement towards greater autonomy and democratic self-government that had started in 1900 and had been lauded by the Supreme Court in *Sanchez Valle* had been severely reversed by the stroke of a congressional pen.

In a separate opinion concurring in the judgment, Associate Justice Sonia Sotomayor – the first and still only member of the Supreme Court of Hispanic, and in her case Puerto Rican, descent – questioned many of the implications of the Court's decision, particularly with regard to the seemingly limitless leeway that Congress has over Puerto Rico under the Territorial Clause. In particular, she questioned the undeniable democratic deficits that characterise the Fiscal Control Board created by the PROMESA statute. Specifically, that a Board with so many broad powers could operate without real participation by Puerto Rican elected officials. In other words, she expressed great concern with the validity of a governance model where Puerto Ricans are not in charge of making the decisions that affect their lives but are instead at the mercy of an appointed junta.

The coup de grâce came in 2022 in a stunningly brief opinion issued by the US Supreme Court in *United States v Vaello Madero*.[7] The controversy in that case was very particular to the Puerto Rican situation: a New York resident, who was the recipient of Supplemental Social Security Income (SSI), moved to Puerto Rico. Eventually, the US government agency in charge of this programme became aware of the move. The problem was that residents of Puerto Rico are

[7] *United States v Vaello Madero* No 20-303.

only entitled to a fraction of the SSI that is available for residents of the 50 states. The US government brought suit to recover the money that was paid in excess.

As noted above, the US Supreme Court had previously ruled that Congress was able to treat Puerto Rico differently from the 50 states with regard to federal programs, as long as there was a rational basis for doing so. In this case, the defendant argued that such rational basis was missing. The federal District and Circuit courts agreed with him.

The Supreme Court, in a six-page majority opinion penned by Associate Justice Brett Kavanaugh, reversed the decision of the lower courts. For the Court, the issue was relatively simple. After reaffirming the rational basis scrutiny that applies to congressional enactments that treat Puerto Rico differently – mostly as inferior – the majority concluded that, as most Puerto Rican residents are exempted from federal income taxes, that differential tax scheme justified Congress's move to deny Puerto Ricans the full benefits of the SSI programme. The Court was not persuaded by the fact that SSI recipients, almost by definition, do not earn enough to pay federal income taxes, regardless of Puerto Rico's tax status.

As with the previous cases discussed so far, the majority opinion seemed to have no moral quarrel with the territorial condition or its real-world effects. Also in line with the previous decisions, the Supreme Court again made no mention of the distinction between incorporated and unincorporated territories, as established by the *Insular Cases*. It was sufficient to characterise Puerto Rico as a US Territory in order to resolve the case before it.

Only two Justices expressed reservations with this state of affairs. First, Associate Justice Neil Gorsuch made surprisingly strong statements condemning the *Insular Cases*, their overtly racist language, and their legally unsupportable conclusions. He rejected the distinction between incorporated and unincorporated territories. But he did not really reveal which definition would prevail were the Territorial Clause to be reunified and the *Insular Cases* reversed. And because no one had asked the Court to review those cases – unlike what happened in the *Aurelius* decision – Gorsuch concurred with the majority decision.

The lone dissenter, again, was Associate Justice Sotomayor. Her dissent sharply criticised the ease with which the majority concluded that the exclusion of up to 300,000 Puerto Rican residents from the full breadth of SSI benefits had any rational basis. But, for the fourth time in a row, colonialism won and Puerto Rico lost. With the *Vaello* decision, a total of four Justices have now penned majority opinions regarding Puerto Rico, and all have come to a very similar conclusion: colonialism is alive and well in US constitutional law.

The end result of this recent line of cases is that Puerto Rico remains an unincorporated territory of the US, subject to the plenary powers of the federal Congress.[8] This means that the 1952 constitutional process did not change the

[8] More explicitly, it remains 'a colony of the United States': PA Malavet, *America's Colony: The Political and Cultural Conflict Between the United States and Puerto Rico* (New York University Press, 2007) 2.

nature of Puerto Rico's status or its relationship with the US. When we combine the legal characteristics of an unincorporated territory with the mostly uncontested fact that Puerto Rico has all the traits of a nation – including a distinct common history, language, traditions, and culture – there can be only one conclusion: Puerto Rico remains a colonial possession of the US.[9]

But Puerto Rico, like the US Virgin Islands and some of the other unincorporated territories of the US, is very different from the territories that existed prior to 1898. As we saw, the territorial condition was premised, in part, on the political disorganisation of the territory. That is why Congress is able to exercise general legislative powers and why one of the requirements for admission to the Union was the adoption of a territorial – soon to be state – constitution.

Puerto Rico has been self-organised politically since 1952; it is not a formless political entity. Puerto Rico has a functioning state government. In that sense, it can be argued that it is an organised political entity – a state in the ordinary use of the word – that has not been incorporated or admitted as a *state of the Union*, but a state nonetheless. This would further strengthen the notion that Puerto Rico's situation cannot be simply addressed by reference to nineteenth century territories.

One final issue warrants attention. For most of the twentieth century, population movement between Puerto Rico and the US was mostly a one-direction phenomenon: in an attempt to escape stagnant economic conditions, thousands of Puerto Ricans migrated to the US. Even before hurricane María accelerated this population flight, it was noted that 'more than 2.7 million Puerto Ricans live on the United States mainland'.[10] Yet, for many decades, '[o]ther US citizens have not moved to Puerto Rico in substantial numbers'.[11] This has changed recently.

The ongoing economic crisis in Puerto Rico led successive local governments to adopt aggressive measures to incentivise foreign capital investment. In 2012, the Legislative Assembly passed a series of statutes, colloquially known as Acts 20 and 22, that gave maximum tax treatment to US-based investors to relocate to the island. This generated a relatively significant influx of, mostly wealthy, non-Hispanics coming in from the mainland.

This influx has had important consequences that have exacerbated the colonial problem. First, it has created a notable national and class divide. There is

[9] Prior to the US Supreme Court cases issued between 2016 and 2020, there was a legitimate debate regarding whether Puerto Rico's constitutional exercise in 1952 was sufficient to overcome its colonial situation. See, eg, J Blocher and M Gulati, 'Puerto Rico and the Right of Accession' (2018) 43 *Yale Journal of International Law* 229, 253 (referring to Puerto Rico as 'a former colony,' in reference to its transition 'from colonial status to self-governance status' in 1952). But after the recent Supreme Court opinions on the subject, it is very difficult to argue that colonialism in Puerto Rico has been extinguished.

[10] Malavet (n 8) 1. The numbers are substantially greater today.

[11] ibid.

a sharp contrast between local, mostly working class Puerto Ricans, and the newly minted wealthy American transplants. This contrast manifests in terms of race, class, and culture. Second, and as a result, there has been a massive acquisition of prime real estate on the island by these wealthy Americans, which has both artificially driven up residential market prices – which has mostly affected working class Puerto Ricans – and deprived locals of access to, for example, the coast and beaches, which are a staple of Puerto Rican life. Resentment has followed and Acts 20 and 22 remain controversial.

B. Solving the Territorial Problem

Even while the US Supreme Court has consistently ruled in recent times that colonialism, under the guise of permanent territorial status, is constitutionally permissible as a matter of US domestic law, it is still politically unsustainable, particularly for most Puerto Ricans. Even defenders of the current Commonwealth status, which the federal Supreme Court has now held is still territorial in nature, argue for a break from colonialism. This flies in the face of what had been previously thought to be a nonpermanent arrangement: 'It is unconstitutional for the United States to remain a colonial power for more than one hundred years'.[12] Apparently, it is not.[13]

This situation brings up two issues: first, what are the viable substantive alternatives in terms of Puerto Rico's relationship with the US? and second, what are the procedural options for choosing between those alternatives? A final question pertains to the current political climate in Puerto Rico and the US: what alternatives are currently politically viable?

i. Substantive Alternatives

One option is the admission of Puerto Rico as a US State. As a matter of pure US domestic law, this would require only an Act of Congress. The power to admit new states is vested exclusively in the federal legislature.[14] As such, the individual states need not be consulted; nor even the Puerto Rican People themselves.

[12] Malavet (n 8) 135.

[13] This may be why Malavet believes that '[w]hile Puerto Ricans talk to one another about the future status of their island, from the perspective of the colonial power the only available alternative to absolute colonial rule has always been the extremely unclear and democratically unsatisfying 'middle-ground' status imposed by the Charter of Autonomy and the current *estado libre asociado* (commonwealth'): Malavet (n 8) 50.

[14] The first clause of Art IV, s 3 reads: 'New States may be admitted by the Congress into this Union'. It is worth mentioning that the Territorial Clause also resides in s 3 of Art IV, strengthening the view that the territorial condition was, historically at least, meant to simply constitute a temporary and transitional condition that eventually culminated in statehood. The *Insular Cases* have completely destroyed that structural connection.

While there could be *international law* problems with the unilateral annexation of a colonised territory without the voluntary and free consent of a majority of its inhabitants, there is no *domestic law* impediment that would stop Congress from unilaterally admitting Puerto Rico as a federated state of the Union.[15]

On the other hand, unilateral annexation is contrary to the principle of self-determination: 'International law no longer gives countries unfettered authority to alter their borders – or even to cede territory voluntarily to another nation'.[16] International law also does not allow for unilateral annexation without the consent of the annexed territory or community.

But that Congress has not, during the past 120 years, exercised its considerable power under its domestic law – regardless of the limitations imposed by international law – is evidence that the main obstacle to Puerto Rico's admission as a state is *political* in nature. The politics of this issue has many dimensions, including the US's standing in the world.

First, the US is not oblivious to the contentious nature of statehood in Puerto Rico and, by extension, to the significant Puerto Rican population that currently resides in the continental US. This has the potential for violent backlash, were the US to admit Puerto Rico without its consent. In fact, Puerto Rico has a significant history of violent resistance to the US imperialist presence, including attempts to achieve independence through armed struggle. This history is not lost on US leaders. If done incorrectly, Puerto Rico could easily become the Northern Ireland of the US.[17]

Armed opposition to the US presence in Puerto Rico dates from its very beginning. The most significant periods of armed struggle were the 1930s – under the leadership of the Nationalist Party – and the 1970s – when many underground organisations coincided with a reenergised independence movement that had adopted a strong revolutionary strategy and a distinct anti-imperialist and socialist outlook.

Second, there is strong domestic resistance in the US to the idea of Puerto Rican statehood. The reasons range from racism to political calculation with regard to the balance of power in Congress and the Presidency. The prospect of a poor, brown, Spanish-speaking island becoming a state of the Union generates

[15] I agree with commentators like Pedro Malavet that public international law will have very little practical significance with regard to the Puerto Rican question, since it 'is totally powerless to enforce any rule against the United States, especially in relation to Puerto Rico's status': Malavet (n 8) 132.

[16] Blocher and Gulati (n 9) 253.

[17] According to Christina Duffy Ponsa-Kraus, an advocate of Puerto Rico being admitted as a state of the Union, 'resistance to statehood [in Puerto Rico] does reflect a concern that statehood would threaten Puerto Rico's culture and, in particular, its language, but any such threat would not come from the Constitution': CD Ponsa-Kraus, 'The "Insular Cases" Run Amok: Against Constitutional Exceptionalism in the Territories' (2022) *Yale Law Journal* 2449 fn 17. Resistance to statehood, however, is not solely based on nationalist considerations, although national identity has been a viable argument against it.

great opposition from mostly conservative and right-wing forces. On the Left, there is a split verdict. Some currents believe that statehood would be beneficial to Puerto Rico's poor and working classes, since it would give Puerto Ricans equal status with regard to entitlement programs and political representation. This is a dominant view within some liberal quarters in the US Democratic Party and has the characteristics of liberal imperialism.

Another view that has historically been defended by the American Left is the recognition of Puerto Rican nationhood and its absolute right to unilateral self-determination, including its decolonisation and independence. This view is more aligned with socialist groups and currents in the US.

Under current international law, independence is an inalienable right that belongs to every people, particularly those who make up a distinct national community that has been subjugated by a foreign power. Few would deny that Puerto Rico fits this profile. As a result, independence is a permanently available option with regard to the status question. Moreover, there seems to be nothing in the *Insular Cases* or current US domestic law which would impede Puerto Rican independence, as happened with the Philippines in 1946.[18] Some, on the other hand, question the compatibility of US domestic law and international law with regard to this subject.[19]

This raises two similar points. First, whether the US can unilaterally relinquish its sovereignty over Puerto Rico and impose independence, regardless of the opinion of the Puerto Rican People.[20] Second, whether Puerto Rico can unilaterally declare independence without US authorisation.

A Puerto Rican declaration of independence should be seen as the result of an internationally recognised exercise of self-determination in the context of colonial possessions. It should not be seen as an unlawful secession, even if done unilaterally. As Milena Sterio explains, while '[i]international law is mostly neutral on the issue of secession',[21] it 'positively allows' for independence if it is exercised by 'colonial peoples,' as opposed to 'a non-colonial minority group'.[22]

[18] Christina Duffy Burnett suggests that the *Insular Cases* can be seen as 'setting forth nothing less than a constitutional theory of secession (albeit of a particular kind)': C Duffy Burnett, 'Untied States: American Expansion and Territorial Deannexation' (2005) 72 *University of Chicago Law Review* 797, 802. Of course, were Puerto Rico to be admitted as a state, it would become a permanent component of the federal Union, making it practically impossible for Puerto Rico to entertain independence in the future. This has been a consistent argument of pro-Commonwealth and pro-independence forces against annexation, on the grounds that it is irreversible. This makes many Puerto Ricans pause before deciding to take that plunge.

[19] See, eg G Lawson and RD Sloane, 'The Constitutionality of Decolonization by Associated Statehood: Puerto Rico's Legal Status Recognized' (2009) 50 *Boston College Law Review* 1123, 1125 (suggesting that the US Constitution 'may constrain the US ability to decolonize Puerto Rico as the People of Puerto Rico choose in accordance with the requirements of international law').

[20] See Ponsa-Kraus (n 17) 2453, in reference to the possibility that the US could de-annex an unincorporated territory. That raises the question, could Congress expel a US state without its consent?

[21] M Sterio, 'Self-Determination and Secession under International Law: The New Framework' (2015) 21 *ILSA Journal of International and Comparative Law* 293, 299.

[22] ibid 293.

In other words, 'nearly everybody agrees that former colonies are the paradigm example' of self-determination under international law.[23]

Another interesting question posed by the Puerto Rican situation is whether the right to independence for colonised nations is conceptually different from secession, or whether it is considered a lawful manifestation of it. Glen Anderson states the question explicitly: 'Is [d]ecolonization [s]ecession?'[24] In any event, the result is the same. Once we conclude that a particular community satisfies UN General Assembly Resolution 1541's definition regarding colonial possessions,[25] the right to independence follows as a legitimate exercise of self-determination.

Of course, there are multiple arrangements that can accompany the independence option. These range from an outright clean break to a gradual process that can take years or even decades. Among the issues that would mostly likely need to be addressed in any independence process are: (1) citizenship; (2) travel and freedom of movement in the US; (3) economic transition, reparation, or assistance; (4) participation in federal programs and application of federal law; (5) currency; (6) US military and law enforcement presence; (7) land ownership transfers; (8) bilateral diplomatic relations; and (9) trade policy. If one takes into consideration the wide variety of variables and possible scenarios, independence ceases to be a single proposition. There are multiple versions of independence, which will depend on geopolitical, economic, and domestic politics both in the US and Puerto Rico, as well as the political and social forces that lead any eventual negotiations.

But after more than 120 years of US presence and control in Puerto Rico, the island has neither been admitted as a State nor has it achieved independence. There is a significant – although waning – sector of Puerto Rican society that opposes both annexation and formal independence. Pro-autonomy movements (*autonomismo*) have been a constant in Puerto Rico since Spanish rule. It could be argued that this current was the dominant view during the greater part of the twentieth century.

Evidently, *autonimismo*, which favours continued relations with the US without becoming either a state or an independent republic, has had a constant and problematic companion: colonialism. As a result, the pro-autonomy movement has been in a constant defensive move against attacks for being apologists for colonialism, to the point that there seems to be very little daylight between the two.

Prior to 1952, there was little doubt that Puerto Rico was a territory of the US subject to Congress's plenary powers. This was the legal equivalent

[23] Blocher and Gulati (n 9) 252. See also Lawson and Sloane (n 19) 1134.

[24] G Anderson, 'Secession in International Law and Relations: What are we Talking About?' (2013) 35 *Loyola Los Angeles International and Comparative Law Review* 343, 373. Sometimes Puerto Rican independence is characterised as permissible secession. See, eg, J Smith, 'Commonwealth Status: A Good Deal for Puerto Rico?' (2007) 10 *Harvard Latino Law Review* 263, 275.

[25] Anderson (n 24) 374.

of a colonial relationship. Even the *autonomistas* of the time criticised this arrangement. Because of a combination of historical, political, and economic considerations, Puerto Rico's *autonomista* movement was unwilling to embrace independence. As such, they attempted to plot a difficult – some would say impossible – middle route: neither a colony nor an independent republic.

The Commonwealth status established in 1952 was the culmination of these attempts. *Autonomistas* heralded the political arrangement adopted in 1952 as a successful process of decolonisation that allowed Puerto Rico to maintain an advantageous relationship with the US with regard to matters such as defence, fiscal, monetary, trade, and economic policy.

As discussed above, that mirage has recently come crashing down. The US Supreme Court's characterisation that the Commonwealth status did not conceptually alter the nature of the relationship between the two countries had the effect of taking the pro-autonomy movement back to square one. As a result, a substantial number of *autonomistas* have attempted to design a new arrangement that allows Puerto Rico to have a continued relationship with the US, but one which falls outside the scope of the Territorial Clause. This includes calls for the exercise of so-called 'creative statesmanship' to identify an arrangement that is both constitutionally sound from the perspective of US domestic law and consistent with international law.[26] This would require probing 'the constitutional boundaries on the rage of permissible forms of governance available to Puerto Rico while still territorially affiliated with the United States'.[27]

So far, those attempts have not been fruitful. All the while, the colonial condition has reverted to a more egregious stage, with the unelected Fiscal Control Board established through the PROMESA statute asserting a dominant role regarding Puerto Rican law and policy. In the end, the pro-autonomy movement seems to be left with only two options: openly embrace the territorial condition with its naked colonialism; or attempt to come up with an acceptable association that would most likely require some sort of independence that regulates Puerto Rico's relation with the US through treaty mechanisms.

ii. Procedural Options

The fact that most status options are simultaneously extremely fluid and almost always mutually exclusive, has created a decades long impasse with regard to this issue. The result of this ideological impasse has been that Puerto Rico's political situation has not changed much in decades. Another problem that further complicates this quagmire is the fact that most status options – including the different manners in which independence can materialise – require the participation and ultimate agreement of the federal government.

[26] Hernández Colón (n 3) 603.
[27] S Issacharoff et al, 'What is Puerto Rico?' (2019) 94 *Indiana Law Journal* 1, 5.

The resistance or indifference of the federal government to intervening or participating in any serious discussion regarding Puerto Rico's political situation can be indicative of many things and also creates contradictory results. On the one hand, I would argue that the US should abstain from interfering with Puerto Rico's exercise of its right to self-determination. To do otherwise could be interpreted as undue meddling from the metropolitan power. On the other hand, the US's lack of engagement with the political process in Puerto Rico adds uncertainty regarding the viability of the different status options. As a result, the political discussion becomes somewhat fanciful, which each status current boasting a maximalist version of their preferred option, regardless of its practical viability or whether the US government would be willing to accept it.

This combination of impasse and uncertainty regarding the federal government's involvement in the process is further complicated by a lack of agreement regarding how to solve the substantive questions and to engage the US in a constructive decolonisation process. Yet, there have been serious attempts by the different currents to, at least, engage one another regarding the procedural question.

To further complicate things, there are ideological differences regarding the substantive requirements that should characterise the decolonisation process itself. The pro-independence sector insists that it is primarily a matter of international law. Other sectors, mostly within the statehood movement, believe it is basically an issue of US domestic law and politics.

Not only does this increase the ideological and conceptual distance between the currents, it is also a source of further impasse, as there can be unsolvable contradictions between international law and US domestic law. To further complicate the matter, we must also analyse whether Puerto Rico has already exercised its right to self-determination.[28] Prior to the US Supreme Court's decisions in the cases discussed above, some authors thought that the 1952 constitutional process was, in fact, a legitimate exercise of this right which, in turn, extinguished Puerto Rico's colonial status.[29]

What are the main requirements of international law regarding Puerto Rican decolonisation? As examined in Chapter 6, the 1952 Constitution allowed the US to remove Puerto Rico from the UN list of territories that had not achieved sufficient self-government. But, during the 1960s, the Puerto Rican question was introduced once again in the UN's agenda, including its Decolonization

[28] To complicate things even further, there is the question of how many times may this right be exercised before the issue is considered settled.

[29] See, eg, Lawson and Sloane (n 19) 1124: 'Postwar decolonization norms and the principle of self-determination of peoples require that Puerto Ricans enjoy the right to "external" self-determination – that is, the right to choose political independence, integration with an existing state, or free association in a referendum expressing the popular will – and, *in theory, Puerto Ricans exercised this right under international law in 1951 by choosing a particular arrangement of free association with the United States*' (emphasis added).

Committee. This could be indicative of the relevance of international law to Puerto Rico's colonial problem.

Some of the theoretical requirements of international law regarding decolonisation procedures are practically difficult, if not impossible. For example, for a true decolonisation exercise to be legitimate, the intervening metropolitan power must recall its military presence from the colonised territory. This is necessary to avoid any question regarding possible coercion or manipulation. The 1952 process did not include UN supervision, gave the Legislature of the metropolitan power final authority over the constitutional text, and required congressional assent for any future change in the relationship.[30] This seems to fail the basic requirements of international law for a lawful exercise of self-determination.

As discussed, the 1952 process – contrary to the PPD's wishes – did not give a final resolution to Puerto Rico's colonial problem. Both the pro-independence and pro-annexation movements have stepped up their criticism and attacks on the Commonwealth model.

In Chapter 6 we discussed the circumstances of the 1967 plebiscite. Since then, plebiscites have been the primary tool used to address the status question, mostly by the statehood movement. There are multiple explanations for this procedural choice.

First, since its original electoral victory in 1968, the PNP has dominated Puerto Rico's government on many occasions. Unable to commit the federal government to either the statehood project or to a binding process to address the issue, the PNP has used its control of the island's governmental structure to adopt *local* legislation to hold several plebiscites. In other words, plebiscites are the easiest mechanism to deploy through local statutory enactment. Such has been the privileged role of plebiscites in the PNP's annexation agenda that, recently, the Puerto Rico Supreme Court's PNP majority held that, because of statehood's 'victory' in the most recent plebiscite, the push for statehood is now official government policy instead of an explicit partisan position.[31]

Second, since these plebiscites are locally designed, the PNP has been able to define the statehood option to its greatest advantage. When one adds to the mix the significant opposition to the current territorial condition and the historic electoral weakness of the pro-independence movement, plebiscites are the ideal mechanism for assessing the support for statehood, consistently defined at its most basic level.

Third, since 1967, plebiscites have become a permanent feature of the status question. Status plebiscites were held in 1993, 1998, 2012, 2017 and 2020. *All of them* were held during PNP administrations.

[30] Keitner and Reisman (n 2) 30.

[31] See *Aponte Rosario v Presidente CEE* 205 DPR 407 (2020). In this case, the Supreme Court held that the push for statehood constituted a legitimate public goal for purposes of the 1952 Constitution's requirement that public funds can only be used for public ends (s 9, Art VI).

iii. Political Reality

The political viability of any change regarding Puerto Rico's colonial status and its relationship with the US depends, in varying degrees, on the current political realities in both countries. This further complicates the goal of agreeing on the procedural and substantive questions associated with Puerto Rican decolonisation.

Historically, the US Democratic Party was a reliable ally of the pro-Commonwealth forces in Puerto Rico. In turn, many pro-statehood supporters turned to the Republican Party, although other sectors began an intense lobbying effort with the Democrats. These paradigms have shifted in recent times.

On the one hand, many important sectors of the Democratic Party have embraced the statehood cause. The reasons for this are varied. First, the statehood movement has been partially successful in persuading leading Democrats, through civil rights language, that the island's colonial situation represents a denial of full citizenship and perpetuates unequal treatment to Puerto Ricans. Second, the Democrats have engaged in political calculation with regard to the electoral consequences of admitting Puerto Rico as a state. In all likelihood, Puerto Rico would elect a substantial number of federal Democratic lawmakers.

On the other hand, the Republican Party has drifted away from the statehood cause, particularly during the Trump era. First, because of the white nationalist shift that has occurred in that party, which does not welcome the integration of a mostly Hispanic state. And second, the Republicans have made the same electoral calculations with regard to Puerto Rico's impact in terms of the composition of Congress and the selection of the Presidency.

This divide affects not only the substantive discussion regarding status alternatives, but it also impacts the debate as to the procedural options. For example, leading Democratic lawmakers have presented competing bills to address the Puerto Rico status question, ranging from an explicitly pro-statehood measure to one that calls for the creation of a convention to directly deal with the issue.

Puerto Rico is also divided, not only on the substantive issue regarding status alternatives, but as to the procedural aspect as well. This double impasse – both in the metropolis and in the island itself – probably means that the status question will continue in its quagmire for the foreseeable future. All the while, the institutional, economic, and political institutions of colonialism are gaining strength, most visibly through the PROMESA statute and the aggressive intervention of the Fiscal Control Board and the federal courts.

Finally, one must consider the deeply embedded economic interests that depend on the island's continued colonial situation. These interests are both American and Puerto Rican. As Malavet points out, the US is 'still invested in the colony'.[32] But it is not just the US government; it is also multinational corporations and hedge funds that benefit from Puerto Rico's territorial condition.

[32] Malavet (n 8) 26.

II. THE 1952 CONSTITUTION'S INTERNAL DEMOCRATIC BLIND SPOTS FINALLY EMERGE

A. The Puerto Rican Summer of 2019

Puerto Rico has been no stranger to mass protests and popular movements calling for social and political change. This directly explains much of the progressive and social content of the 1952 Constitution. The Puerto Rican labour, student, feminist, and environmental movements, in particular, have been a constant feature of the island's daily life and collective history. Anti-colonial and anti-war struggles have also characterised the modern political landscape. This includes important social movements against the Vietnam and Iraq wars, the US Navy presence in the island-city of Vieques, environmentally harmful developments – particularly with regard to the island's shoreline and beaches (which have constitutional protection) – as well as labour deregulation and unpopular privatisation projects and austerity measures. The full list is substantial.

While the importance and impact of social movements in the preceding decades should not be undermined, nothing comes close to the scale of the events of the summer of 2019. The 'Summer of '19' (*Verano del 19*) constituted the largest moment of social mobilisation in the island's modern history. The background was austerity and corruption. The immediate context was an erosion of democratic legitimacy. The catalyst was a leaked chat detailing governmental insensibility and manipulation. The result was a constitutional crisis.

Puerto Rico has been in economic recession since at least 2005. This is the result of a total exhaustion of the colonial capitalist economic model, based on foreign capital, production aimed at export and tax exemption, in exchange for job creation. This approach has totally displaced local capital, required massive amounts of imports to satisfy the internal market, and depleted the public coffers. The revenue generated from the taxation of wages has not compensated for the massive loss in potential revenue because of the generalised tax breaks to foreign – mostly US – capital.

The response by successive Puerto Rican governments from both main political parties – the PPD and the conservative, pro-annexation New Progressive Party (PNP)[33] – has been repeated rounds of austerity measures. This has led

[33] As has been noted above, the PNP was established in 1967 as a breakaway of the Republican Statehood Party (PER). The PER was the longstanding standard bearer of the pro-annexation movement, including the 1952 constitutional process. The PNP won the 1968 general election, and the PER was totally wiped out. It should also be noted that the left-wing, pro-annexation Socialist Party (PS), which during the 1930s was one of the strongest electoral forces in the island, disbanded in 1956, after two decades of eroding electoral support. This means that only the PPD remains in terms of the political parties that participated in the 1952 constitutional process. The other main political party at the time, the Puerto Rican Independence Party (PIP), still exists, although its electoral support has remained minimal for several decades, save for the momentous electoral results of 2020.

to massive layoffs of public employees, more taxation on wage-earners, drastic cuts in pension benefits, and substantial roll-backs in labour protections in the private sector.

This austerity has co-existed alongside widespread corruption. During the economic boom of the 1990s, corruption became a household phenomenon. Several leading members of the government at the time were indicted by federal prosecutors for diverse corruptions schemes. This culture spilled over when economic expansion rapidly transformed into permanent recession. While corruption was sort of socially acceptable during the good times, it became absolutely unbearable during periods of economic crisis.

This combination of austerity and corruption was soon met with an erosion of democratic legitimacy. Puerto Rico has not re-elected a Governor since 1996. Since then, all elected chief executives have only been able to serve one-year terms at most. Since the adoption of the 1952 Constitution, the two main political parties have been able to consistently obtain more than 95 per cent of the vote between them. In fact, from 1952 to 2016, the lowest combined electoral support was in 1984, when the PPD and PNP only obtained a combined 92.3 per cent. This was due to the brief appearance of a fourth political party that was set up by the PNP mayor of San Juan who was denied the opportunity to mount a primary challenge to the sitting PNP Governor at the time.

The election of 2016 substantially strayed from that paradigm. Due to the strong showing of two independent candidates, combined with the vote totals of two additional minority parties, the PPD-PNP combination was only able to muster some 80 per cent of the vote. This constituted an electoral earthquake. While the *losing* candidate for Governor in 2008 received 41.29 per cent of the vote, the *winning* candidate in 2016 obtained 41.80 per cent of vote.

As a result, Governor Ricardo Rosselló took office with a serious democratic deficit: nearly 58 per cent of the public voted for someone else. This was the lowest percentage for a winning candidate for Governor in the history of Puerto Rico until 2020.

Rosselló's governorship was not popular. It presided over the implementation of many austerity measures required by the Fiscal Control Board mentioned above, as well as other unpopular actions, such as the approval of a labour deregulation bill which slashed decades-long protections for workers.

In September 2017, hurricanes Irma and María hit the island. The latter was a category 5 hurricane that ripped through the country. Although Puerto Rico is certainly no stranger to tropical storms and hurricanes, María was a 'once in a century' storm that hit the island directly, at a moment of great vulnerabilities, including the weakened power grid.

The Rosselló government's response was negligible and wholly insufficient. It highlighted the fact that many of those in positions of leadership in the government were neophyte partisan loyalists who lacked experience and expertise. While few people actually died during the storm event itself, the government's incompetent response resulted in the death of thousands during the aftermath.

At least there was a sense that we were all in the same boat. But then a disgruntled partisan loyalist decided to leak the contents of a chat that included the Governor and his closest allies, most of them young men who hailed from privileged backgrounds.

The leaked chat transcript was quite revealing: it was full of juvenile jokes, racist and misogynist comments, shady dealings, and plans to viciously attack political opponents and to purposely mislead the public on several matters. It was a bombshell. But the coup de grâce was a series of messages where these senior executive officials, including the Governor, made fun of those who had died during María. This was the straw that broke the camel's back.

Massive popular mobilisations followed, calling for the Governor's resignation. It was the culmination of decades of collective frustration with the political system and its leadership. Although all sectors of society participated in this process, there was a notable presence of young people and women.

The fact that the calls were for the Governor's resignation, and not his impeachment, reveals the structural deficiencies of the 1952 Constitution. As with Article VII modifications, impeachment is an exclusively legislative weapon. There is no recall option to remove a government official. And because there are no direct mechanisms for the public to initiate or require legislative action – including impeachment proceedings – there was an immediate consensus that the only viable alternative to the political crisis was resignation and that popular mobilisation was the most useful mechanism to achieve this end result.

The 1952 Constitution established a specific impeachment process in order to remove a sitting Governor. It is very similar to the federal structure. First, the exclusive power to initiate an impeachment proceeding against any governmental official, including justices of the Supreme Court,[34] belongs to the House of Representatives. But, unlike their federal counterpart, the House can only pass articles of impeachment with a two-thirds majority vote. The reason for this supermajority is that impeachment should be reserved only for those instances where members of the official's own party recognise the need to remove them. In other words, it is reserved for extraordinary circumstances that generate cross-party agreement.

The causes for impeachment are treason, bribery, other felonies (*delitos graves*) and those felonies that implicate moral turpitude (*depravación*). It is worth noting that, although the Spanish text used in the 1952 Constitution indicates that the alleged conduct must be contrary to the criminal law, it is clear that the ultimate judgment as to what is an impeachable offence is a political one.

If the House of Representatives passes articles of impeachment, the Senate acts as the jury in a trial presided by the Chief Justice if it pertains to the Governor. This is indicative of pure copying from the federal text, since there is no equivalent in Puerto Rico to the situation in the US where the Vice President

[34] Lower court judges can only be removed by the Supreme Court in the manner established by statute: Puerto Rico Constitution, Art V, § 11.

also presides over the Senate, thus creating a conflict of interest with regard to the trial. In Puerto Rico, the Senate President is not in the line of succession. Yet, the framers opted to emulate the federal practice and have the Chief Justice preside over the Governor's impeachment trial.

With regard to Rosselló's case, the legislators began to feel the pressure. Since the Governor had decided to hunker down and wait out the storm, the public started to focus on the problem of legislative inaction on this matter. The PNP majority in the House of Representatives finally turned on their party president. The House Speaker announced the imminent introduction of articles of impeachment, which would be supported by a substantial majority of the PNP caucus, not to mention the minority PPD and PIP delegations. The die was cast. After doing the maths, the Governor finally decided to resign.

But there was a problem. One of the participants in the leaked chat was the Secretary of State. As we saw earlier, this official is the first in line in terms of gubernatorial succession, as there is no lieutenant governor. Unlike Governor Rosselló, the Secretary of State resigned shortly after the chat's contents were published.

The vacancy generated by the Secretary's resignation created two options if the Governor were to resign or be removed. If the vacancy persisted, the next in line would be the Attorney General. But the Governor could attempt to fill the office of Secretary of State and then resign, thus directly selecting their successor.

But there was another problem. The Legislative Assembly was not in session. So, if the Governor appointed a Secretary of State, it would be through a recess appointment that required the calling of an extraordinary legislative session to consider the nomination before any resignation or removal took place. In the meantime, because it would be a recess appointment, the designee would be able to fill the spot while the Legislature considered the nomination during the extraordinary session. The open question was: what would happen if the Governor resigned or was removed while the Secretary was still functioning as a recess appointment and had not yet been confirmed by both legislative houses?

As discussed above, precisely because of the absence of a lieutenant governor, the 1952 Constitution requires that the Secretary of State, unlike the rest of the members of the Cabinet, be confirmed by both legislative chambers. While hundreds of thousands of people marched in the streets, the Legislative Assembly held an extraordinary session in order to consider Governor Rosselló's appointment to the post of Secretary of State. Because it was widely believed that the Governor would not last in his post for long, the confirmation of Pedro Pierluisi as Secretary of State was the equivalent of naming a new Governor. Unlike a sudden vacancy, where the issue of succession is incidental, here the stakes were higher: Rosselló wasn't really naming a Secretary of State; he was choosing his successor.

By the slimmest of margins, the House of Representatives confirmed Pierluisi as Secretary of State. The Senate was another matter. Because of political rivalries that are beyond the scope of this book, the majority PNP delegation opposed Pierluisi's nomination, even though they all belonged to the same political party.

While the Senate stalled on Pierliusi's confirmation and after determining that impeachment was imminent, Rosselló finally resigned. While thousands cheered in the streets, an immediate legal question arose: who would be sworn in as Governor? On the one hand, Pierluisi was the acting Secretary of State by virtue of his recess appointment. On the other hand, he had not been duly confirmed to that post by both legislative houses, which would mean that the next in line, the Attorney General, should be sworn in.

Shortly after Rosselló resigned, the Senate finally acted on Pierluisi's nomination as Secretary of State. But they did not reject his nomination directly. Instead, they chose to close the legislative session without an affirmative vote on consent. As such, the Senate proposed, it had rejected the nomination, given that Pierluisi was a recess appointment and had also not become Governor, since he needed senatorial conformation in order to do that. Because the Legislature started and ended a session, any recess appointee required affirmative confirmation in order to remain in their post. As the Senate had withheld its consent, the recess appointment lapsed.

Nonetheless, Pierluisi was sworn in as Governor. The Senate immediately filed suit to challenge Pierluisi's accession to the governorship. Their contention was simple: the constitutional text, and most importantly, the intent of the framers as memorialised in the formal adoption history of the 1952 Constitutional Convention,[35] clearly stated that a *sine qua non* requirement for a Secretary of State to accede to the governorship was confirmation by both chambers of the Legislative Assembly. Because Pierluisi had not been confirmed by the Senate at the time of Rosselló's resignation, the Senate argued, he was constitutionally ineligible to become Governor. At most, he had remained an interim Secretary of State because of his recess appointment, which lapsed the moment the Senate adjourned without affirmatively confirming him to the post.

While the legal and constitutional question was being channelled through the courts, popular attention focused on two important aspects: first, the widely-held belief that Pierluisi should not become Governor, since he had clearly violated even the democratically deficient constitutional structure by bypassing senatorial confirmation; and second, that, since the People – not the Legislature through impeachment – got rid of Governor Rosselló, the People should be able to select his replacement through some sort of election. The former required judicial correction; the latter required constitutional amendment and political action.

It seemed totally ironic that after weeks of intense popular mobilisation, a new Governor could simply come in out of the cold, hand-picked by the

[35] As noted in Chapter 6, the historical practice of the Supreme Court of Puerto Rico has been to give determinative weight to the expressed intent of the framers, as stated in the official transcripts of the Constitutional Convention. See JM Farinacci-Fernós, 'Originalism in Puerto Rico: Original Explication and its Relation with Clear Text, Broad Purpose and Progressive Policy' (2016) 85 *Revista Jurídica Universidad de Puerto Rico* 203.

disgraced former Governor just prior to his resignation, without even a hint of democratic consent. The fact that Pierluisi could succeed Rosselló without Senate confirmation seemed a bridge too far, even for a constitutional structure that, to begin with, was not wholly democratic on this issue.

It would seem that the undemocratic nature of the whole structural constitution converged in a single event: first, the fact that a candidate won the governorship with little less than 42 per cent of the vote, because of the plurality rule and the absence of a second-round structure; second, the unavailability of a recall mechanism that would have allowed the People to directly remove an elected official when they betrayed the public trust; third, the unresponsiveness of the Legislative Assembly to popular indignation, in order to trigger impeachment proceedings. The hundreds of thousands in the streets were not chanting 'Impeach Ricky' (the nickname of Governor Ricardo Rosselló) and trusting in the formal constitutional structure for removal of a sitting Governor. Instead, the rallying cry was 'Ricky, resign!', which is, evidently, a very informal political mechanism; fourth, the unavailability of a democratic mechanism for the selection of a new Governor, particularly under these circumstances. The People wanted to have to a say in who would govern next.

In other words, the formal constitutional structure failed to address, in the most basic democratic fashion, both the issue of gubernatorial removal and substitution. That structure envisioned an active Legislature who would impeach the Governor and affirmatively consent to the successor, even if only through prior confirmation of the Secretary of State and other Cabinet members. It also envisaged a passive People, limited to watching their elected legislators carry out their functions. But the Summer of '19 demonstrated the opposite: it was the People who were active and the legislatures who lagged behind. The constitutional structure seemed wholly inadequate for the new political reality.

The Supreme Court of Puerto Rico has not been immune to hyper-partisanship, particularly in a situation in which there is no real ideological divide between the main political parties, except as to the specific issue of Puerto Rico's relationship with the US. It is a situation akin to sports rivalry: the loyalty to our own side is unlimited and the hatred of those opposite side is irrational and arbitrary. Through a combination of sudden death, constitutionally required forced retirements, the failure of divided government during the 2004–2008 term, and a nakedly partisan move to expand the membership of the Court in 2010, the PNP was able to appoint six of the nine Justices of the Supreme Court. The remaining three members of the Court had been named by PPD administrations. A fiercely fragmented and politically charged Court has been a constant since, at least, 2009.

But in *Senado v Pierluisi*,[36] the Supreme Court ruled unanimously. This was rather welcome news, given the absolute failure of the other constitutional

[36] *Senado v Pierluisi* 2019 TSPR 138.

actors to adequately address the political crisis that had been brewing and the apparent breakdown of the constitutional order by way of an illegal usurpation of power. The Court's unanimity allowed its ruling to have much more acceptance and to give some level of legitimacy to whoever finally acceded to the governorship.

The question before the Supreme Court was: could a recess appointee to the post of Secretary of State become Governor after a vacancy in that office, without having first obtained confirmation by both houses of the Legislative Assembly? As if this wasn't complicated enough, there was an additional wrinkle that needed to be addressed.

In 1952, shortly after the Constitution was approved, the Legislative Assembly adopted Act No 7 (Act 7-1952), establishing a comprehensive line of succession to complement and implement the provisions of Article IV, Section 7 of the Puerto Rico Constitution. In 2005, an amendment was approved by way of Act No 7 (Act 7-2005). This amendment allowed for *temporary* substitutions of the Governor – for example, if they physically left the Commonwealth – by Cabinet members who would otherwise not meet the constitutional requirements to become Governor, including age, residency and confirmation. In other words, recess appointees could become *interim* Governor in situations of *temporary* absence.

What about permanent vacancies, such as the present case? For some inexplicable reason, Act 7-5005 allowed an *unconfirmed* Secretary of State to become Governor, even in situations of a permanent vacancy, unlike other Cabinet secretaries that were included in the order of succession. Act 7-2005 seemed to be in direct contradiction of Section 5 of Article IV and, as noted above, with the explicit intent of the Constitutional Convention.

Accordingly, the Court looked to the official adoption history of the 1952 Constitution. The debates during the Convention revealed an explicit position: no Secretary of State can become Governor without first obtaining confirmation by both legislative houses. Full stop. As discussed above, this double-confirmation requirement was meant to offset the democratic deficit that would characterise any substitution of an elected Governor with an unelected Cabinet secretary. The Court held that Act 7-2005's alteration of that equation was contrary to the Constitution. As such, it found the statute to be unconstitutional.

As a result, the Supreme Court concluded that Pierluisi was ineligible to become Governor when Rosselló resigned. At that precise time, Pierluisi had yet to receive confirmation by the Senate. Therefore, the Attorney General, as next in line, needed to be sworn in. Pierluisi accepted the result and shortly after the ruling left the Governor's mansion he had been inhabiting for the previous couple of days.[37]

[37] The Attorney General, Wanda Vázquez, was sworn in as Governor. Even though she had stated that her goal was to serve out the remainder of Governor Rosselló's term and she would not seek her party's nomination, eventually she changed her mind and ran for election, seeking to head up

While the Supreme Court's decision in *Senate v Pierluisi* addressed the egregious constitutional crisis of a hand-picked, last minute recess appointment becoming Governor without the requisite legislative confirmation, the broader structural crisis persisted. Even after the swearing in of the Attorney General as Governor, the democratic deficiencies of the constitutional structure remained crystal clear. Puerto Rico would now be governed by an unelected official, second in line, and appointed by a Governor who, in turn, had received less than 42 per cent of the vote and had now resigned in disgrace. Hardly the stuff of vigorous democratic popular self-rule.

The political events of the Summer of '19 transcend the legal focus of this chapter. But many of the constitutional questions that were raised then are still relevant today. The same constitution that protected the Puerto Rican People's right to march, protest, assemble and peacefully topple a disgraced Governor, failed them in terms of democratic governance. A national conversation on constitutional reformed followed, if only to eventually peter away because, unless there is legislative initiative, no reform can happen. And in order to achieve legislation action on the constitutional reform front, the individual members of the Legislative Assembly require sufficient political incentive to do so. The democratisation of the political structure laid out in the 1952 Constitution was not in their own self-interest.

B. The Erosion of the Two-party System and Proposals to Democratise the Puerto Rican Constitutional Structure

Which ideas emerged from the Summer of '19 in terms of constitutional reform? As we are about to see, most of them share one important characteristic: democratisation and expansion of direct popular participation in governance.

First, the replacement of the plurality regime for, at least, gubernatorial elections. It should be noted that Section 4 of Article VI of the Constitution, which spells out the plurality rule, applies to all elected offices, including legislators. Would an amendment to replace the plurality rule apply across the board or would it only be applicable to post of Governor? It would seem that, even though the main driver of the amendment was the question relating to the governorship, a successful amendment in this regard would apply to all elected officials as well.

One alternative that has been consistently discussed is the holding of a second round of balloting among the top two finishers during the first round.[38] This would have enormous democratic and political consequences.

the PNP ticket. Ironically, Pedro Pierluisi challenged her to a primary for the PNP nomination. After a very hard fought and bitter primary contest, Pierluisi came out on top. Governor Vázquez made a strong showing, but not enough to be victorious. In the 2020 election, Pierluisi was elected Governor of Puerto Rico, but with a very weak mandate, having only obtained 33 per cent of the vote.

[38] Another model that has been discussed, although much less, is the ranked vote system used, for example, in New York City and Ireland.

From a democratic point of view, it would make sure that whoever wins a singular office, particularly when it comes to the first Executive, has a strong majoritarian mandate. This would give their term greater democratic legitimacy.

From a political point of view, this could dramatically alter the already-shifting two-party system. For example, it would strengthen third parties in the first round and allow them to negotiate from a position of strength, pressuring the top parties to, for the first time since the 1952 Constitution was adopted, engage in negotiations for some sort of coalition government.

As we saw above, from 1952 until 2016, the two main political parties consistently obtained more than 90 per cent of the vote between them. In 2016, that combination was substantially reduced to barely 80 per cent. Given the winner-takes-all system, it was a remarkable feat that other forces were able to garner 20 per cent of the vote, and then a whopping 35 per cent of the vote in 2020. Such was the level of discontent with the traditional two-party system. The 2016 election was supposed to be a wake-up call for the established parties.

For the PNP – a party used to obtaining massive numbers of votes, even when it lost an election – the 2016 results were devastating. Never had the party received so few votes, particularly when coming into an election as the opposition party. For example, in 2008 it obtained close to 53 per cent of the vote in what was considered to be a landslide against the incumbent PPD administration. We should not forget that, since 1992, the PNP had lost its legislative majority only twice (2000, 2012).

The fact that the PNP only managed to obtain less than 42 per cent of the vote was nothing less than a debacle. Still, it managed to win the governorship and retake the majority of both legislative chambers. But, as described above, the events of 2019 severely weakened the PNP as the historically largest party in Puerto Rico since the latter half of the twentieth century.

If the 2016 election was bad for the PNP, it was even worse for the PPD. The once-mighty party, which was able to obtain majorities hovering over 60 per cent during the 1950s and 1960s, only managed to receive a little less than 39 per cent of the vote for Governor. That a major Puerto Rican political party had received less than 40 per cent of the vote was something unheard of since the dawn of the modern two-party system in 1968. The PPD also lost its legislative majority in both chambers. Its main strength remained in municipal contests, particularly the larger cities.

While 2016 constituted an electoral earthquake, its main beneficiaries were not the existing third parties, either the historical PIP (founded in the 1940s) or the newcomer Working People's Party (PPT).[39] On the contrary, the main beneficiaries of the changes in electoral winds were two independent gubernatorial candidates who, between them, managed to obtain nearly 17 per cent of

[39] The PPT was founded in 2010, mostly by members of the Movement towards Socialism (MAS), itself the product of the fusion between several left-wing groups that had 'survived' the nationalist turn within the independence movement during the 1990s.

the vote. Moreover, for the first time in Puerto Rican electoral history, an independent candidate managed to secure election to the Legislative Assembly. José Vargas Vidot topped the poll for the 11 available at-large seats for the Senate, obtaining almost 11 per cent of the total vote.[40] Outside the PNP-PPD, only the PIP managed to elect members of the Legislative Assembly: one Senator and one Representative, both through the at-large seats.

In 2020, the earthquake that had started in 2016 became a tsunami. The 2020 election results were radically different from any other electoral contest on the island since the adoption of the 1952 Constitution and the emergence of the current two-party system in 1968. The historical characteristics of the 2020 elections require detailed analysis. Four main events deserve further attention.

The first major event relates to the results for the governorship. As we have seen, the combined vote of the PNP-PPD for this position in 2016 was barely 80 per cent. By itself, this would have constituted the lowest amount of combined support for the major parties since the 1952 Constitution was adopted. In 2020, that combined vote was only 65 per cent. This marks a 15 per cent drop from the previous result which was, in turn, a 15 per cent drop from the 2012 election. In other words, in just eight years, the two-party system went down from 95 per cent to 65 per cent.

The *winning* candidate in 2020 received far less than the *losing* candidate in 2016: 33 per cent compared to 39 per cent. That the PNP, a party that had received 53 per cent of the vote as recently as 2008, had only managed to obtain a third of the vote was truly momentous. There were no big celebrations on election night. The winning candidate was Pedro Pierliusi, the same person who was the protagonist of the Secretary of State debacle in 2019.

The PPD candidate only managed to obtain a little less than 32 per cent of the vote. It seemed that the PPD continued on its long decline, which appeared to move faster than the PNP. In other words, every time the PNP fell hard, the PPD seemed to fall even harder.

Where did the other 35 per cent of the vote go?

The first major beneficiary of the momentous decline of the two-party system was the recently established Citizen's Victory Movement (MVC). This new political party was formed as a sort of coalition of diverse progressive currents and forces, including – but not limited to – the PPT, the Sovereigntist Unity Movement (MUS), VAMOS, and Alexandra Lúgaro, one of the two independent candidates in 2016, who single handedly managed to receive more than 11 per cent in that election. It also benefited from high-profile defections by progressive leaders from both the PPD and the PNP. The MVC adopted an explicitly progressive political programme that rejected neoliberal measures and

[40] As we saw in Ch 4, both the Senate and the House of Representatives have 11 at-large seats. By statute, each political party can only nominate up to six candidates, thus making it relatively easier for other political forces – whether independent candidates or smaller third parties – to enter parliament. Each voter can select only one at-large candidate for each legislative chamber.

austerity. Again running for Governor, this time under the MVC banner, Lúgaro came in third with 14 per cent of the vote.

The second major beneficiary of the 2020 election for Governor was the PIP. Its candidate, Senator Juan Dalmau, obtained an impressive 13.5 per cent of the vote, coming in a close fourth. If one considers that the highest result obtained by a PIP gubernatorial candidate since 1968 was 5.7 per cent in 2000, the 2020 total was a historical feat for the party.[41]

Finally, a fifth party also obtained respectable results in the 2020 race for Governor, particularly considering the historical two-party dominance of that office. The Dignity Project (PD) is a fundamentalist religious party that, while nominally communitarian when it comes to socioeconomic issues, has more and more taken on a distinct right-wing ideology. Most of its support came from disaffected, traditionalist PNP voters who object to that party's moderate embrace of LGBTTQ rights. The PD's candidate for Governor obtained 6.8 per cent of the vote, higher than any other third party since before 2020.

The second major event of the 2020 elections was the result for the Legislative Assembly. The first thing that stood out was that it was the PPD, not the PNP, who managed to scrape a legislative majority, but only just. In the House of Representatives, the PPD elected 26 of the 51 seats, a slim majority of one. The PPD 'won' its majority by barely edging out the PNP in key district races. In the 11 at-large seats, the PPD only elected two representatives to the PNP's five.

On the Senate side, the PPD elected only 12 of the 27 seats, short of an overall majority, but still emerging as the largest party. The PNP obtained 10. Again, the PPD secured its plurality because of favourable district results, since it only managed to elect two at-large seats, compared with the PNP who elected four of the 11 that were available. In the end, the PPD managed to elect the presidencies of both chambers, effectively gaining control of the Legislative Branch, thus ushering in the second instance of divided government in the past 30 years. But the relative strength of the major parties is very different from the 2004 experience. Then, the PPD won the governorship with 48 per cent of the vote, compared to the PNP's 33 per cent in 2020. Moreover, in 2004 the PNP won 17 of 27 senators and 32 of 51 representatives, compared to the PPD's 12 senators and 26 representatives. It is a particular version of divided government, with both traditional parties considerably weakened in their respective positions.

Again, third parties fared far better in 2020 than in previous electoral contests. The MVC elected two senators and two representatives, with the PIP and PD electing one in each house. Independent Senator Vargas Vidot secured reelection. As a result, six political currents gained representation in the Puerto Rican Senate, the most diverse ever, while the House has five different delegations. In the Senate, notwithstanding the two-party system's stranglehold over

[41] It should be noted that, while the gap between their respective candidates for Governor was razor-thin, there was a more significant difference between the MVC and the PIP with regard to their results under their respective party tickets: the MVC obtained 12 per cent to the PIP's 7 per cent.

the district seats, the alternative political forces make up more than 18 per cent of the chamber. While impressive, it still constitutes considerably less than the 35 per cent obtained by the MVC, PIP, PD, and independent candidate in the at-large category.

In that sense, the structure established in the 1952 Constitution mostly benefited the two traditional parties. For instance, *all* of the successful third party and independent candidates that managed to secure their election did so through the at-large seats. Of the 11 available at-large seats in the Senate, the PNP won four, the PPD and MVC two each, and the PIP, PD, and Independents one each. Of the 11 available at-large seats in the House of Representatives, the PNP won five, the PPD and MVC two each, and the PIP and PD one each. In other words, although receiving a combined 35 per cent of the vote, none of the third parties managed to obtain a single one of the 40 district seats for the House or the 16 district seats for the Senate.

In fact, it could be argued that the 1952 two-party system actually worked exactly as it was designed to, securing minority representation through the at-large seats, while favouring the major parties through the district seats. There is no mathematical way to obtain a majority in each chamber exclusively through the at-large seats, and the first-past-the-post formula still works as a powerful guardrail against the emergence of a real multi-party system, regardless of a substantial increase in support for alternative parties or currents. In other words, the first-past-the-post model allowed the PPD, with just under a third of the overall vote, to take control, by itself, of the Legislative Assembly.

But the 2020 election almost made even more history with regard to the district seats, both in the House of Representatives and the Senate. On the House side, MVC candidate Eva Prados nearly caused the greatest upset in Puerto Rican electoral history by failing to win her district seat by a mere 128 votes (0.52 per cent) of the more than 24,600 ballots cast.[42] Her second-placing 8,251 votes (34.64 per cent) represent the highest tally by a district candidate not hailing from the PNP or PPD.[43] On the Senate side, one of the MVC district candidates for Senate for San Juan beat the PPD into third place.[44]

The third major event of the 2020 election was the San Juan mayoral race. As the capital of Puerto Rico, San Juan is the country's major city and seat of government. At least two San Juan mayors have become Governors and many others have been their party's nominees for that post. In that sense, San Juan stands out among the 78 municipalities in Puerto Rico. The mayoral election

[42] The 2020 election was marred by widespread irregularities, particularly with regard to the San Juan races, including Prados' 3rd District. Many believe that, in fact, Prados won her seat.

[43] Similarly, MVC candidate Alberto Derkes also made history in his District by coming in second, behind only the PNP candidate.

[44] Recall that Senate district seats are not single-member. Each district elects two Senators, with each voter entitled to select up to two candidates. In that sense, there are always two winning candidates. The MVC candidate in San Juan (Rosa Seguí), while nominally finishing third, can be said to have come in in second place.

is a national issue, unlike the other municipal elections which are more local in nature.

The San Juan mayoral election of 2020 was historic. As with Eva Prados in her House district seat race, the MVC candidate for mayor almost made history by barely losing out to the winning PNP candidate. It would have been the first time ever that a third party had won the capital's mayoral race. MVC candidate Manuel Natal obtained 33.87 per cent, well ahead of the PPD's candidate, who received just 23 per cent.[45] The PNP won with 36.60 per cent.

The final major event was also a mayoral race. While not as significant as the San Juan contest, the situation in Guánica – a small town in the southwest – is worth mentioning. In 2020, a write-in candidate, Edgardo Cruz, lost the election by only a few dozen votes.

There is a high probability that a second round would have handed Prados, Natal, and Cruz resounding electoral victories in their respective races. In that sense, a two-round electoral model, or even a ranked choice system, could be the final deathblow to the two-party system, allowing the emergence of a new political culture of pluralism in terms of electoral options that reflects the current makeup of Puerto Rican society.

For decades, the political debate in Puerto Rico during election season has been dominated by the 'useful vote' argument. This is a version of the 'lesser of two evils' rationale. This argument has been used by the PPD in particular. The PPD has attempted to position itself as a bulwark against the more right-wing and assimilationist PNP, which is crucial, given that most, though certainly not all, third-party alternatives tend to originate in progressive or anti-statehood sectors of society. The 'useful vote' rationale is the classic argument in a two-party system and is meant to artificially reproduce that system, even when its constituent parties have lost a considerable amount of political favour.

With a two-round system, smaller parties could very well not remain small for too long. That is because the pressure of 'strategic voting' during the first round would disappear, allowing the growing sector of the population that has had enough of the main parties to support new alternatives, without running the risk of indirectly producing an electoral victory for their less preferred option among the two main parties. On the contrary, the system encourages electors to select their preferred alternative on the first round, and then shift to strategic voting in the second round if they so choose.

This model could substantially elevate the vote totals of third parties that, until now, have been victims of strategic voting within a winner-takes-all two-party system. This has important consequences. First, it would greatly strengthen their hand when the two parties that make it to the final round attempt to secure their support. It could lead to official agreements that, under a plurality scheme,

[45] It should be noted that the PPD was the incumbent party in the San Juan City Hall, having won both the 2012 and 2016 mayoral elections. For his part, Natal was a former Representative of the PPD.

are hard to come by, given the strong negotiating position of the larger party. Second, it could actually allow one of the new parties to displace one or even both traditional alternatives, thus producing, even within the two-party logic, an electoral reality that is better reflective of current popular preferences.

Curiously enough, in the long run, one of the main beneficiaries of the two-round system could be the PPD itself, if their argument concerning the lesser of two evils is actually true. Of course, it could come at the cost of negotiating agreements with third parties from a position of relative weakness. There is a significant difference between a major party that is able to obtain 45 per cent of the vote being able to persuade the potential backers of smaller parties to shift their vote for strategic purposes without having to give up much, and a major party that, because of a two-round system, only obtains 30 per cent of the vote and now must formally engage a third party that was able to garner, for example, 15 per cent of the vote. In the latter scenario, the larger party would not be able to impose their will through the argument of 'useful voting'. Their weakened position of 35 per cent and the other party's strengthened position of 15 per cent creates a whole new dynamic that can see the latter's positions actually be agreed upon formally by the major party attempting to receive their support during the second round of voting.

The second main target of reform has been proportionality in terms of legislative seats.[46] It is a natural outgrowth of the rejection of the plurality rule with regard to the first-past-the-post system in single member constituencies. As noted above, under the current system, a political party can obtain nearly two-thirds of a legislative chamber with as little as 40 per cent of the vote. Moreover, a political party can obtain 10 per cent or more of the vote and still be relegated to one or two members of either the House of Representatives or the Senate.

The Constitutional Convention wanted to avoid coalitions as much as possible. There are historical and partisan reasons why the PPD, the main political force in 1952, wanted to avoid that outcome and, instead, favour single-party governments.

As to their support for single-party governments, the reason seems obvious: for decades the PPD was able to muster electoral majorities above 50 per cent. This feat was a combination of real popular support and the artificial benefits

[46] This issue has become even more important when considering the fact that in the 2020 election, the PPD and PNP only managed to obtain two and four of the 11 available at-large seats in the Senate, respectively, and two and five of the 11 available at-large seats in the House of Representatives. As we saw above, the current statutory scheme allows parties to nominate a maximum of six candidates for the at-large seats in each legislative chamber. The PPD's results in 2020 will most likely result in that party nominating less than the maximum allowed five in the 2024 election, becoming the first major party to do so in the history of the two-party system. In other words, the major parties will probably go after the at-large seats to reverse the gains by the emerging third parties. If we add the fact that no third party has yet to win a district seat in either house, it becomes quite clear that the current system that combines at-large seats with first-past-the-post district seats is no longer suitable for the current preferences of the Puerto Rican electorate.

of first-past-the-post. An electoral system based on proportionality could erode that support and allow a multi-membered opposition to attempt and constitute a Frankenstein government.

This brings us to the historical reasons for their rejection of a proportional system. During the 1930s, the PPD's predecessors, particularly the Liberal Party, were the main political force on the island. But they were not able to secure 50 per cent support. The remaining parties, the Republican Union and the Socialist Party, could only beat the Liberals if they joined together. This led to a Coalition between these two parties that obtained legislative majorities in Puerto Rico from 1932 until 1940.

On the one hand, the Coalition made perfect sense: neither the Republican Union nor Socialist Party could ever dream of obtaining an electoral majority individually. In that sense, the Coalition was a marriage of convenience. It helped matters that both parties hailed from the pro-statehood sector of the population and that they loathed the Liberals.

On the other hand, the Coalition made no sense at all: the Republican Union was a very conservative party that represented the interests of employers, industrialists and other business interests, while the Socialist Party was the party of organised labour with a distinctive left-wing tongue. As a result, the legislative programme of the Coalition from 1932 until 1940 was characterised by contradiction, tension and incoherence.

For the PPD, which was born out of the Liberal Party, the Coalition revealed two lessons. First, it was important to avoid the smaller parties being able to team up and edge out a legislative majority. It should be noted that the ability of the Republican Union and the Socialist Party to obtain electoral majorities from their combined support was not the result of a proportional system. It was not a matter of adding up their respective legislative seats, obtained proportionally from their respective shares of the vote.

The Coalition was possible because, under the statutory regime that was adopted at the time, parties could form electoral alliances by which a single candidate could run under two or more party columns. This allowed the allied parties to measure their relative strength – by tallying the vote the candidate received under either column – while making sure that there was no vote splitting between them, thus ensuring the common candidate's election. A proportional system of legislative allotment would produce a similar result, in that it would allow parties to combine their electoral support. Under a proportional system, each party would be able to elect legislators according to their respective individual strength, and then be able to combine them under a common legislative programme.

The second lesson that the PPD took away from the experiences of the Coalition during the 1930s was the advantage of single-party government in terms of ideological and programmatic coherence and consistency. Even the former parties of the Coalition stated publicly that they would not join forces again. Actually, there were several direct clashes between the delegates of the

Republican Statehood Party – successor of the Republican Union – and the Socialist Party – by then a mere shadow of its former self.

Since 1940, there has never been a formal or informal coalition government in Puerto Rico. The 1952 Constitution was designed to generate that result, not only in terms of the Executive, but in terms of the need to produce a legislative majority in both chambers.

Curiously enough, through 2004–2008 there was a hint of how a legislative coalition would look. In the 2004 elections, the PNP easily won majorities in the House of Representatives and the Senate. However, by the narrowest of margins, the PPD candidate for Governor was elected. It was the first experience in terms of divided government in, at least, a generation. Curiously, the 2020 elections produced a second instance of divided government.

Of course, divided government and legislative coalitions as the result of proportional representation and the presence of several parties in the Legislature are not synonymous. But one of the more interesting consequences of the experience of divided government in 2004 was that the PNP's senatorial delegation *split* in terms of cooperation with the PPD Executive.

This split was aided by the fact that the defeated PNP candidate for Governor – former Governor Pedro Rosselló[47] – managed to get a PNP Senator to resign to his post so that Rosselló could take his place. His stated objective was to become President of the Senate and use the PNP's legislative majorities to bypass the PPD Executive as much as possible.

But the PNP Senate leadership resisted Rosselló's attempts. This generated an interesting scenario: the anti-Rosselló block of the PNP delegation was in a minority. But, if it was added to the minority PPD delegation in the Senate, they could out-vote the rump PNP majority. And thus an *informal* deal was struck: the PPD Senators would support the anti-Rosselló block, in exchange for a more moderate tone in terms of cooperation with the Executive. The PPD's main objective was to deprive the Rosselló-led PNP from taking over the Senate and making life impossible for the PPD Governor.

If we add to the mix the single PIP legislator, that would mean that the 2004 Senate included *four* political parties, *none* of which was large enough to single-handedly dominate the chamber. Although it was the result of palace intrigue during divided government, its effect was similar to what would happen in a proportional system for legislative seats: negotiation and cooperation between minority factions that could muster up a workable majority. This outcome would have even greater democratic benefit if it was the result of *popular will* where different political parties are able to obtain sufficient electoral support to participate in the Legislature but not enough to govern by themselves. The main argument remains: a single political party should only hold a legislative majority if it also holds a comparable electoral majority.

[47] Pedro Rosselló was a two-term Governor, serving 1993–2001. In 2004, he was nominated again for the post. He is also the father of Governor Ricardo Rosselló, who resigned in disgrace in 2019.

The electoral situation in 2020 further highlighted this point. The new parties and the independent candidate, although they collected 35 per cent of the at-large vote, controlled only 18 per cent of the legislative seats. While district representation is still regarded as necessary, there is an emerging consensus that this lack of proportionality is democratically unacceptable. One alternative is to transform district seats into a two-round or ranked vote system, and to expand the at-large seats with a purely proportional mechanism. Another possibility is to create multiple-member districts that distribute their seats proportionally.

The third main lesson from the Summer of '19 was the benefits of a recall mechanism for elected officials. Instead of having to occupy the streets by the hundreds of thousands, including incidents of physical clashes with the police, the People would have been able to activate a formal legal mechanism to remove the Governor electorally.

But the 2019 experience also highlighted another democratic deficit of the 1952 Constitution: how the new Governor is selected. The 1952 Constitution adopted a model based on a pre-determined line of succession, without any direct participation by the electorate. One alternative that has been discussed is that, except for vacancies that may happen shortly before a general election, if a Governor resigns, dies, or is removed, an interim Governor will temporarily lead the Executive Branch while a special election is held to select a permanent substitute to serve out the rest of the original term.

As we have seen throughout this book, the 1952 Constitution gave the leading role with regard to policy to the Legislature and not the People. One direct consequence of this approach is the total absence of initiative mechanisms, even for statutory issues. Unlike other jurisdictions in the US, Puerto Rico has no mechanism that allows ordinary citizens to directly enact or repeal ordinary legislation.

The experiences of the 2019 events have unleashed many other ideas regarding democratisation of the political process. Among these are the possibility of electing more officers of the Executive Branch, particularly the Secretary of State who doubles as the lieutenant governor in terms of the line of succession.

Other ideas deal with the political class, like the establishment of term limits. While Puerto Rico has yet to re-elect a single Governor in more than 25 years, there is a generalised view that the political class has become too self-entrenched. The most egregious example of this phenomenon relates to mayors. Puerto Rico has an unfortunate culture of mayors who serve for decades only to have their son or daughter take over upon their retirement. The good news is that mayors are not constitutional officers, which means that term limits could be adopted through an ordinary statute.

The issue of bicameralism has also been present in the public discission regarding constitutional reform. The nature of the debate, however, varies considerably, ranging from superficial populism that believes that fewer legislators would be a good thing – with the ironic result of giving the remaining legislators more power because there would be less of them – to a more profound argument regarding the need to avoid additional veto points to transformative legislation and to empower the Legislative Branch as opposed to the unitary Executive.

Like asking a genie for infinite wishes, another possibility could be modifying the amendment procedure itself to make it easier for the People to enact future amendments. There are multiple articulations of this idea.

First, the procedure could be changed to allow for more than three amendments per referendum. Truth be told, the requirement that no more than three amendments can be submitted to the People at a time does not establish how many times per year this exercise can be carried out. There is always the possibility that the Legislative Assembly might adopt several sets of amendments that can be considered by the People in successive referendums. But the current political and legal tradition is that referendums should be rare and that an amendment process in general should be limited to three proposals.

As a result, instead of potentially abusing the constitutional silence regarding the maximum of three-amendment referendums that can be carried out in any given year, one alternative is to increase the three-amendment maximum to, say, five or seven. This allows for greater flexibility in terms of modifying the constitutional text, without running the risk of too much change too quickly.

Second, another option could be to eliminate the Legislature's monopoly on initiating the amendment process. As we have seen, while the People have the last word on whether an amendment will be adopted, the Legislative Assembly has the sole power to propose an amendment in the first place. One possibility would be to allow for citizens to initiate an amendment process by, say, obtaining sufficient signatures from the public.

This would increase the democratic legitimacy of the amendment process. By having the amendment process start and end with the People, one could even argue that an amendment to the constitution would mark an exercise of some sort of constituent power, since the People can rarely be characterised as a constituted power. Of course, by agreeing to use the amendment process established by the current constitution, it could be argued that the People are temporarily casting aside the full constituent power they possess as the sovereign – a problematic proposition in a colonial society – thus requiring compliance with the current legal order.

But the point remains: giving the People the power to initiate and culminate an amendment process would be a democratic leap forward, addressing one of the main democratic flaws of the 1952 Constitution, ie the passive role given to the People in terms of developing the constitutional project. Of course, an initiative mechanism should make sure that the amendment proposals obtain sufficient popular support so as to reflect a true preference on the part of the public.

This alternative has particular democratic appeal because, by addressing that democratic flaw, it allows for the People to correct many of the structural aspects of the 1952 Constitution that deal with legislative and electoral processes. As has been noted above, it is particularly difficult to correct these structural flaws if, in order to fix them, one has to obtain the consent of the same institutional actors who benefit from those flaws and who are able to retain their positions precisely because of them. The democratisation of the amendment process by bypassing the Legislature could allow the People to democratise the political structure as a whole.

Third, there is the possibility of requiring periodic consultations of the People on whether the constitution should be revised or, at least, to assess whether it still commands popular support. A constant reaffirmation of the constitutional project by the current generation helps to resolve many of the issues associated with the so-called dead-hand problem. In these circumstances, the constitution's legitimacy and authority is reaffirmed and even strengthened.

On the other hand, if a periodic consultation reveals eroding support, or even majoritarian rejection of the current constitution, it opens the way for a new constituent process without the need to speculate as to whether the constitution is still valid at any particular historical moment. In the end, it is a win-win scenario: either the current constitution is strengthened by the periodic consultation, or its lack of support is demonstrated, which will probably generate a popular process and debate with regard to the construction of a new constitutional project.

In any event and regardless of the particular modifications that are made to Article VII of the 1952 Constitution, the goal should be to democratise the amendment process so that the People are able to improve, develop, and adapt *their* constitutional project. When this happens, there is a greater chance that the constitution will truly reflect the current views of the social majority in Puerto Rico, thus allowing Puerto Rican constitutionalism to continue to develop and mature.

III. THE CONSTITUTION, CLASS STRUGGLE, AND POLICE POWER DURING THE PANDEMIC

Puerto Rico has been in economic recession since 2006. This has led to the imposition of numerous austerity measures that have exacerbated social conflicts. This, in turn, has led to social unrest and popular mobilisations against these measures. The neoliberal proposals that have been implemented in the island during the previous decades seem at odds with the progressive constitution that was adopted in 1952. Although marginally, the labour and popular resistance to these measures imply a questioning of that gap and the vindication of the social aspects of the 1952 Constitution, particularly its labour rights provisions.

As detailed in Chapter 6, the unwillingness of institutional actors to fully implement these provisions has also created a climate where those rights are no longer present in the public discourse. The historic erosion of the labour movement, similar – though more dramatically – to what has transpired in the

US, has also led to a backsliding on important parts of the social constitution. This creates a vicious cycle that has stripped the most progressive provisions of the 1952 Constitution down to their normative bare bones, with the additional ideological, historical, and social consequences of doing so. The labour rights provisions, particularly the collective ones, have been the main victims of the conservative version of Puerto Rico's living constitutionalism.[48]

But other aspects of the social constitution still endure, particularly those that relate to the government's broad police powers. More recently, these powers have been deployed during humanitarian emergencies, such as the devastating hurricanes that hit the island in 2017 and the COVID-19 pandemic that has raged since early 2020. These two events require individual treatment.

As a tropical island in the middle of the Caribbean, Puerto Rico has been no stranger to hurricanes, including devastating ones. Once every generation, a particularly powerful storm hits Puerto Rico, causing considerable material destruction. The list includes hurricanes such as San Ciriaco (1899), San Felipe (1928,), San Ciprián (1934), Santa Clara (1956), Hugo (1989), and Georges (1999). But not since the 150 plus miles an hour storms of the early twentieth century had a hurricane delivered such a blow as Maria in 2017.[49]

While the first effects of Maria related to property and infrastructure destruction, the government's inept response to the crisis led to more than 3,000 deaths. As explained above, this was one of the catalysts for the massive 2019 protests that led to the resignation of Governor Rosselló. It also revealed both the current substantial economic gaps in Puerto Rico – literally revealing numerous neighbourhoods whose poverty was concealed by nature – and the negative impacts of decades of neoliberal measures.

For example, the state-owned energy company originally established in 1940 – during the heyday of direct governmental intervention in the economy through the creation of profitable state-owned entities – had been considerably hollowed out through the years through crushing debt, subcontracting, lack of proper maintenance, and inept partisan management. This meant that the island's power grid was enormously vulnerable when hurricane María hit. During the first days after the event, most services, including internet, mobile phone communication, and even water, were scarce. But the reestablishment of power to most of the population was an endeavour that lasted many months. And even then, the system was weaker than ever and subject to intermittent blackouts, which became commonplace during 2021.

The central government's failure, after decades of neoliberal erosion, to adequately address the fallout from hurricane María led many people to turn to their own communities and neighbours as their safety net, including cleanup, groceries, childcare and even security. This rudimentary collectivist response

[48] See Farinacci-Fernós (n 35).

[49] Barely a week before María hit, hurricane Irma – another powerful category 5 storm – barely missed the island.

served as a reminder of the social constitution's ideological project. More importantly, it served as a dress rehearsal for the historic pandemic that struck the world in early 2020.

Serving almost as the opposite of the María response, Puerto Rico became a posterchild regarding its COVID-19 response. In addition to the considerable sums of federal funds that were channelled to ordinary Puerto Ricans – which, in turn, strengthened the contradictions of Puerto Rican colonialism and the island's continued dependence on federal dollars as a response to the imposition of a dysfunctional colonial economy – the local government quickly made use of its considerable police powers. Combined with the collectivist approach inherited from María, the result was mostly positive.

As with many US states during the early days of the COVID-19 pandemic, Puerto Rico's Governor made extensive use of the emergency powers delegated previously by the Legislative Assembly to address emergencies. Adding to the irony, from March 2020 until January 2021, the executive orders were issued by Wanda Vázquez, the former Attorney General who had succeeded Governor Rosselló after his departure in 2019. In other words, the Governor with the weakest democratic mandate in modern Puerto Rican history was wielding the most extensive powers ever used during the 1952 Constitution's reign.

Most of the normative force exercised by the executive orders came from the Legislature, which, according to Section 19 of Article II, is the main recipient of the government's police powers, particularly with regard to matters associated with public safety, public health, and general welfare. That explains why there were very scarce legal challenges to most of the pandemic responses made by the government, and why virtually none of them were successful.

Once effective vaccines against the novel coronavirus became available, Puerto Rico became one of the most vaccinated jurisdictions within the US and around the world. This was done, even though transportation to Puerto Rico is not as efficient as it is within the continental US. The spectre of the botched US response to hurricane María was still fresh in the minds of the public.

This success story has two explanations: first, the historical collectivist culture in Puerto Rico that was heightened by the experiences of Irma and María. In other words, a substantial segment of the Puerto Rican People responded positively to the vaccination drives and voluntarily innoculated themselves; second, the assertive use by the government of its police powers through mask mandates and vaccination requirements to access important public goods and services.

IV. FINAL THOUGHTS

It seems almost impossible to deny the contradictory and paradoxical nature of the Puerto Rican constitutional project, currently centred around the text that was adopted in 1952. Neither is this circumstance limited to that document. On the contrary, Puerto Rican history is full of these contradictions, which emanate from: centuries of colonialism, and resistance to it; a problematic relationship with practical democracy, and attempts to achieve it; and a deep desire for social justice, and the difficulties in attaining it.

Probably the most dominant *external* feature of the Puerto Rican constitutional project has been its colonial nature. Colonialism has been everywhere: the general development of the island's legal system, first under Spanish domination and then under US control; the denial of true home rule; the constant intervention by the imperial powers with regard to the operation of its constitutional structures, the absolute control over Puerto Rico's economic system, with its dysfunctional effects; and the political repression of dissenting movements, specifically the pro-independence forces.

As we have seen, the 1952 Constitution was authorised, conditioned, approved and permanently influenced and directed by US colonialism. This includes the Jones Act, Public Act 600, the elimination of Section 20 of the Bill of Rights, the creation of economic conditions that frustrated its transformative provisions, and the overarching influence over its institutions that underenforced them.

For its part, democracy has been an inconsistent companion of colonialism and an unreliable – sometimes absent – ally of social justice. In terms of internal contradictions, the democratic factor stands on top. As this book has made clear, Puerto Rico's constitutional project is full of instances of great democratic aspirations coupled with substantial democratic deficits. From a historical perspective, Puerto Rico's exposure to democracy has been limited, recent, and full of tensions. Authoritarianism has not been absent from island life, and even during its more modern 'democratic' era, Puerto Rican democracy has been characterised by, at the very least, a distrust of popular self-rule.

Probably the most intense and explicit instance of democratic contradictions is in the 1952 constitutional process itself and the document it produced. As has been explained, the drafting process included both anti-democratic (repression of the independence movement) and democratic (selection of delegates and encouragement of popular engagement) features. Yet, in the end, the political and governmental structures, institutions, and mechanisms that resulted from the framing process were largely hierarchical and showed little enthusiasm for active popular participation in the democratic process, aside from voting.

The democratic element, including its shortcomings, has acted as the conceptual wildcard with regard to the remaining issue: the social and progressive content of the Puerto Rican constitutional project. During moments where democracy was broadened and strengthened, the social and progressive aspect of the constitutional project have thrived. Examples of this phenomenon were the inclusion of transformative and pro-working-class provisions in the 1952 Constitution and the removal of Governor Rosselló in 2019. But during moments of limited democratic spaces, these aspects have been severely hindered. This phenomenon was witnessed repeatedly during Spanish rule and in key moments after the US intervention in 1898. But we have also demonstrated that undemocratic processes resulted in some progressive outcomes, such as the legalisation of divorce and labour unions by the military rulers after the 1898 invasion.

Social transformation in the direction of greater economic justice has been an instinctive goal that has rarely turned into reality. Puerto Rico has been, and continues to be, a society plagued with inequality, exploitation, dysfunction, violence, poverty, and deprivation, among other similar social ills. This state has existed parallel to important movements and attempts to correct them. The 1952 Constitution was supposed to be an ally of the latter, but it has sometimes been highjacked to assist the former.

Here is a radical proposal: maybe more democracy and less colonialism is the crucial formula for the unleashing of the 1952 Constitution's transformative potential and of Puerto Rico's quest for a fairer and more just society. The 1952 Constitution is far from perfect. In fact, it is not even close to being complete or finished. The formal restoration of Section 20 of the Bill of Rights would be an important first step in this direction. Much more needs to be done.

But the constitutional project that began well before 1952, and that was partially and contradictorily formalised that year, constitutes an important phenomenon that is worthy of attention, analysis, and encouragement. Where Puerto Rico goes from here is anyone's guess. Let us hope that we can finally shake off colonialism, embrace a more robust democratic system, and build a better place for all.

Bibliography

ARTICLES AND BOOKS (SPANISH & ENGLISH)

Achiume, ET and Carbado, DW, 'Critical Race Theory Meets Third World Approaches to International Law' (2021) 67 *UCLA Law Review* 1462

Álvarez González, JJ and García Saúl, AI, 'Derecho Constitucional' (1991) 65 *Revista Jurídica Universidad de Puerto Rico* 799

Anderson, G 'Secession in International Law and Relations: What are we Talking About?' (2013) 35 *Loyola Los Angeles International and Comparative Law Review* 343

Arato, A, 'Forms of Constitution Making and Theories of Democracy' (1995) 17 *Cardozo Law Review* 191

del Carmen Baerga Santini, M, '"¡A la Organización, a Unirnos Como un Solo Hombre!": La Federación Libre de Trabajadores y el Mundo Masculino del Trabajo' in Pérez Velazco, E (ed), *100 Años de Sindicalismo Puertorriqueño* (Ediciones Callejón, 2007) 149

Baldwin, SE, 'The Constitutional Questions Incident to the Acquisition and Government by the United States of Island Territory' (1899) 12 *Harvard Law Review* 393

Blocher, J and Gulati, M, 'Puerto Rico and the Right of Accession' (2018) 43 *Yale Journal of International Law* 229

Colón-Ríos, J and Hevia, M, 'The Legal Status of Puerto Rico and the Institutional Requirements of Republicanism' (2011) 17 *Texas Hispanic Journal of Law and Policy* 1

Doyle, O, 'The Boundaries of Constituent Authority' (2019) 20 *German Law Journal* 161

Duffy Burnett, C, 'Untied States: American Expansion and Territorial Deannexation' (2005) 72 *University of Chicago Law Review* 79

Elkins, Z, Ginsburg, T and Blount, J, 'The Citizen as Founder: Public Participation in Constitutional Approval' (2008) 81 *Temple Law Review* 361

Elkins, Z, Ginsburg T and Melon, J, *The Endurance of National Constitutions* (Cambridge University Press, 2009)

Farinacci-Fernós, JM, 'Originalism in Puerto Rico: Original Explication and its Relation with Clear Text, Broad Purpose and Progressive Policy' (2016) 85 *Revista Jurídica Universidad de Puerto Rico* 203

—— 'Post-Liberal Constitutionalism' (2018) 54 *Tulsa Law Review* 1

—— 'Curious In-Laws: The Legal Connections between Montana and Puerto Rico' (2018) 79 *Montana Law Review* 187

—— 'Looking Beyond the Negative-Positive Rights Distinction: Analyzing Constitutional Rights According to their Nature, Effect and Reach' (2018) 41 *Hastings International and Comparative Law Review* 31

—— 'Cómo cambiar nuestra Ley Suprema: Un análisis del Artículo VII de la Constitución de Puerto Rico' (2019) 2 *Amicus Revista de Política Pública y Legislación Universidad Interamericana de Puerto Rico* 153

—— 'The Constitution is Dead, Long Live the Constitution! The Creation, Endurance and Modification of Modern Revolutionary Constitutions' (2020) 25 *Barry Law Review* 35.

Farinacci-Fernós, JM and Rivera-Vega, G, 'Los Usos de Fuentes Transnacionales en el Derecho Puertorriqueño (Parte I)' (2015) 51 *Revista Jurídica Universidad Interamericana de Puerto Rico* 189

Fernós-Isern, A, *Original Intent in the Constitution of Puerto Rico: Notes and Comments Submitted to the Congress of the United States* (LexisNexis, 2002) 21

Gathii, JT, 'Imperialism, Colonialism, and Ingternational Law' (2007) 54 *Buffalo Law Journal* 1013

Ghai, Y and Galli, G, *Constitution Building Process and Democratization* (Institute for Democracy and Electoral Assistance, 2006)
Goldsworthy, J, 'Australia: Devotion to Legalism' in J Goldsworthy (ed), *Interpreting Constitutions: A Comparative Study* (Oxford University Press, 2007) 109
Gorrín Peralta, CI, 'La Declaración Universal de los Derechos Humanos en la Jurisprudencia del Tribunal Supremo de Puerto Rico' (2010) 44 *Revista Jurídica Universidad Interamericana de Puerto Rico* 1
Henkin, L, 'A New Birth of Constitutionalism: Genetic Influence and Genetic Defects' in M Rosenfeld (ed), *Constitutionalism, Identity, Difference and Legitimacy* (Duke University Press, 1994) 52
Hernández Colón, R, 'The Evolution of Democratic Governance under the Territorial Clause of the US Constitution' (2017) 50 *Suffolk University Law Review* 587
Issacharoff, S et al, 'What is Puerto Rico?' (2019) 94 *Indiana Law Journal* 1
Kay, RS, 'Constituent Authority' (2011) 59 *American Journal of Comparative Law* 715
Keitner, CI and Reisman, M, 'Free Asociation: The United States Experience' (2003) 39 *Texas International Law Journal* 1
Lawson, G and Sloane, RD, 'The Constitutionality of Decolonization by Associated Statehood: Puerto Rico's Legal Status Recognized' (2009) 50 *Boston College Law Review* 1123
Lerner, H, *Making Constitutions in Deeply Divided Societies* (Cambridge University Press, 2011)
Lugo del Toro, K, *Nacimiento y Auge de la Confederación General de Trabajadores 1940–1945* (Universidad Interamericana de Puerto Rico, 2013)
Malavet, PA, *America's Colony: The Political and Cultural Conflict between the United States and Puerto Rico* (New York University Press, 2007)
Otaño, JA 'Puerto Rico Pandemonium: The Commonwealth Constitution and the Compact-Colony Conundrum' (2004) 27 *Fordham International Law Journal* 1806
Picó, F, *History of Puerto Rico: A Panorama of Its People* (Markus Wiener, 2014)
Ponsa-Kraus, CD, 'The "Insular Cases" Run Amok: Against Constitutional Exceptionalism in the Territories' (2022) *Yale Law Journal* 2449
Purdy, M, 'An Alternative Road: How the West can Draw from China's Belt and Road Initiative to Improve the Efficiency of Western Foreign Aid to Africa' (2022) 30 *Michigan State International Law Review* 125
Ramos González, CE, 'La Inviolabilidad de la Dignidad Humana: Lo Indigno de la Búsqueda de Expectativas Razonables de Intimidad en el Derecho Constitucional Puertorriqueño' (2011) 45 *Revista Jurídica Universidad Interamericana de Puerto Rico* 185
Reed, TG, 'Fair Use as Cultural Appropriation' (2021) 109 *California Law Review* 1373
Rodríguez Rodríguez, A, 'Palabras de la Hon. Anabelle Rodríguez Rodríguez en ocasión del acto de cierre editorial de la Revista de Estudios Críticos del Derecho de la Universidad Interamericana de Puerto Rico' (2015) 11 *Clave Revista de Estudios Críticos Del Derecho* 1
Serrano Geyls, R, 'The Territorial Status of Puerto Rico and its Effects on the Political Future of the Island' (2005) 39 *Revista Jurídica Universidad Interamericana de Puerto Rico* 13
Smith, J, 'Commonwealth Status: A Good Deal for Puerto Rico?' (2007) 10 *Harvard Latino Law Review* 263
Sterio, M, 'Self-Determination and Secession under International Law: The New Framework' (2015) 21 *ILSA Journal of International and Comparative Law* 293
Trías-Monge, J, *Historia Constitucional de Puerto Rico*, vol 3 (Editorial de la Universidad de Puerto Rico, 1982)
Tushnet, M, 'Constitution-Making: An Introduction' (2013) 91 *Texas Law Review* 1983

INTERNATIONAL SOURCES

Universal Declaration of Human Rights (1948)
American Declaration of the Duties and Rights of Man (1948)
UNGA Resolution 748 (VII) (27 Nov 1953) UN Document A/RES/748(VIII)

Index

www.ingramcontent.com/pod-product-compliance
Ingram Content Group UK Ltd.
Pitfield, Milton Keynes, MK11 3LW, UK
UKHW020816290926
15470UKWH00003B/1193

9 781509 953462